The programmer's guide to C++

for Alice, Gillian and John

The programmer's guide to C++

Adrian P. Robson
The University of Northumbria at Newcastle

First published in 1996 by UCL Press

UCL Press Limited
University College London
Gower Street
London WC1E 6BT

The name of University College London (UCL) is a registered
trade mark used by UCL Press with the consent of the owner.

British Library Cataloguing-in-Publication Data
A CIP catalogue record for this book is available from the British Library.

ISBN: 1-85728-437-2

Typeset in Palatino and Courier.
Printed and bound in Great Britain by
Biddles Ltd., Guildford and King's Lynn, England.

Contents

CHAPTER 1

Introduction

This book is written for students and professionals who can already program in a language like Ada, Modula-2, Pascal, C or Fortran, and want to move to C++ because of its object oriented programming features. It will also be useful to programmers familiar with C++ who want a guide that covers some of the most recent features of the language. It does not attempt to teach programming to beginners. However, it can be used by students learning to program with C++, as a companion to supplement their main text book.

All important features of the language are explained, including templates, exception handling, run-time type information, and the new cast operators. The C++ string class is used throughout the book. However, other parts of the standard class and template libraries are beyond the scope of this book.

There are exercises at the end of each chapter, which reinforce and further explore the ideas and techniques of C++ programming. There are model solutions in appendix A for almost all of these exercises.

1.1 The C++ language

C++ was designed and originally implemented by Bjarne Stroustrup, who works for AT&T Bell Telephone Laboratories. The language began as C *with classes* in 1982, and was first called C++ in 1983. It was being used by AT&T researchers in 1984 and was distributed to universities and throughout AT&T in early 1985. The AT&T C++ translator Cfront version 1.0 was released to the public in late 1985.

Commercial compilers began to appear in 1988 from companies like Zortec and GNU. C++ moved into the mainstream of programming languages with Cfront version 2.0 in June 1989, and major manufacturers started providing C++ products for their platforms. Borland released a C++ compiler in 1990, followed by Microsoft in 1992. Cfront version 3.0 was released in 1991 with templates, and a version supporting exception handling followed in 1992.

An ANSI C++ committee was formed in late 1989. One of their first actions was to approve templates and exception handling. Since then, the committee has added name spaces, run-time type information, and many minor features to the language.

The design of C++ was influenced by many other computer languages. C provided the basic syntax and semantics. Classes came from Simula 67. Operator overloading and embedded declarations are features of Algol 68. Ada and Clu influenced C++ templates, and Ada, Clu and ML influenced the design of C++ exception handling.

C++ supports nearly all the features of ANSI C. It is link compatible with the standard C libraries. Unlike standard C, C++ will only allow ANSI C syntax, so C++ is a strongly typed language. Some C++ programmers ignore the object oriented aspects of C++, and use it as an improved C. This is acceptable, but C++ is at its best when its object oriented features are used to the full.

There are many excellent C++ compilers available. However, some do not conform to the draft ANSI C++ standard. This is not a criticism, but it does mean that certain features discussed in this book will not work with some compilers.

1.2   Object oriented programming

Object oriented programming is a method of making software. In general, it approaches software design by building a program from a number of objects that communicate by exchanging messages. An object has a state that can change when messages arrive. Objects are instances of classes. A class has a data part, which stores state, and a set of allowed messages that can be sent to an instance of that class. Any number of instances of a particular class can be created. Bjarne Stroustrup, the original designer of C++, defines the object oriented programming paradigm as:

> Decide which classes you want; provide a full set of operations for each class; make commonality explicit by using inheritance.

In C++, a class defines a public interface for an object in the form of a set of functions, and a private implementation in the form of functions and data. The separation of interface and implementation means that an object's user does not have to know about its internal working. This abstraction promotes good program design. New classes can be defined by inheriting the attributes of existing classes.

Object oriented programming supports a form of *polymorphism*. Different objects can understand the same message, although they may respond to it in different ways. In addition, messages can be sent to an object without knowing its exact type. Polymorphism is further supported by classes that are defined with parameterized attributes. In C++ these are called template classes, and they are used as general purpose or utility classes.

The list of features said to identify an object oriented programming language varies, depending on the language being described. However, there are some features that most authors agree must be present: objects, classes, abstraction and inheritance. To get full benefit from object oriented programming polymorphism is also required.

C++ is a *hybrid* object oriented language. It combines the features of a traditional third generation language with object orientation. Some languages, such as Smalltalk, are totally based on an object oriented approach. These are called *pure* object oriented languages. There is much debate about which sort of language is best for particular applications. At the moment, hybrid languages are preferred for the development of production applications, whereas pure languages are very good for fast prototyping.

1.3 Overview of chapters

Chapter 2 The basics
The form of a simple C++ program is explained. Comments, names, the fundamental types, constants and simple input and output are discussed.

Chapter 3 Variables and expressions
Variables, operators and expressions are explained in this chapter. All the important C++ operators are discussed. How to use the standard C++ string class is explained. Type conversion and side effects are also discussed.

Chapter 4 Controlling execution
The control statements available in C++ are described. These include `if`, `switch`, `while`, `do` and `for` statements.

Chapter 5 Compound types
The use of structures and arrays is explained. Pointers and memory management are introduced. Other material covered in this chapter includes `typedef` names, reference types, and old C style strings.

Chapter 6 Functions
Functions and their use are explained. The different sorts of parameters and return values that can be used with functions are described. Recursive functions are discussed.

Chapter 7 Classes
This introduces the concept of classes and shows how class objects can be used to build programs. Constructors and destructors are explained.

Chapter 8 More about classes
This chapter introduces more material on classes. Inlining, static members, constant objects and members, nested classes and separate compilation are amongst the C++ class features discussed.

Chapter 9 Friends and operators
Friend functions and classes are explained, and operator overloading is introduced.

Chapter 10 Inheritance
This extends the previous chapters by showing how inheritance can be used to build class hierarchies. Single and multiple inheritance and some aspects of C++ design style are discussed.

Chapter 11 Virtual functions
Some of the more advanced aspects of C++ programming are considered in this chapter. The concept of polymorphism is introduced. Virtual functions and pointers to objects are presented as one method of supporting poly-morphism in C++.

Chapter 12 Templates
This chapter introduces templates as an important feature of C++. Function templates are explained. Generic and container classes are discussed, and C++ class templates are introduced to support these concepts.

Chapter 13 Advanced features
This chapter introduces some of the newer features of C++. Exception handling, casting, run-time type information and name spaces are all discussed. In particular, casting is explained in detail because of the dangers associated with its use.

Chapter 14 More input and output
The standard C++ input and output streams have already been introduced, but this chapter provides much more detail. Topics discussed include the

standard streams, setting flags and parameters, named files, and how to detect and manage stream errors and end of file conditions.

Appendices
The appendices include worked solutions for almost all the chapter exercises. There is a detailed description of the standard C++ string class, and a list of some other useful libraries.

1.4   Additional reading

Learning to program with C++

Barclay K. A. & B. J. Gordon 1994. *C++ problem solving and programming.* Englewood Cliffs, New Jersey: Prentice-Hall.
Graham, N. 1991. *Learning C++.* New York: McGraw-Hill.
Lippman, S. 1991. *A C++ primer,* 2nd edition. Reading, Mass.: Addison-Wesley.
Winder, R. 1992. *Developing C++ software,* 2nd edition. Chichester: John Wiley.

The C++ language

Coplien, J. O. 1992. *Advanced C++ programming styles and idioms.* Reading, Mass.: Addison-Wesley.
Ellis M. A. & B. Stroustrup 1990. *The annotated C++ reference manual.* Reading, Mass.: Addison-Wesley.
Plauger, P. J. 1995. *The standard C++ library.* Englewood Cliffs, New Jersey: Prentice-Hall, 1995.
Stroustrup, B. 1991. *The C++ programming language,* 2nd edition. Reading, Mass.: Addison-Wesley.
Stroustrup, B. 1994. *The design and evolution of C++.* Reading, Mass.: Addison-Wesley.

The C language

Banahan, M., D. Brady, M. Doran 1991. *The C book: featuring the ANSI C standard.* Reading, Mass.: Addison-Wesley.
Kernighan, B. & D. Ritchie 1984. *The C programming language,* 2nd edition. Englewood Cliffs, New Jersey: Prentice-Hall.

Object oriented analysis and design

Booch, G. 1993. *Object-oriented analysis and design with applications,* 2nd edition. Menlo Park, California: Benjamin-Cummings.
Rumbaugh, J., M. Blaha, W. Premerlani, F. Eddy, W. Lorensen 1991. *Object-oriented modeling and design.* Englewood Cliffs, New Jersey: Prentice-Hall.

CHAPTER 2

Getting started

2.1 A simple C++ program

Let us start by considering the following C++ program:

```cpp
// file: demo.cpp
// Demonstration program - print numbers

#include <iostream.h>

const int MAX = 10;

void main()
{
  int count = 1;
  while ( count <= MAX ) {
    cout << "counting " << count << endl;
    count = count + 1;
  }
}
```

This program does not do very much. It just prints a list of numbers from zero to ten.

The lines beginning with // are comments. They do not affect the operation of the program, and are used to make the program easier to understand and maintain. In this case, they briefly tell us what the program does, and where it is stored. The line beginning with #include is a preprocessing directive. Its use allows the standard C++ I/O library <iostream.h> to be used in the program.

The body of the program is given in main, between the outer set of braces, { and }. This is the executable part of the program. It is composed of

statements, which end with semicolons. All normal C++ programs have a
main function.

A C++ program can communicate with its environment by receiving
data from the command line and returning a status value. The word void
in front of main indicates that the program will not return a status value
when it finishes, and the empty parentheses () mean the program will not
expect any information from its environment at run-time.

In main, the first line defines an integer variable called count, giving
it an initial value of one. This is followed by a while statement, which
repeatedly executes the block after it. It stops when the expression
counting <= MAX evaluates to false. The name MAX is a constant, defined
above main, with the value 10. So when count becomes greater than
10, the loop will stop. Each time the loop executes, a message is printed on
the computer's screen, and count is incremented by one. This happens ten
times.

The identifier cout names the standard output stream, and the symbol
<< means insert into the stream. Together, they output data to the screen.
First "counting ", which is a string literal, is printed, followed by the
value in count. Finally, endl is a manipulator that causes the output
stream to start a new line.

The symbol = is the assignment operator. It puts the value of the expression on its right-hand side into the variable on its left-hand side. It is used
here, with the + operator, to add one to count.

A C++ program ends when main is finished. In this program there is
nothing after the while statement. So when the loop finishes so does the
program.

The demonstration program is stored in a file called demo.cpp. The file
type cpp is the default for Borland's C++ compiler. A different file type
may have to be used with other compilers. The exact way to turn this program into an executable form will depend on the operating system and
compiler that are used.

2.2 Program structure

A C++ program consists of one or more files containing definitions
of classes, variables, constants and functions. These are compiled, and
the resulting machine code is linked together to form an executable program. Large programs are broken down into separate, independently
compilable, components stored in separate files. Simple programs, which
include most of the examples in this book, are written as a single file.
However, even the simplest program normally uses some components
from the standard libraries that come with the C++ language.

When a separate component is used, an #include directive obtains a specification of its interface, and this is used by the compiler to check, in a limited way, that the component is being used correctly. The procedure for compiling and linking a C++ program depends on the compiler and operating system being used. Most will automatically link the standard libraries into your program, but application specific components have to be explicitly managed. The use of header and source files to support separate components is explained in §8.9.

There are a number of ways to organize the layout of a C++ program. One of the simplest and most effective is as follows:

```cpp
// Introductory comments ...

// Standard libraries ...
#include <iostream.h>

    . . . . . . . . .

// Application specific components ...
#include "applic.h"

    . . . . . . . .

// Global constants ...
const int MAX = 100;

    . . . . . . . .

// A few functions used only in main ...
void startupmess( ostream& os )
{
    os << "hello" << endl;
}

    . . . . . . . .

// The main program ...
void main()
{
    // Local variables ...
    int pagecount;

        . . .
    // The main part of the program ...
    startupmess(cout);

        . . .
}
```

Class declarations (see Ch. 7) are usually put in separate files, but during initial development, and for most of the exercises in this book, it is okay to put them in the same file as the main program. The simplest approach is to put all class related declarations before main.

2.3 Comments

Any text following //, until the end of the line is a comment. A comment can also be enclosed between /* and */. This sort of comment can span more than one line. For example:

```
// this is a comment line
    a = b;   // this is a comment at the end of a line
/* this is also
    a
    comment */
```

Comments are used to document a program so it is easier to understand and maintain. They do not affect a program's operation.

2.4 Identifiers

Names or identifiers in C++ consist of letters, digits and the underscore character. Identifiers must begin with a letter or an underscore. Upper and lower case characters are distinct. All identifiers must be declared before they can be used. A declaration introduces one or more identifiers into a program and gives them meaning. Some examples are:

```
const float RANGE = 3.6; // declare a constant called RANGE
char ans;                // declare a variable called ans
float range;             // range not the same name as RANGE
int max( int a, int b ); // name a function called max
```

2.5 Variables and types

Variables are storage locations that hold a program's data while it is running. They can be given names that are used to access the values they store, or they can be accessed with pointers that hold their location. For the moment we will concentrate on named variables, and leave pointers to §5.1. Variables are used in expressions (see Ch. 3) and to pass data into and out of functions (see Ch. 6). All C++ variables have a *type* that stipulates the form of data they can hold. This can be a *fundamental* type or a *class* type. The fundamental types are built into the language. Class types are supplied as parts of the standard libraries, or they are programmer defined as part of a C++ program. This chapter describes the fundamental types. A discussion of classes begins in Chapter 7.

A type is specified when a variable is created:

```
int count;    // a variable that holds a whole number
string name;  // a variable that holds a string of characters
```

Here, int and string are types, and count and name are identifiers that
are the names of the variables.

2.6   The fundamental types

There are a number of simple types built into the language. There are *integral* and *floating* types, which are collectively called *arithmetic* types. There
is a Boolean type for storing true and false values. And there are *enumerations*, which are similar to integers.

The integral types, in increasing size, are given in Table 2.1. Notice that
char is an integral type. This means that, although variables of type char
are normally used to store single characters, they can explicitly store
numerical values, and be used in arithmetic calculations.

All the integral types can be signed or unsigned. For example,
unsigned int or signed char. Unsigned integers cannot represent negative numbers, but they can represent a larger positive value than can be
stored in the equivalent signed type. The signed integer types are synonyms for their plain versions, so signed int is the same as int. The integral type normally used for arithmetic is int.

Table 2.1   Integral fundamental types.

Type name	Purpose
char	A character
short int	A short integer number
short	The same as short int
int	An integer number
long int	A long integer number
long	The same as long int

Storage size increases, or is equal, from top
to bottom of list.

There are implementation dependent limits on the size of a number that
can be stored as an integer. The size of the number that can be stored generally increases from char, short, int to long, but on some computers
short and int are the same. The standard header file <limits.h> contains information about the minimum and maximum values for the integral types. Some values for a typical C++ compiler are given in Table 2.2.

An integer *overflows* if an attempt is made to store a number that is too
large. If this happens, the stored value will be incorrect but an error will not
be reported. However, many C++ compilers will issue a warning if overflow is possible, for example when a long value is assigned to an int variable. An overflowing signed integer incorrectly changes sign. So adding

Table 2.2 Typical integral type ranges.

Type	Minimum value	Maximum value
char	−128	127
short	−32768	32767
int	−32768	32767
unsigned int	0	65535
long	−21474836648	2147483647

one to the maximum positive value for a particular integral type will give a negative result. An overflowing unsigned integer wraps through zero, so adding one to a maximum value produces zero.

Values of type `bool` can be either `true` or `false`. This is an integral type, and `bool` values generally behave as signed integers, although it is unwise to use them as such. If a `bool` variable or constant is used in an arithmetic expression, `false` is converted to zero and `true` to one. Some older C++ compilers do not support a `bool` type. In this case, `int` can be used instead, with zero representing `false` and any non-zero integer representing `true`.

The varieties of floating point numbers, in order of increasing precision, are given in Table 2.3. The characteristics of the real numbers are implementation dependent. Details of their ranges can be found in the standard header `<float.h>`.

Table 2.3 Floating point fundamental types.

Type name	Purpose
float	a floating point number
double	a double precision floating point number
long double	a long floating point number

Precision increases, or is equal, from top to bottom of list.

An enumeration is a user defined set of named integer constant values. Each enumeration is a different type. Each of the constants has the type of its enumeration. They look like this:

```
enum Colour { RED, YELLOW, GREEN };
```

In this example, the name RED represents the value 0, YELLOW is 1 and GREEN is 2. Enumerated names can be given specific integer values, which can be calculated from other constants:

```
enum Grade { GOOD = 100, AVERAGE = GOOD / 2, POOR = 0 };
```

A conventional style is to use capitals for the names of constants, and to begin user defined type names with a capital. Hence the names GOOD and Grade. Enumerations are not integral types but they are promoted to integers when required. Integral types can be converted to enumerations.

Enumerations can be declared without a type name:

```
enum { MIN = 20, MAX = 40 };
```

If this is done, the enumeration's constant names are of type int, and they behave like named integer constants (see §2.8).

2.7 Strings

A string is a sequence of characters that can include spaces and special characters such as tabs. There are two ways to store a character string in C++: in an array of characters, or in a string object. Character arrays are the way strings are handled in C programs, and they can also be used in C++. However, string objects are the best way to manage strings in a C++ program because they are safer and easier to use.

The type of a string object is string, and it is used in much the same way as a fundamental type. If string is used in a program, a header file called <string> or its equivalent must be included like this:

```
#include <string>
...
string name;
name = "abc";
```

Character arrays are sometimes referred to as *C strings* while string objects are called *C++ strings*. C strings are explained in §5.3, and C++ strings in §3.3.

2.8 Constants

Constants are values that do not change. They can be literals, which are actual values, or named constants. A literal is just a value of a specific type. Literals are used in expressions and declarations:

```
price =  cost + 6.4; // literal is 6.4
cout << "Alice";      // literal is "Alice"
int count = 0;        // literal is 0
```

It is often convenient to give a value a name, and use this instead of a literal. This makes programs much easier to understand and maintain. Named constants are defined like this:

```
const MIN = 50;            // type is int by default
const int MAX = 100;
const Colour STOP = RED;   // an enumerated type
```

```
const float PI =  3.142;
const float MAX_AREA = MAX * MAX * PI;
const string TITLE = "Management Report";
const char YES = 'Y';
```

For integers, enumerations are an alternative way to define constant values. Enumerations and named constants must be declared before they can be used.

There are literals corresponding to each of the fundamental types and a string literal. The following are examples of integer literals: 1249234, 99, 0, 345U, 16777215L, 45UL, 0XFF and 010. Decimal, hexadecimal or octal notation can be used. Integers beginning with a non-zero digit are decimal. The prefix 0x or 0X indicates hexadecimal notation, and numbers beginning with zero are octal. So the number twelve can be written as 12, 0xC, 0Xc or 014. Commas are not allowed. A suffix can be used to indicate a preferred type: U or u for unsigned, and L or l for long. The actual type of an integer literal depends on its prefix, value and suffix. The type is chosen to use the most compact internal representation. Table 2.4 shows the possible choices.

Table 2.4 Integer literal types.

Literal format	Choice in order of preference			
	1	2	3	4
0xFFFF or 0777	int	unsigned int	long int	unsigned long int
999	int	long int	unsigned long int	
999U	unsigned int	unsigned long int		
999L	long int	unsigned long int		
999UL or 999LU	unsigned long int			

Character literals are written like this: 'a', 'D', ' ', '\n' and '\xaa'. The \ character starts an escape sequence. An escape sequence specifies a single character. A list of valid sequences is given in Table 2.5. In the examples above, \n is a new line character and \xaa is the character represented by the decimal number 170.

Real or floating point literals are written like this: 3.127, .001, 5.6E3, 2e5L and 4e-10F. Scientific notation can be used, where 5.6e3 means 5.6×10^3. An F suffix indicates a float and L a long double. The type is double if no suffix is given.

String literals are sequences of characters in double quotes:

```
"This is a string literal. It will sound the bell \a"
```

Table 2.5 Character escape sequences.

Use	Sequence
new line	\n
horizontal tab	\t
vertical tab	\v
backspace	\b
carriage return	\r
alert (bell)	\a
form feed	\f
back slash	\\
question mark	\?
single quote	\'
double quote	\"
octal code	\ooo
hex code	\xhh

A string literal has the same type as an array of characters. This is called a C string, and is described in §5.3. If two string literals are put next to each other, they are concatenated even if there is a line break between them. So these two are the same:

```
cout << "This "
        "and this" << endl;
cout << "This and this" << endl;
```

The Boolean literals are true and false, and have the type bool:

```
bool found = false;
```

2.9   Simple input and output

Input and output are fully explained in Chapter 14, but the following shows how simple data can be input from a computer's keyboard and written to its screen. Input and output operations are performed using the standard stream library. To use this, <iostream.h> must be included in the program.

Use the << insertion operator with cout for output. The statement

```
cout << count << endl;
```

will print the value of count and start a new line. The exact format of the output will depend on the type of count. Output can be controlled by *manipulators* like endl and hex. The statement:

```
cout << hex << count;
```

15

Table 2.6 Some useful output manipulators.

Manipulator	Purpose
dec	convert to decimal
hex	convert to hexadecimal
endl	add end of line and flush
setw(int w)	set output field width

Remember to include <iomanip.h> if setw is used.

will print the value of count in hexadecimal notation. Some useful manipulators are given in Table 2.6. Take care; the effect of some manipulators lasts after the statement in which it is used. For example, if decimal output is needed after hex has been used with cout, then dec must be used before the value is output.

Use the >> extraction operator with cin for input. For example, the following statement will input a value for the variable bookno:

```
cin >> bookno;
```

The following example program illustrates the use of the >> and << operators by looking at some literals and constants:

```
#include <iostream.h>

const float PI = 3.142;

enum Grade { GOOD, AVERAGE, POOR };

void main()
{
  cout << "I said \"Lets look at some constants\"." << endl;
  cout << "This is a two line string\nSecond line" << endl;
  cout << "This "
          "and this" << endl;
  cout << "This and this" << endl;
  cout << "Some integers are " << 0xff << ", "
          << -1 << ", " << -1U << " and "
          << hex << -1U << '\n';
  cout << "Some characters are " << '\x61'
          << " = " << 'a' << '\n';
  cout << "Now some floating point values" << endl
          << 2.5 << ' ' << 0.25E10 << ' ' << 9E20 << ' '
          << 123456789.0 << endl;
  cout << "Grades are " << GOOD << ' '
          << AVERAGE << ' '<< POOR << endl;
  cout << "PI is " << PI << endl;

  double width, depth;
  cout << "Give width and depth: ";
```

```
    cin  >> width >> depth;
    cout << "width is " << width
         << " and depth is " << depth << endl;
}
```

This program produces the following output:

```
I said "Lets look at some constants".
This is a two line string
Second line
This and this
This and this
Some integers are 255, -1, 65535 and ffff
Some characters are a = a
Now some floating point values
2.5 2.5e+09 9e+20 1.23457e+08
Grades are 0 1 2
PI is 3.142
Give width and depth: 3.5 6.7
width is 3.5 and depth is 6.7
```

2.10   Exercises

1. (a) Type the demonstration program shown in §2.1 into an appropriately named file on your computer. Compile and run it. You might
   have to do a bit of research to find out how use the C++ compiler and
   program editor on your computer.
   (b) You may have managed to write this program without any problems. To see what kind of faults can occur, try the following with
   copies of your demonstration program:
   i.   Remove the semi-colon from one of the statements in main.
   ii. Remove the #include line.
   iii. Change main to Main.
   There is no model solution for this exercise.
2. Write a program that asks for your first name and then prints a hello
   message with your name in it. Define a C++ string in main to hold the
   name and include <string> or its equivalent.
3. Write a program that asks for two numbers and prints out their sum.
   Define two float variables to hold the input data with float a, b.
   The addition operator is +.

CHAPTER 3
Variables and expressions

3.1 Variables

A variable is an area in memory where information is stored and can be manipulated. A data value can also be stored as a named constant, as discussed in §2.8, but a constant cannot be modified. A variable has an address, which is its location in memory. It has a type, which specifies what sort of data it can hold and how they can be used. It can have zero, one or more names, and it has a value. A variable can be accessed, and its value changed, by using one of its names or through a *pointer*. A pointer is a variable that contains the address of another variable or named constant. Pointers are explained in §5.1. In this chapter we will look at named variables. Variables without names are discussed later in §5.8.

A variable must be defined before it can be used. This gives it a type and optionally an initial value:

```
int seats;
int count = 0;
float total;
int i, j, k;
float  area = 3.4;
double x = 0.0, y = 0.0;
```

If an enumeration is given a type name, this can be used to define a variable:

```
enum Colour { RED, YELLOW, GREEN };
...
Colour door = YELLOW;
```

Once a variable has been declared it can be used. It can be assigned values of the appropriate type:

```
count = 6;
total = 12.5;
area = 10;
door = RED;
```

And it can be used to calculate another value:

```
area = 10.5 * count;
```

A variable's *scope* describes the places in a program where it can be used. A variable can be used after it has been declared, but it cannot be used outside the *block* in which it is declared, where a block is a number of statements and declarations enclosed in braces, { and }. The full scope rules include control statements, functions, classes and name spaces, which are all discussed in later chapters. But for the moment, the implications of scope are that a variable declared inside main can only be used in main after its declaration. We say it has *local* scope within main. A variable declared outside a block is said to have *global* scope, and is available throughout the program after its declaration. Variables are normally declared locally in main, but named constants are often declared globally at the top of the program. A variable can be declared anywhere in main before it is used. However, many programmers declare all the variables together at the beginning of a block because this usually makes the program easier to understand. If a name is used locally and globally, the local name hides the global name. However, the global name can still be accessed by prefixing the name with the : : operator as shown in the following short program:

```
#include <iostream.h>

const int MIN = 0;              // global constants
const int MAX = 100;

void main()
{
    int count = 3;              // local variable
    cout << count << endl;
    cout << distance << endl;   // error - not declared
    float distance = 25.7;
    cout << distance << endl;   // okay now

    const int MIN = -20;        // hide global name
    cout << MIN << endl;        // use local
    cout << MAX << endl;        // use global
    cout << ::MIN << endl;      // use global
}
```

3.2 Operators and expressions

An expression is a sequence of operators and operands that specifies a computation. It may result in a value and it may have side effects. Nearly all the operators work with one or two operands: they are unary or binary. In general, an operand can be a constant, a variable, a function, or another expression. There are a lot of operators in C++. Some may be familiar, such as the arithmetic operators + and *, which are addition and multiplication. Other are more unusual. For example, there are operators for creating and destroying dynamic objects, and for using pointers. In this section we will look at the operators most often used to perform arithmetic or logical calculations. Other operators will be discussed in later chapters when appropriate. A full list of C++ operators is given in Appendix C.

An expression's computed value depends on how its operands and operators are grouped together. An operator's behaviour is affected by its precedence, which defines the relative priority of different operators, and by its associativity, which defines the grouping of operators with the same precedence. In the expression 3 * 4 + 3 the operator * has a higher precedence than +, so the grouping is (3 * 4) + 4. The expression 3 – 4 + 5 is similar but the operators + and – have the same precedence and have left-to-right associativity, so the grouping is (3 – 4) + 5. As this shows, the rules in C++ are compatible with the rules of normal arithmetic. There are rules for all the operators. For example, the assignment operator = has right-to-left associativity, so a = b = c groups a = (b = c).

The above examples use parentheses to show how expressions group. But parentheses are actually used in expressions explicitly to form groups, possibly overriding the default rules. The expression 3 + 4 * 5 is equal to 23, but (3 + 4) * 5 is equal to 35. Parentheses are very important. Except in the simplest cases, use parentheses to make expressions easy to understand. The full rules are difficult to memorise, and parentheses can help to improve clarity.

In general, the order of calculation is not defined. The grouping of operators with operands does not precisely define the order of evaluation. For example, the expression a * b + c * d groups (a * b) + (c * d) but we cannot predict if a * b or c * d will be calculated first.

Functions are often used in expressions. A function has a name, takes zero or more arguments, and produces a value. There are functions that do not return a value, but these are of no use in an expression. There are a number of useful mathematical functions available in the standard library. They can be used if the <math.h> header file is included in a program. For example, the positive difference between two floating point numbers can be calculated with the expression fabs(before-after). A full explanation of functions is given in Chapter 6.

3.2.1 Arithmetic operators

The arithmetic operators are shown in Table 3.1. The operands of all these operators must have arithmetic type. When an arithmetic operator has a mixture of operand types, automatic conversions are performed. These are called the "usual arithmetic conversions" and are given in Appendix D. The purpose of the conversion is to yield a common type for the calculation. Put simply, it converts the operands to a type than maintains the precision of both operands. How divide by zero and overflow are handled depends on the compiler and computer being used. Most C++ implementations just ignore overflow.

Addition, subtraction, multiplication and unary minus are simple:

```
count + increment      // addition
count - 4              // subtraction
width * height         // multiplication
width * -depth         // and with a unary negative
```

The division operator / is not quite as simple. It can be applied to floating point and integer operands with different results. When it is used with int operands it gives the quotient. That is the whole number of times the right-hand operand goes into the left-hand operand. But if one or both of the operands is a double or a float the result will be a floating point number. So, 7.0 / 2 gives 3.5, while 7 / 2 gives 3. In the floating point calculation the int constant 2 is converted to a double. Ensuring that a floating point division happens when two int objects are involved needs a conversion. Given that a and b are type int, the expression a / double(b) will force a floating point division. The % operator gives the remainder after division. For example, 7 % 2 has the value 1. Both operands must be integers, so 7.0 % 2 is an error.

Table 3.1   Arithmetic operators.

Operator	Purpose
+	addition
−	subtraction
*	multiplication
/	floating point division
/	integer division – quotient
%	integer division – remainder (modulo)
−	unary minus

3.2.2 Assignment operators

The result of an expression can be assigned to a variable object with the = operator, provided object and expression have compatible types. For example, the following statement takes `tax` from `grosspay` and puts the result in `netpay`:

```
netpay = grosspay - tax;
```

An assignment operation has a result which has the type and value of its left-hand operand. This can be used like the result of any other expression. So the following are valid:

```
x = y = z
cout << ( x = 6 )
```

The first example assigns the value of z to x and y. In the second, the value 6 is assigned to x and inserted into the output stream. In this case, the parentheses must be used. Without them the expression would group (cout << x) = 6, which does not make sense.

Any expression can form a valid statement. So this is a statement that does nothing worthwhile because its result is not used:

```
total + 9;
```

C++ provides an abbreviated form for expressions like x = x + 6, where a variable is used to calculate a new value for itself. The expression x = x + 6 can be written as x += 6, and there are similar abbreviations for other operators. Table 3.2 gives a list of all the assignment operators.

The left-hand side of an assignment operator can be any expression that computes to something that can be assigned a value. Simple variables meet this criterion, but so do references and dereferenced pointers. Anything that can be used on the left-hand side of an assignment is called an *lvalue*. In a similar manner, an expression that is valid on the right-hand side of an assignment is called an *rvalue*.

Table 3.2 Assignment operators.

Expression	Purpose	Equivalent
a = b	simple assignment	
a += b	add and assign	a = a + b
a -= b	subtract and assign	a = a - b
a *= b	multiply and assign	a = a * b
a /= b	divide and assign	a = a / b
a %= b	remainder and assign	a = a % b
a <<= b	shift left and assign	a = a << b
a >>= b	shift right and assign	a = a >> b
a &= b	AND and assign	a = a & b
a |= b	OR and assign	a = a | b
a ^= b	EOR and assign	a = a ^ b

3.2.3 Increment and decrement operators

The operator ++ adds one to, or increments, and -- subtracts one from, or decrements, a variable of arithmetic type. They can be used before or after a variable name with different effect. For example,

```
data = count++;
```

assigns the value of count to data, and then adds one to count. But the expression

```
data = ++count;
```

adds one to count, and then assigns this new value to data. The decrement operator -- behaves in a similar way. Never use an incremented or decremented object more than once in an expression. For example, after

```
i = 6 + i++;
```

the value of i is undefined. Table 3.3 is a summary of the increment and decrement operators.

Table 3.3 Increment and decrement operators.

expression	equivalent
a = n++	a = n; n = n + 1
a = ++n	n = n + 1; a = n
a = n--	a = n; n = n - 1
a = --n	n =n - 1; a = n

3.2.4 Bitwise operators

The bitwise operators allow individual bits in an integer to be altered. This kind of processing is unnecessary in most programs, but these operators can be very useful to systems programmers working with low level software components, such as device drivers. The bitwise operators are summarized in Table 3.4.

The bitwise AND operator is &. In the expression expr & mask, each bit in mask is combined with the equivalent bit in expr using an AND operation. If both bits are one, the result is one, otherwise the result is a zero bit. This is useful for switching selected bits to zero. Bitwise OR and exclusive OR are used in the same way. The OR operator is |. With this, if either bit in the operands is one, the resulting bit is one, otherwise it is zero. This is useful for setting selected bits to one. The exclusive OR operator is ^. It produces a one bit if one, and only one, of the bits being processed is one, otherwise the result is a zero bit. This is useful for inverting the value of

Table 3.4 Bitwise operators

Operator	Purpose
<<	shift left
>>	shift right
&	bitwise AND
|	bitwise OR
^	bitwise exclusive OR
~	one's complement

selected bits. The one's complement operator ~ is unary. It inverts the state of every bit in its operand. The following examples show how these bitwise operators can be used:

```
iobyte = iobyte & 0x0F;  // 4 low order bits unchanged
                         // all higher order bits set to 0
iobyte = iobyte | 0x0F;  // 4 low order bits set to 1
                         // all higher order bits unchanged
iobyte = iobyte ^ 0x0F;  // invert 4 low order bits
                         // all higher order bits unchanged
iobyte = ~iobyte;        // invert the state of every bit.
iobyte = ~0xF0;          // low order byte set to 0x0F
                         // all higher order bits set to 1
```

The shift operators << and >> move bits left or right respectively. Their operands must be of integral type, and the result is the type and value of the left operand shifted by the number of bits given by the value of the right operand. The right operand must not be negative, or greater than or equal to the number of bits in the biggest supported integer. Bits shifted out in either direction are discarded. Shifting left puts zeros in the vacated low order bits. Shifting right will put zeros in the high order bits if the right operand is an unsigned type or has a non-negative value, otherwise the result is undefined. To protect against this, the right operand should be declared as an unsigned type, or it should be converted for the shift:

```
unsigned int iobuff;
int signedbuff;
iobuff = iobuff << 2;    // shift iobuff left 2 bits
iobuff = iobuff >> count; // shift iobuff right count bits
signedbuff = unsigned(signedbuff) >> 4; // safe shift right
```

The << and >> symbols have two meanings: shift left and right, and stream insertion and extraction. The compiler can normally identify which operation is required from its context. However, if the two uses are mixed in the same expression, parentheses have to be used to ensure correct grouping.

3.2.5 Relational and logical operators

C++ has a Boolean type called `bool` that can have two values: `true` and `false`. All the relational and logical operators produce results of type `bool`. Boolean expressions are used in conditional statements, which are described in Chapter 4.

Some C++ compilers do not have a `bool` type, but `int` can be used instead. The integer value 0 represents `false`, whereas any non-zero integer value represents `true`. So, for example, the expression n - n evaluates to false, and 3 * 6 is always true. Values of type `int` can be converted to type `bool`.

The simplest relational operator is ==, which tests for equality. The expression 7 == 7 is true and 3 == 7 is false. Take care, a very common mistake, which your compiler might not catch, is using the assignment operator = instead of ==. The inverse of == is the not equal operator ! =. The other relational operators are listed in Table 3.5. These operators compare left operand with right operand. So a > b, is read as a greater than b.

Relational expressions and Boolean variables or constants can be combined using the logical operators shown in Table 3.5. For example, n == 1 || m > 6 tests the assertion that n is equal to one or m is greater than six. Parentheses are not required in this case because || has a lower precedence than == or >. However, parentheses can be used for clarity, so the above expression might be written as (n == 1) || (m > 6). As with arithmetic expressions, parentheses can be used explicitly to control grouping. For example, ! (a && b) is not the same as !a && b (it is actually the same as !a || !b). Take care not to use the bitwise operators by mistake, a & b is not a Boolean expression.

The left operand of || or && is always evaluated first, and the right-hand operand is not evaluated unless it has to be. For example, 1 || n is always true and n is not evaluated, while 0 && n is always false and n is not evaluated.

3.2.6 The conditional expression

This is a rather strange expression with three operands. It has the form:

expression-c ? *expression-t* : *expression-f*

When it is evaluated, *expression-c* is always calculated first. If the condition represented by this sub-expression is true, the whole expression has the value of *expression-t*, otherwise it has the value of *expression-f*. The types of *expression-t* and *expression-f* must be compatible. An example that prints a different message depending on a being even or odd is:

```
cout << ((a % 2 != 0) ? "odd" : "even");
```

26

Table 3.5 Relational and
logical operators

Operator	Purpose
==	equal
!=	not equal
<	less than
<=	less than or equal
>	greater than
>=	greater than or equal
!	NOT
||	OR
&&	AND

3.2.7 The comma operator

The comma operator is not used very often. Nevertheless, this operator should be understood because it is easy to use by mistake, in a way that will slip past the compiler.

A pair of expressions separated by a comma operator are evaluated left to right and the value of the left expression is discarded. The type and value of the result are those of the right operand. All side effects (see §3.5) of the left expression are applied before the right operand is evaluated.

In the context where the comma has a special meaning, such as a list of arguments to a function, the comma operator can only appear in parentheses. This very strange function call is valid: `f(a,(t=3,t+2),c)`. There are three arguments. The value of the second argument is 5, and the function call assigns the value 3 to `t`. Using a comma operator this way is not the kind of thing a sensible programmer does and it should be strenuously avoided. The only reasonable use for a comma operator is with a `for` statement, which is discussed in §4.2.3.

3.3 Strings

C++ variables of type `string` store a sequence of characters. The header file `<string>` or its equivalent has to be included if `string` variables or named constants are used. Do not confuse this with `<string.h>` which has a different purpose. Strings are declared and initialized like this:

```
#include <string>
...
string name;
string errormess = "bad data";
string address1, address2;
```

27

String values can be assigned to `string` variables:

```
name = "Alice";
address1 = address2;
errormess = "";
```

Strings can be compared with the standard relational operators (see §3.2.5). For example:

```
if   ( address1 == address2 )
   cout << "addresses are the same";
if   ( name >= "Alice" )
   cout << "value in name is greater than or "
            "equal to Alice";
```

Strings are compared character by character, starting with their leftmost characters. The comparison uses the character's numerical code value. The strings are equal if they are the same length, and all the compared characters are equal. If two characters are not equal, the string containing the character with the numerically larger code value is the greater. If the end of only one of the strings is reached with no unequal characters being found, the longer string is greater. This may seem complicated, but it is just *alphabetic* ordering. For example, `"bigger"` is greater than `"big"`, `"alice"` is greater than `"Alice"`, `"hello "` is greater than `"hello"`, and `"bun"` is greater than `"ban"`.

Variables and constants of type `string` can be joined together with the + operator. This is called concatenation:

```
fullmess = name + " is " + errormess;
```

The length of a `string` can be obtained and an individual character in a string can be accessed, as the following demonstrates:

```
for ( int i = 0; i < name.length(); i++ )
   if ( name[i] == 'a' )
      name[i] = 'A';
```

Here, every occurrence of a in `name` is changed to A. The length of the stored string is provided by `name.length()`, and the individual characters are accessed using the subscript operator `[]`. Exactly how `for` and `if` statements work is explained in Chapter 4. The dot notation `name.length` can be used because `name` is actually a class object. This is fully explained in Chapter 7.

Input and output is simple using insertion and extraction operators:

```
string name;
cout << "Give your first name: ";
cin >> name;
```

```
cout << "Your name is " << name << endl;
```

However, reading in a string using >> will only input characters up to the first space. To read in a string containing spaces, the function getline can be used like this:

```
cout << "Give your full name: ";
getline(cin,name);
```

This inputs a complete line, including spaces, and stores it in the string variable name.

There is an alternative method of managing strings as an explicit array of characters. This is the way strings are handled in C, and it is explained in §5.3. However, the recommended approach is to use string variables as described above. More information about the operations that can be performed on string variables is given in Appendix B.

3.4 Type conversions

C++ allows mixed mode expressions such as 2 + 3.5, which has an integer and a floating point operand. Both operands must be the same type for the computation, so implicit conversions are performed. Conversions are also used if needed during initialization and passing arguments to functions. These are the "usual arithmetic conversions" and are described in detail in Appendix D.

Sometimes it is necessary to force a value to be converted to a particular type. For example, when both arguments are integers, float(a) / b performs a floating point division. The expression float(a) converts a from int to float. There are standard conversions defined in the language for most of the fundamental types. But take care, conversions can throw away information. This may be okay. For example, converting a floating point number to an integer with int(3.6) discards the decimal part to give a value of 3. However, some conversions can produce rubbish. If a long integer is converted to an int, significant digits might be lost.

Enumerated types are automatically converted to integers when required, but integers have to be explicitly converted to an enumerated type to avoid an error or warning message. Floating point numbers can also be explicitly converted to enumerated types. The conversion changes them to int and then to the enumerated type.

Some conversions are not allowed. A constant, for example, cannot be converted to a variable type. If absolutely necessary, this sort of thing can be done with a cast. Casts are expressions that can be used to override the normal type checking rules of C++. However, one form of cast, called a static_cast, can be used for conversion. Casts are explained in §13.2.

3.5 Side effects

A side effect occurs when an object is modified by the evaluation of an expression. For example,

```
sum = sum + i++;
```

adds the value of i to sum and, as a side effect, increments i. Technically, an assignment has the side effect of modifying its left-hand operand, but normally we do not treat this as a side effect.

The vague ordering of operations in C++ expressions can cause problems. For example, we cannot predict the value of i after `--i + i` or `i = 6 + i++;` and we do not know the argument values in `f(--i, i++)`. There is some help. All side effects are guaranteed to happen:

- At the end of an expression statement.
- At a comma, `||`, `&&` or `? :` operator, after the leftmost operand is evaluated. The left operand is always evaluated first.
- To argument expressions before a function is entered. The order of evaluation of arguments is not defined.

3.6 Exercises

1. Value added tax (VAT) is 17.5%. Write a program that asks for a value, then prints out this value, the VAT amount and the total cost. Make the VAT percentage a constant, so that it is easy to change by editing the code.
2. Write a program to calculate the area and circumference of a circle. The area of a circle is given by a $= \pi r^2$, and its circumference by c $= 2\pi r$. Where r is the radius of the circle and π is approximately 3.1416.
3. If a = 6, b = 2 and c = 9, what are the values of the following expressions?
   (a) `b + c * 6`
   (b) `c % b`
   (c) `c / b + 4`
   (d) `c / b + 4.0`
   (e) `a - 4 != 3`
   (f) `c / (a - 3 * b)`
   (g) `a == 6 && b == 3`
   Write a small program to check your answers.
4. Given these declarations:

   ```
   int i = 5;
   int j = 1, k = 6;
   ```

   What are the values of i after each of the following assignment statements?

```
i = j++ - --k;
i = k * -i;
i = j * i++;
```

Write a small program to check your answers.

5. An int called motor controls the operation of an electric motor. The low order bit (bit 0) selects the direction: 1 is forward and 0 is reverse. The next bit (bit 1) switches the motor on and off: 1 is on. All the other bits should be set to 1. Write expressions to:

   (a) Initialize the motor control word.
   (b) Switch the motor on in the forward direction.
   (c) Switch the motor off without changing the direction bit.
   (d) Switch the motor on without changing the direction bit.
   (e) Change the direction of the motor to the opposite of its current state.

CHAPTER 4

Controlling execution

4.1 Selection statements

The ability to choose which statements are executed, based on some condition, is one of the most important features of a programming language. C++ provides two ways to do this: the `if` statement and the `switch` statement.

4.1.1 If statement

An `if` statement is used to optionally execute a statement, or to choose between two statements, depending on a condition. There are two formats for an `if` statement:

```
if ( condition ) statement-t
if ( condition ) statement-t else statement-f
```

In the first case, *statement-t* is only executed if *condition* evaluates to `true`. In the second, either *statement-t* is executed if *condition* is `true`, or *statement-f* if it is `false`. In both cases execution continues with the statement following the `if` statement. The statements *statement-t* and *statement-f* can be replaced by a block (also called a compound statement). So several statements can be used where one is expected:

```
if ( amount <= 10 )
   cout << amount << " items will be delivered" << endl;
else {
   cout << "Too many items for one delivery" << endl;
   amount = 10;
}
```

An `if` substatement can be another `if` statement. This is called a nested `if` statement:

```
if ( ... )        // if#1
   if ( ... )     // if#2
      ...;
   else           // else if#2
      ...;
```

In a nested `if` statement an `else` is connected to the nearest previous `if` without an `else`. So, in the above example, the `else` is connected to `if#2`. A block can be used to override this relationship. So the `else` associates with `if#1` in the following:

```
if ( ... ) {     // if#1
   if ( ... )     // if#2
      ...;
}
else             // else if#1
   ...;
```

A variable or named constant declared in an `if` substatement has local scope, even if it is a single statement. This means that we cannot have conditional declarations. After

```
if ( ... )
   int i;
```

the object `i` is not in scope and cannot be used. However, if a block is used the object is available within that local scope:

```
if ( ... ) {
   int i;
   // i can be used
}
// i is not defined
```

The draft ANSI standard proposes that a variable can also be declared in the *condition* of an `if` statement. Such a variable must be initialized and it cannot have the same name as any declaration in the substatements of the `if` statement. The name is in scope from the declaration to the end of the statement. The value of the *condition* is the value of the initialized variable.

4.1.2 Switch statement

In a `switch` statement control is passed to one of a number of statements depending on a condition. It has the form

`switch ( ` *condition* ` ) ` *statement*

where *condition* is an integral type (or a class object that can be converted to an integer). The body of the `switch` is *statement*. This is a block containing a number of statements and `case` labels. A `case` label is

```
case constant-expression :
```

There can also be one `default` label:

```
default :
```

Control is passed to the `case` label that has a *constant-expression* equal to *condition*. Duplicate `case` labels are not allowed in the same `switch` statement. If no match is found, control is passed to the `default` label or to the statement after the `switch` statement.

A `case` or `default` label defines an entry point. A `switch` statement does not finish when the next label is encountered. To terminate the execution of a `switch`, a `break` statement must be used. This may sound very complicated, but in practice it is simple:

```
switch ( ans ) {
case 'y':
case 'Y':
   cout << "Resetting totals" << endl;
   stock_total = 0;
   break;
case 'n':
case 'N':
   cout << "Totals not modified" << endl;
   break;
default:
   cout << "Invalid reply. Please try again" << endl;
}
```

Take care, if a `break` statement is missed out by mistake, execution will fall through into the next `case` label's statements. There will be no compilation error generated.

Names can be declared in the body of a `switch` statement. They are in scope from the declaration to the end of the `switch` statement. The draft ANSI standard proposes that variables can also be declared in the *condition* of a `switch` statement. Such a variable must be initialized, and this value is given to the *condition*.

4.2   Iteration statements

Iteration statements control the repeated execution of particular parts of a program. They are *loops*. There are three in C++: the `while`, `do` and `for` statements. To some extent these are interchangeable, but they are specialized to be useful in different situations. All of these statements check a Boolean expression to see if the iteration should continue. The value of this expression should be affected by the execution of the loop. If it is not, once the loop starts it can never finish.

4.2.1 While statement

A `while` statement executes a statement, or block of statements, zero or more times, while a condition evaluates to `true`. Its form is

```
while ( condition ) statement
```

The body of the `while` loop can be a single statement or a block, which is executed as long as *condition* evaluates to `true`. The condition is evaluated before each execution of the loop. If it evaluates to `false` the first time, the body of the `while` statement will not be executed. For example, the following calculates the sum of a sequence of numbers entered at the terminal:

```
int number = 0, sum = 0;
cout << "To stop enter a negative number" << endl;
while ( number >= 0 ) {
    sum += number;
    cout << "number: ";
    cin >> number;
}
cout << "Sum is " << sum << endl;
```

Names, such as variables and named constants, can be declared in the body of a `while` statement. They are in scope from their declaration to the end of the `while` statement. They are created and initialized during each pass through the loop and destroyed at the end of that iteration. The draft ANSI standard proposes that variables can also be declared in the *condition* of a `while` statement. Such a variable must be initialized, and this value is given to *condition*.

4.2.2 Do statement

A `do` statement executes a statement, or block of statements, one or more times, until a condition evaluates to `false`. Its form is as follows:

```
do statement while ( condition );
```

The body of the `do` loop can be a single statement or a block. This is executed once before *condition* is evaluated. If *condition* has the value `true`, the body of the loop is repeated. The condition is evaluated at the end of each iteration, and the loop repeats until it becomes `false`. As an example, here is a do statement that inputs a value for an integer variable called number:

```
int number;
bool goodnumber;
do {
    cout << "Give a whole positive number: ";
    cin >> number;
    if ( number >= 0 )
       goodnumber = true;
    else {
       cout << "Incorrect, number must be positive."
            << endl;
       goodnumber = false;
    }
} while ( !goodnumber );
```

Take care, the last line of a do statement can easily be confused with a while statement.

4.2.3 For statement

The for statement has the following form:

for (*dec-or-expr* ; *condition* ; *expression*) *statement*

where *dec-or-expr* is either a declaration or an expression, and *condition* is a Boolean expression. This, with a minor difference relating to the continue statement discussed in §4.3 is equivalent to a while statement that looks like this:

```
dec-or-expr;
while   (condition) {
        statement
    expression;
}
```

First, and only once, the expression or declaration *dec-or-expr* is performed. Then *condition* is checked. If it evaluates to `false` the first time, the body of the for statement is not executed. If *condition* is `true`, the body of the for statement is performed and *expression* is executed. Then *condition* is checked again, and so on until *condition* evaluates to `false`.

The *condition* or *expression* parts of a for statement can be omitted, but if *condition* is not present the for will loop forever. The scope of any names declared in *dec-or-expr* extends only to the end of the for statement.

Unfortunately, some compilers do not implement this ANSI C++ scope rule, and a variable name declared in *dec-or-expr* will exist outside the body of the `for` statement.

The `for` statement is most useful for loops using a variable that changes from a starting value, in fixed steps to a final value. This is very common when processing arrays (see §5.2), but for a non-array example consider:

```
for ( int i = 1; i <= 5; i++ )
    cout << i << ' ' << (i * 2) << endl;
```

Here, the integer variable `i` is declared and given an initial value of 1. Before each iteration the value of `i <= 5` is calculated. If this is `true`, the body of the `for` statement is executed. When this is done the value of `i` is incremented by one with `i++`. The effect of this loop is to execute an output statement five times, each time providing a new value of `i` counting from 1 to 5.

As with the other iteration statements, variables and named constants can be declared in the body of a `for` statement. As a matter of style, the controlled variable declared in the *dec-or-expr* part of a `for` statement should not be modified in the body of the loop.

Nested `for` loops are useful when more than one controlled variable is needed:

```
for ( int i = 1; i <= 2; i++ )
    for ( int j = 5; j <= 6; j++ )
        cout << i << " with " << j << endl;
```

This generates a sequence of `i` and `j` pairs: 1 with 5, 1 with 6, 2 with 5, and 2 with 6.

Comma operators are sometimes used with `for` statements. For example, the following produces 1 with 5 and 2 with 6:

```
int i, j;
for ( i = 1, j = 5; i <= 2; i++, j++ )
    cout << i << " with " << j << endl;
```

However, this is not very easy to understand. The following, without the commas, is much better:

```
int j = 5;
for ( int i = 1; i <= 2; i++  ) {
    cout << i << " with " << j << endl;
    j++;
}
```

4.3 Jump statements

A break statement can be used in a switch, while, do or for statement
to terminate its execution. When a break statement is encountered control
passes to the statement following the terminated statement. Use of the
break statement, except in a switch statement, should be treated with
suspicion. It can confuse the structure of a program. In most cases, the condition that will cause a break to be executed can be incorporated in the
condition part of the statement.

A continue statement can be used with a while, do or for statement
to skip to the end of its current iteration. In a do or while statement control
is passed immediately to the *condition* part of the statement. In a for
statement the *expression* part is performed before *condition* to ensure that
controlled variables are managed consistently. Take care when using a
continue with a while or a do. A continue can bypass the part of a
loop that modifies the variable tested in the loop's *condition,* causing unexpected behaviour.

The following for statement illustrates how break and continue
work:

```
for ( int i = 1 ; i <= 20 ; i++ ) {
    if ( i == 2 ) continue;
    if ( i == 5 ) break;
    cout << "i is " << i << endl;
}
```

Here, the for statement is specified to loop twenty times, with i going
from 1 to 20. However, when i is equal to 2, a continue is executed and
the rest of that particular iteration is skipped, so i is not printed. The for
statement continues until i equals 5, when a break statement is executed
which terminates the for statement. Thus, the variable i is only printed
when it has the values 1, 3 and 4.

C++ has a goto statement that will unconditionally pass control to a
labelled statement in the same function:

```
void silly()
{
    cout << "silly entered" << endl;
    goto end;
    cout << "will not print" << endl;
end:
    cout << "silly finished" << endl;
}
```

The goto statement should only be used under exceptional circumstances.
The ill considered use of goto statements can produce very poor programs

that are difficult to test and maintain. In almost every case the use of a selection or iteration statement is a much better choice.

4.4 An example

The following program prints multiplication tables. It uses while, do, for, if and switch statements. The overall structure of the program is simple. The outer while loop controls the printing of a whole multiplication table. First the user of the program is asked which table is wanted. This is done with a do loop. The table is actually printed with a for loop. Finally the user is asked if another table is wanted. The reply is processed by a switch statement that sets the condition controlling the outer while loop.

```
#include <iostream.h>
#include <iomanip.h>

const int TOP = 12;

void main()
{
   cout << endl;
   cout << "Tables Print Program" << endl;
   cout << "--------------------" << endl << endl;

   bool more = true;
   while ( more ) {
      int table;
      bool goodans;
      do {
         cout << "Give required table (2 to 12): ";
         cin >> table;
         if (table >= 2 && table <= 12)
            goodans = true;
         else {
            cout << "Table must be in range 2 to 12, "
                 "please try again" << endl;
            goodans = false;
         }
      } while ( !goodans );
      cout << endl;
      for ( int i = 1; i <= TOP; i++ ) {
         cout << table << " x " << setw(2) << i
              << " = " << table * i << endl;
      }
      char ans;
```

```
        cout << endl << "Another table ( y or n ) ";
        cin >> ans;
        switch ( ans ) {
        case 'Y':
        case 'y':
           more = true;
           break;
        default:               // 'n' and 'N'
           more = false;
        }
    }
}
```

4.5 Exercises

1. Write a program to calculate the sum of the integers between two values input at the terminal.
2. Calculate the factorial of a value input at the terminal. The factorial of an integer n is given by n! = 1 × 2 × 3 × ... × n. By convention 0! = 1.
3. Write a short program to print out a character's binary code. You may assume that a `char` is 8 bits long. For example, given the character S, the program should print 01010011 on a machine using ASCII coding. (A hint: the rightmost bit of a negative number is 1.)
4. Iteration can be used to solve some mathematical problems numerically. For example, the values of x for which $x^3-x-1=0$ can be found using Newton's method. In this case, the method involves finding successive values of x using the formula:

$$x_{n+1} = x_n - \frac{x_n^3 - x_n - 1}{3x_n^2 - 1}$$

The result will converge to the required value of x. Write a program to perform this calculation. Stop when the difference between successive values of x is less than or equal to 0.001. To calculate the difference use the standard function `fabs`, which returns the absolute value of a floating point number. Include the standard mathematics library `<math.h>` for this function.
5. Write a program that prints a multiplication matrix, like this:

```
     1  2  3  .  12
     2  4  6  .  .
     3  6  9  .  .
     4  .  .  .  .

     .  .  .  .  .
    12  .  .  .  .
```

CHAPTER 5

Compound types

5.1 Pointers

A pointer is an object that holds the location of another object. It is typed, so it can only point to objects of a particular type. To declare a pointer, an * is used with a type name. So the following declares a pointer to an integer:

```
int* pntr2int;
```

To use a pointer it must first be given a value, which is the address of a suitably typed object. The prefix & operator can be applied to the name of a variable or constant to get its address. This can be assigned to a pointer of the correct type, or used to initialize it. A pointer can also be used to assign or initialize another pointer of the same type:

```
int anint;                  // an integer variable
float afloat;               // a floating point variable
int* pntr2int;              // a pointer to an int
pntr2int = &anint;          // assign a pointer
pntr2int = anint;           // error - anint is not a pointer
pntr2int = &afloat;         // error - afloat is not an integer

float* pntr2float = &afloat;    // initialized pointers
int* anotherpntr = pntr2int;    // initialized pointer
```

To access the object being pointed at, a pointer must be *dereferenced*. This is done by preceding the pointer name with an *. The type of a dereferenced pointer is the type of the object being pointed at. For example,

```
*pntr2float = 6 * *pntr2int;
```

Here, an integer value is multiplied by six, and the result is assigned to a floating point variable. Take care, arithmetic can be performed directly on a pointer. So the expression `*pntr2int++` is valid, but it adds the physical length of an `int` variable to the pointer rather than adding one to the `int` object pointed to. Parentheses are used to resolve the problem like this: `(*pntr2int)++`. There are a number of ways a pointer can be combined with an increment or decrement operator. Table 5.1 shows the possibilities. However, pointer arithmetic normally only makes sense in the context of arrays, and this is explored in §5.2.1.

Table 5.1   Pointers and increment operators.

Equivalent syntax		Meaning
`++(*p)`	`++*p`	pre-increment object pointed to
`(*p)++`		post-increment object pointed to
`*(++p)`	`*++p`	access via pointer that has been incremented
`*(p++)`	`*p++`	access via pointer, post-increment pointer

The value of a pointer can change while a program is running. So the same dereferenced name can refer to a different object at different times:

```
int count1, count2;
int* counter = &count1;
*counter = 3;              // refers to count1
counter = &count2;
*counter = 6;              // refers to count2
```

This feature is very useful for implementing dynamic data structures (see §5.4), and for supporting polymorphism with class objects (see Ch. 11), but it can be very confusing if used carelessly.

A pointer that temporarily points to nothing can be given a zero value. This is called a *null* pointer. Any attempt to dereference a null pointer will cause a run-time error:

```
int* p2int;          // pointer value undefined
p2int = 0;           // a null pointer
*p2int = 294;        // run-time error - invalid pointer
p2int = &count       // assign a valid address
*p2int = 294;        // okay now
p2int = 375;         // error - non-zero integer
```

The `const` qualifier can be used with a pointer to restrict its behaviour. We can have a constant pointer, a pointer to a constant object, or both. Table 5.2 shows the possible combinations. Like any other constant, a `const` pointer has to be initialized, and it cannot be modified. A pointer to a `const` object can hold the address of a constant or non-constant object, but in either case the object cannot be modified via the pointer. The address of a `const` object cannot be stored in a pointer to a non-const object. The following demonstrates these restrictions:

Table 5.2 Constant pointer declarations.

Declaration	Type of p
`T* p;`	pointer to an object of type `T`
`const T* p;`	pointer to a constant object of type `T`
`T* const p;`	constant pointer to an object of type `T`
`T const *P;`	constant pointer to an object of type `T`
`const T* const p;`	constant pointer to a constant object of type `T`

```
int anint, anotherint;
int* const constp2int = &anint; // constant pointer must be
                                //    initialized
constp2int = &anotherint;       // error - cannot modify
                                //    constant pointer

const int* p2constint;          // a pointer to a constant
p2constint = &anint;            // okay to point to a
                                //    non-constant
*p2constint = 37;               // error - cannot modify it
const int CONSTINT = 10;
int* p2int;
p2int = &CONSTINT;              // error - cannot assign
                                //    const int* to int*
```

When a pointer is being declared, the * operator actually associates with the object name rather than the type name. So in

```
int* p2int1, p2int2; // possible mistake
```

`p2int2` is an `int`, not a pointer to `int`. The compiler will catch this when the variable is used, and it is easy to fix. Either declare each pointer as a separate statement, or write it like this:

```
int *p2int1, *p2int2;
```

The use of pointers with arrays and structures is discussed in §5.2.1 and §5.4.1.

5.2 Arrays

An array is a collection of objects of the same type. Each element of an array is accessed using one or more subscripts, depending on the dimension of the array. For example, a one dimensional array of five integers called `total` is declared like this:

```
int total[5];
```

The elements of `total` are accessed using the subscript operator `[]`:

```
total[3] = 5 + total[2];
```

The first element of an array has the subscript zero. The last element has a subscript one less than the declared size of the array. So for example, `total[0]` and `total[4]` are the first and last elements of the above array. C++ arrays are not bound checked, so it is easy to read or write off the end of them, with unpredictable results. This can damage data or even crash a program. It is likely that the emerging ANSI standard for C++ will include one or more libraries that provide bound checked alternatives to ordinary C++ arrays.

An array object cannot be modified as a whole. In particular, one array cannot be assigned to another, even if it has the same type and size. This kind of operation has to be done on an element by element basis:

```
float insidetemp[10];
float outsidetemp[10];
...
insidetemp = outsidetemp;               // error
for ( int i = 0; i < 10 ; i++ )         // okay
    insidetemp[i] = outsidetemp[i];
insidetemp++;                           // error
for ( int j = 0; j < 10 ; j++ )         // okay
    insidetemp[j]++;
```

An array can have an initializer, which is a list of values for array elements in subscript order:

```
int total[5] = { 3, 5, 2, 5, 8 };
```

If the initializer has too few items to fill the array, zeros are added. It is an error to have too many items, and the list must contain at least one item:

```
int total1[5] = { 23, 65 }; // is the same as
int total2[5] = { 23, 65, 0, 0, 0 };
int total5[5] = {0};          // all elements are zero
int total3[5] = { 23, 65, 0, 0, 0, 0 }; // error - too many
int total4[5] = {};           // error - must be at least one
```

The size of the array can be omitted if an initializer is used. So the following declares an array of three double numbers:

```
double size[] = { 3.7, 5, 2 };
```

An array can be declared as a constant. None of the elements of such an array can be modified:

```
const double MAXSIZE[3] = { 1.5, 2.5, 3.5 };
MAXSIZE[0] = 3.6;          // error
```

Multidimensional arrays are easy to define. For example, the following is an initialized array with three rows and two columns:

```
int matrix[3][2] = {{1,2},{3,4},{5,6}};
```

Like its one dimensional counterpart, a multidimensional array initializer does not have to be complete, and missing elements are given a zero value. However, only the first dimension size can be omitted:

```
int matrix1[3][2] = {{1},{3,4}};
int matrix2[][2] = {{1,2},{3},{5,6}};
int matrix2[][] = {{1,2},{3,4},{5,6}}; // dimension error
```

Access to an element of a multidimensional array needs as many subscripts as there are dimensions. For example,

```
matrix[1][0] = matrix[2][1] + 6; // access and assignment
// add one to every element of matrix ...
for ( int row = 0; row < 3 ; row++ )
   for ( int col = 0; col < 2 ; col++ )
      matrix[row][col]++;
```

5.2.1   Pointers and arrays

Pointers and arrays have a special relationship. An array can be converted into a pointer to the first element of the array, and a pointer to an array can be used as though it were an array name:

```
int test[10];
int* p2test = test;      // convert array to pointer
*p2test = 24;            // change test[0]
p2test[2] = 32;          // use pointer as array
```

If an array is declared as const, any associated pointers must be declared as pointing to a constant object:

```
const int carray[] = {1,2,3,4,5};
const int* p2carray = carray; // this is okay
int* p2carray = carray;  // error - not a pointer to const
*p2carray = 99;          // error - array is const
```

Simply demonstrated, an ability to treat a pointer as though it were an array name may appear to be useless, but it makes managing dynamically allocated arrays easy. How this is put into practice is discussed in §5.8.

Arithmetic can be performed on pointers that automatically takes account of array element size. This is simplest for one dimensional arrays. For example, given an integer array declared as int test[ASIZE], the following will print it out:

```
int* p2array = test; // address of test array
for ( int i = 0; i < ASIZE; i++ )
   cout << *p2array++ << ' ';
cout << endl;
```

Here, the location of an integer array is converted into the pointer p2array. Then, in the for loop, the expression *p2array++ dereferences the pointer to print the value of an array element, and then increments p2array to point at the next element of the array. Table 5.1 shows the ways in which pointers and increment operators can be combined. However, the use of pointer arithmetic instead of subscripts is not recommended. Pointer arithmetic is popular with some traditional C programmers because it can be quicker, but subscripts are much easier to understand, and in practice the gain in efficiency is often marginal.

If pointer arithmetic has to be used, then a knowledge of how arrays are physically stored is required. Array elements are stored in consecutive memory locations. For multidimensional arrays, the elements are stored so that in effect the rightmost subscript varies fastest. So for int a[4][3], which is an array with four rows of three integers, the first three elements in store are the first row's int values in subscript order. These are followed by the second row's elements, and so on. Handling a multidimensional array is further complicated because it does not automatically convert into a pointer to its first element, so an explicit reinterpret_cast is required (see §13.2.3.)

5.3   C strings

A C *string* is a sequence of characters stored in an array of char of sufficient length. The sequence is terminated by a NUL character which is written as '\0'. So this is a C string:

```
char dog[5] = { 'C', 'l', 'e', 'o', '\0' };
```

It is much more convenient to used string literals for initializing character arrays. The literal must be able to fit into the array:

```
char dog[5] = "Cleo";            // just enough room
char littledog[5] = "Moss";      // more than enough room
char terrier[] = "Penny";        // array size is 6
char anotherdog[7] = "Brollie";  // error literal too long
```

Be careful when choosing the length of a char array. It must be at least one character longer than the longest string it will have to store, because it must be able to store a terminating zero. If special characters, like \n, are used in a string, they are stored in a single character.

Like any other array, a string cannot be directly assigned to another string. A string has to be explicitly copied character by character. However, there is a standard C string library that offers a number of useful string functions, including strcpy, which copies one string to another, strcmp, which compares strings, and strlen, which gives the length of a string, excluding its terminating NUL character. The header file <string.h>, not to be confused with <string>, must be included if these functions are used. The following shows some of the ways that C strings can be used in C++:

```
#include <string.h>

char dog1[10] = "Cleo";
char dog2[] = "Brollie";
char dog3[10];

// Explicit string copy from dog2 to dog3
int i = 0;
while ( dog1[i] != '\0' ) {
   dog3[i] = dog1[i];
   i++;
}
dog3[i] = '\0';

// Using string library copy function to copy dog2 to dog3
strcpy(dog3,dog2);

// Using string compare
if ( strcmp(dog1,"Cleo") == 0 )       // strings equal
   cout << "Cleo found" << end;
if ( strcmp(dog1,"Cleo") < 0 )        // dog1 < "Cleo"
   cout << "Cleo after" << end;
if ( strcmp(dog1,"Cleo") > 0 )        // dog1 > "Cleo"
   cout << "Cleo before" << end;

// Using string length
cout << strlen(dog1) << end;
```

C strings can be declared as constants, which must be initialized:

```
const char TERRIER[] = "Penny";
strcpy(TERRIER,dog2);  //    error - cannot modify constant
```

C strings can be formed into arrays. An array of C strings can be defined as a two dimensional array of characters like this:

```
char [5][10] dogs;
char [5][10] moredogs = {"Rover","Fido"};
```

Both of the above are arrays of five strings each able to hold up to nine characters. An alternate, and preferred, style is to introduce a `typedef` name. These names are discussed in §5.6, but the following shows how one can be used for a C string:

```
typedef char DogString[10];
DogString dogs[5];
DogString moredogs[5] = {"Rover","Fido"};
```

C strings are very common in C++ programs, but they have limitations such as no bounds checking, and restricted copy semantics. C++ string objects, described in §3.3, are much safer and easier to use. If it is necessary, a C++ `string` variable or constant can be converted to a C string like this:

```
char newdog[20];                  // C string
string mydog = "Penny";           // C++ string
strcpy(newdog,mydog.c_str());     // conversion to string
```

5.4   Structures

Many languages offer a record type. In C++ this is called a structure. In an array all the elements are the same type, but in a structure the elements (or members) can be of different types. For example, the following is a structure of type `Account` that has two data members:

```
struct Account {
    int number;
    float balance;
};
```

Members cannot be given initializers in a `struct` declaration, but an initializer can be specified when an instance of the structure is defined. This gives values for the structure's members in the order they appear in its declaration. A instance of a structure can also be used as an initializing value. So for example, instances of `Account` can be defined like this:

```
Account myaccount;
Account savings = myaccount;
Account expenses = { 1293, 12.56 };
const Account SPECIAL = { 9999, 10.00 };
```

The members of a `struct` object are accessed with a *dot* operator:

```
myaccount.balance = 56.02;
current = expenses.number;
cout << SPECIAL.balance;
```

```
SPECIAL.number = 7893;      // error - cannot modify constant
```

Structures of the same type can be assigned to each other, which applies a copy operation to each member in turn. However, most other operations are not supported:

```
myaccount = expenses;             // assignment okay
if ( myaccount == expenses )      // error
    ...;
myaccount++;                      // error
```

There is an alternative way to define an instance of a `struct`. A `struct` declaration can be immediately followed by an instance name. The `struct` name can be omitted if no other instances of the structure are wanted:

```
struct {
    int amember;
} aninstance;
```

Structures and classes have a lot in common. Class features, such as member functions and constructors, can also be used with structures. (A structure is actually just a class with default public access.) There is much more about classes later, starting in Chapter 7.

5.4.1 Pointers and structures

Structures can be accessed with pointers. This is done by explicitly dereferencing the pointer and using the dot operator, or by using the `->` operator:

```
Dog* p2dog = &mydog;      // pointer to a Dog
(*p2dog).age = 4;         // dot notation
p2dog->age = 4;           // -> notation
```

Here, the two assignment statements are equivalent. If the `*` operator is used, the dereferenced pointer must be enclosed in parentheses. Failure to do this will generate an error because the dot operator will be applied directly to the pointer, which is not a structure. The `->` operator is the preferred method because of its simplicity.

A structure can contain a member that is a pointer to an instance of itself:

```
struct Node {
    int data;
    Node* next;
};
```

Such a pointer is used to connect two instances of the structure:

```
Node node1, node2;
node1.next = &node2;
node1.next->data = 67;
```

Here, the `next` member of `node1` is used to modify the `data` member of `node2`.

5.5   Unions

A `union` looks similar to a `struct`, but the different members of a union are alternatives stored in the same place. So only one member can be stored in a union at a time. For example the following structure can store a `float`, an `int` or an array of `char` in its `union` part:

```
enum Vdatatype { VFLOAT, VINT, VNAME };

struct Vardata {
   Vdatatype utype;
   union {
      float afloat;
      int   anint;
      char  name[8];
   };
};
```

Here, the `utype` member indicates what type of data is currently being stored in `union`. But there is no automatic check, so a union can be misused:

```
Vardata store;
store.utype = VNAME;
strcpy(store.name,"fred");
store.afloat += 1.2345;      // valid but ...
   // whoops - assigning the wrong type of data to union
```

A union can be also be given a name and used like a structure in its own right:

```
union Dataunion {
   float afloat;
   int   anint;
   char  name[8];
};

Dataunion udata;
udata.anint - 5;
```

Unions are dangerous because it is very easy to access data using the wrong member. However, they can offer considerable space optimization for variant data. In general they are best avoided. But if they are used, encapsulate them in a class, and provide safe access via member functions as explained in Chapter 7.

There are some restrictions on how a union can be specified and used. It can have member functions, like a C++ class (see Ch. 7), but it cannot have virtual functions (see Ch. 11). It cannot have a base class or be used as a base class (see Ch. 10). A union cannot contain data members that are instances of classes with constructors (see §7.2), destructors (see §7.3), or user defined assignment operators (see §9.2.2).

5.6 Typedef names

Alternative type names can be declared using a typedef specifier. A typedef name is just a synonym for another type, and it can only be used in the same way as the original. The original type name is still available, and a single type can be given several different typedef names. A typedef does not introduce a new type in the way a class, structure or enumeration does. For example, given these typedef statements:

```
typedef char* Cstring;
typedef int Vector[3];
```

The following pairs of declarations are equivalent:

```
Cstring a;              char* a;
Cstring b, c, d;        char *b, *c, *d;
Vector v;               int v[3];
```

A typedef name obeys the same scope rules as other names. A typedef name can be declared more than once in the same scope if the declarations are identical. Otherwise typedef names must be unique within their scope. The following example shows how these rules work:

```
struct Mystruct {
    typedef float Value;    // local to Mystruct
    Value avalue;           // type is float
};

void funct()
{
    typedef char Value;     // local to funct
    Value avalue;           // type is char
}

typedef int Value;
```

```
typedef Value Anothername; // okay  - a typedef can use a
                                      typedef name
typedef int Value;          // okay  - typedef can be
                                      repeated
typedef float Value;        // error - different type to
                                      previous typedef
typedef int Mystruct;       // error - name already declared

void main()
{
    Value avalue;           // type is int
}
```

The use of `typedef` is generally a matter of style. Some programmers use them a lot, others not much, if at all. They can help with the definition of C strings and the dynamic allocation of multidimensional arrays, as shown in §5.3 and §5.8. A `typedef` is often used to hide the explicit use of `*` in pointer definitions. They can be used to introduce meaningful type names, and they are often used in libraries to improve portability.

5.7   Reference types

A reference is an alternative name for an object. They are normally used with function parameters (see §6.2), but they can be used independently. A reference type is specified by putting `&` after a type name. So `X&` means reference to X. For example,

```
int i = 2;
int& r = i;      // r and i refer to same variable
int j = r;       // j = 2
r = 6;           // i = 6
```

References must be given a value when they are defined. A variable reference must be initialized to an lvalue, but a constant reference can be initialized to a constant:

```
int& i = 2;        // error
const int& j = 2;  // ok
```

Do not confuse pointers and references. They can sometimes be used to achieve the same result, but it is best to make a clear distinction to avoid confusion. Use reference types for function parameters and return values, and use pointers for memory management and dynamic data structures.

5.8   Memory management

Pointers and dynamic memory management are closely related. Computer memory can be explicitly allocated and deallocated while a program is running, and pointers store memory locations. Memory is allocated by creating objects with the new operator, which returns the location of the created object. This location is stored in a pointer of the correct type:

```
int* p2int = 0;                 // pointer initialized as null
p2int = new int;                // allocate memory for an int
float* p2float = new float(67.3); // an initialized float
Dog* mydog = new Dog;           // a Dog struct
```

Most objects created with new can be given an initial value, as show with p2float. Structures, like classes, can be given an initial value, but this involves constructors which are described in §7.2 and §8.3. It is often important to be able to identify a pointer that does not currently hold the location of an object. This is done by giving the pointer a zero value, which is called the null pointer.

   A dynamically allocated object has no name and can only be accessed with a pointer that holds its location. The pointer is simply dereferenced to gain access to the object's data. If the object is a structure (or a class), the -> operator is used to access its members:

```
*p2int = 45 + *p2int / 5;
mydog->age = 2;
```

   An object created with new has *dynamic storage duration*. This means that its lifetime is not limited to its scope. It exists for the lifetime of the program, or until it is destroyed with the delete operator. This operator is used on a pointer to the object to be destroyed:

```
delete p2int;    // destroy an integer
delete mydog;    // destroy a Dog structure
```

Never use a pointer *value* after it has been used with a delete operator. A delete operator can only be applied to pointer values created with new, or to a pointer with a zero value. Applying delete to a zero pointer has no effect. A delete operator cannot be used with a pointer to a constant object.

   There is no automatic *garbage collection* in C++. Destroying a pointer or overwriting a pointer value will not destroy the object pointed to, or reallocate its memory. A delete operator must be used before a pointer value is thrown away. Failure to do this will cause a *memory leak*. Always remember that in itself the definition of a pointer does not allocate any storage for the target object. A common error is to define a C string as say char* name, and then fail to load it with a pointer value. This looks like a valid string, so it can be used with something as simple as `strcpy(name,"abcd")`, which will seriously damage the program.

If a `new` operation fails, most compilers will throw an exception called something like `alloc` or `bad_alloc`. Exceptions are explained in §13.1, but here it is enough to know that if nothing is done to manage the exception the program will be terminated.

As an example of how to use `new` and `delete`, the following demonstrates how a dynamic data structure can be built using a `struct` and some pointers. It is a *stack* implemented as a *linked list*. A stack is a data store that has first-on last-off behaviour. Putting an item into a stack is called a *push* operation, and the removal of an item is called *pop*. So a pop retrieves the most recently pushed item from a stack. A linked list is a sequence of dynamically allocated structures (or classes) connected by pointers.

In practice, a dynamic data structure like this would have the *push* and *pop* operations implemented as member functions of a class (see Ch. 7). But to show the basic technique, this will do:

```
struct Node {
   int data;
   Node* next;
};

Node* stack;   // global stack root

void main()
{
   Node* temp;

   // initialize stack as empty
   stack = 0;
   ...
   // push item on stack
   temp = new Node;
   temp->data = 1;
   temp->next = stack;
   stack = temp;
   ...
   // pop item off stack
   int data;
   if ( stack == 0 )
      cout << "stack empty" << endl;
   else {
      data = stack->data;
      temp = stack;
      stack = stack->next;
```

```
    delete temp;
  }
  cout << data << endl;
}
```

Here, the variable `stack` points to the top of a linked list of Node structures. To push an integer value onto the stack, a Node is created using new.
The value is stored in this, which is then inserted at the front of the linked
list. The example shows the first item being pushed onto the stack. Later
items can use exactly the same algorithm. The pop operation is the reverse.
It removes a Node from the linked list, leaving the root pointer `stack`
pointing at the front of a list of the remaining instances of Node.

   C++ has some very sophisticated ways of modifying the standard way
of managing memory. In particular the behaviour of new and `delete` can
be modified. This and other features of these operators are discussed in
§9.2.6.

Dynamic arrays

Arrays can be dynamically allocated and deallocated using the new and
`delete[]` operators. One dimensional arrays are created like this:

```
Dog* dogset = new Dog[5];    // an array of 5 Dog structures
int* count = new int[size];  // an array of size integers
```

   The new operator returns the location of the array. For a one dimensional
array this is a pointer to the first element of the array. Hence the int* type
for count in the above example. The number of elements in the array must
be given, but the value can be supplied as a variable. So it is possible to
decide on the size of a dynamic array at run-time. An array cannot be
explicitly initialized when it is created with new. But if the element type is
a structure or a class, and a default constructor is defined (see §7.2), it will
be invoked for each element of the array.

   Dynamically allocated arrays are accessed just like normal arrays using
subscript notation:

```
int* vector = new int[3];
vector[1] = 4;
```

There is nothing special about this. As explained earlier in §5.2.1, any
pointer to an array can be used as though it were an ordinary array name.
There are some differences. Unlike static arrays, a dynamic array name can
be used with an assignment operator. However, only the pointer is copied
not the dynamically allocated array. This is called a shallow copy.

   Multidimensional arrays can cause problems, but a typedef can help.
A statically defined two dimensional array can be declared like this:

```
typedef int Vector[3];
Vector matrix1[5];            // same as int matrix[5][3]
```

Dynamically allocating a similar array needs a pointer, and this is declared using the `typedef` name:

```
Vector* matrix2 = new Vector[5];
Vector* matrix3 = new int[5][3];
```

Both of these are equivalent, but the first is preferred. The first dimension can be a variable, but the size used in the `typedef` must be a constant. We are in effect allocating a one dimensional array of `Vector` arrays:

```
typedef int Vector[3];
Vector* matrix4 = new Vector[size];
```

Dynamically allocated multidimensional arrays can have only one variable dimension, all other dimensions must be fixed at compile-time. However, this restriction can be avoided by simulating a multidimensional array with a dynamically allocated one dimensional array and a mapping function. The function supports multidimensional behaviour by converting a list of subscripts into an offset for an element in the one dimensional array. This method is demonstrated in the solution to Exercise 8.4 given in Appendix A.

Accessing a dynamically allocated multidimensional array is the same as for its static equivalent:

```
matrix4[2][3] = 24;
```

To destroy a dynamically allocated array, use the `delete[]` operator with the pointer like this:

```
delete[] matrix4;
```

As with other dynamically allocated objects, never use a pointer *value* after it has been used with a `delete` operator. Do not use `delete[]` on non-array objects, and do not use `delete` without `[]` on arrays. The `delete` operators can only be applied to pointer values created with `new`, or to a pointer with a zero value. Applying `delete[]` to a zero pointer has no effect. The `delete[]` operator cannot be used with a pointer to a constant array. If the element type of the array is a structure or class, and a destructor is defined (see §7.3), it will be invoked for each element of the array before the memory is deallocated.

5.9 Exercises

1. Write a program that inputs five floating point numbers and stores them in an array. After all the numbers are input, the program should print them out. Then calculate and print the average of the values stored in that array.

2. Write a program that inputs a word and checks if it is a palindrome. A palindrome is a word, the letters of which when taken in the reverse direction read the same. Use C strings. The <string.h> functions strlen and strcmp might be useful.

3. Consider the stack example given in §5.8. Write short algorithms in C++ to:
   (a) Print out all of the data items stored in the stack.
   (b) Destroy the whole stack.

4. A linked list is used to store names and account numbers. A node in this list is an instance of the structure:

```
struct Node {
      string name;
      int account;
      Node* next;
}
```

The address of the first node in the list is stored in a pointer called accountlist. Write an algorithm in C++ that creates an independent copy of this list. The new list should be in the same order as the original, and the location of its first node should be stored in a pointer called duplicate.

5. A dynamically created array called height contains 10 floating point numbers. Unfortunately it is too small. Write an algorithm in C++ that will double the array's size without losing any of the stored numbers.

CHAPTER 6
Functions

A function is an executable sub-unit of a program. It has a name; it can be given arguments to operate on and it can return a value. A function typically takes data from one or more input arguments, and passes back data by way of either output arguments or as the return value of the function. For example, we can define the following function:

```
double max( double a, double b )
{
    if ( a > b )
        return a;
    else
        return b;
}
```

This has the name max, and it has two parameters, a and b. It returns a value of type double, which is the larger of a or b. It might be used in an expression such as:

```
total = 6.3 + max(10.3,invalue) * 0.25
```

When this expression is evaluated the function max is *called* with arguments 10.3 and invalue. These values are passed to the function as its parameters. When the function's execution is complete, its returned value is used in the rest of the expression.

Functions are a very powerful design concept. A program can normally be separated into a number of parts, each represented by a function. A function's behaviour can be specified in terms of its parameters and return type. It can then be written and tested in isolation from the rest of the program. Functions can often be reused in different parts of the program. Groups of related functions can be written as program components stored in a file separate from the main program. General purpose functions can be written to be used in a number of programs. Indeed, there are standard libraries, such as <string.h> and <math.h>, that provide lots of useful functions.

A function must be declared before it is called. This can be done by providing a full function definition, or just by giving a declaration. A function declaration, or prototype, is the part of the function that specifies how it can be called. So for the max function defined above, a declaration is:

```
double max( double, double );
```

As this shows, names do not have to be given for parameters in a declaration. A definition matching this declaration must be supplied somewhere else in the program. A function can be declared, but not defined, inside another function.

The primary part of a C++ program takes the form of a function with the name main. This can have parameters and a return value as explained in §6.8. However, it cannot be used like a normal function. It is automatically invoked just once when the program is executed, and it cannot be explicitly called like other functions.

The structure of a program with functions can take a number of forms. Some programmers put the declarations for all the functions in a program before main, and the matching definitions after main. Others make the declarations local by putting them in the functions where they are used. As before, they still put the declarations at the end of the program after main.

Both of these approaches are okay, but a simpler and perfectly satisfactory way is to put all function definitions *before* main, and not to use declarations unless absolutely necessary. If one function calls another, the called function must be defined before the calling function. Very rarely two functions will call each other, in which case a function declaration will have to be used as a *forward reference*. This is the approach used in this book. Larger programs are normally split into separate files, and function declarations are very useful in this context (see §8.9).

6.1 Scope and duration

Variables are commonly declared inside a function. These variables can only be used inside the function after their declaration. They are said to have *local* scope within the function. In general, locally declared variables are destroyed when a function ends. Their duration is the same as their scope. Parameter names have local scope.

Variables declared outside a function have *global* scope, and these can be used in any function defined after their declaration. The duration of a global variable is the lifetime of the program. If a local variable has the same name as a global variable, the local variable is accessed when the name is used. However, the global variable can be specified by putting : : in front of the name.

These scope rules also apply to named constants, enumeration and typedef names. For example, in the following function the local name SCALEFACT hides the global constant of the same name:

```
const float SCALEFACT = 3.6;
const float PI = 3.142;

float transform( float before )
{
    const float SCALEFACT = 1.5;
    float prescale;
    prescale = 2 * before * PI ;
    return prescale * SCALEFACT;      // local constant used
}
```

A local variable declared as static is initialized once in the lifetime of the program, and it is not destroyed at the end of the function. This feature has limited use, but it can be used to count the number of times a function is called. For example, this function counts up from eight:

```
int demo()
{
    static count = 8;
    return count++;
}
```

6.2   Parameters

A function parameter can be declared for input and output, or for input only. A parameter has a type, which specifies what sort of object can be used as an argument for that parameter when the function is called. Input–output parameters are distinguished from input-only parameters by being suffixed with an &. This makes them reference types, which are described in §5.7. For example, the following trivial function triples the value of its first parameter, returning the output value through its second parameter. It does not return a function value, so its function type is void:

```
void triple( int in, int& out )
{
    in *= 3;
    out = in;
}
```

Here, both parameters are modified inside the function, but the effects are different. An input-only parameter can be modified, but the argument in the calling function will not change because a *copy* of the argument is passed to the called function. However, when an input–output parameter is modified the argument in the calling function is changed. We say that input-only arguments are *passed by value* and that input–output arguments are *passed by reference*.

The type of the arguments used when the function is called must match the parameters in the function definition. Constants can be used as input-only arguments. So `triple` can be called like this:

```
int input = 4;
int output1, output2;
triple(input,output1);
triple(42,output2);
triple(input,6);           // error - 2nd argument constant
triple("hello",output2);   // error - 1st argument not int
```

A function can be defined with no parameters by giving it an empty parameter list. But parentheses must still be used when it is called:

```
void print_copyright()
{
    cout << "(c) A.P.Robson 1996";
}

print_copyright();
```

6.2.1   Structures

A structure (or class) can be used as a parameter in the same way as a fundamental type:

```
struct Stockitem {
    int id;
    int quantity;
};
void merge( Stockitem s1, Stockitem& s2 )
{
    s2.quantity = s2.quantity + s1.quantity;
}
```

It is often more efficient to pass a large structure by reference rather than by value, even if is only being used for input, because it will not be copied. However, such a parameter should be declared as constant:

```
void print( const Stockitem& sitem )
{   // sitem cannot be modified
    cout << sitem.id << ":" << sitem.quantity << endl;
}
```

6.2.2 Pointers

A pointer can be specified as a parameter in a number of ways. For example,

```
void funct1( Node* list )
void funct2( const Node* list )
void funct3( Node*& list )
```

Here, funct1 can modify the Node object pointed to by the parameter, but it cannot change the pointer argument. The function funct2 cannot modify the object or the pointer. If the pointer is going to be modified, use a reference as shown with funct3, which also allows modification of the object pointed to by the parameter.

A pointer parameter is treated in the same way as any pointer object. In particular, its argument must be the name of a pointer of the same type, or the address of a suitable object.

6.2.3 Arrays

Arrays can be used as function parameters, but they behave in a different way from other types of parameter. For example,

```
void copy_cstring( const char sin[], char sout[] )
{
    int i = 0;
    while ( sin[i] != 0 ) {
        sout[i] = sin[i];
        i++;
    }
    sout[i] = 0;
}
```

Here, the first parameter sin is input only because it is defined with const. But the second parameter sout is input–output, so it can be modified.

Array parameters are modifiable by default. This is different from non-array parameters, where an input–output parameter has to be identified with an &. The above function can be called with array names or a literal as arguments:

$$(\text{int} \& \ a) \quad \equiv \quad (\text{int} * \ a)_{65}$$

$$a = b \qquad\qquad *a = b$$

```
char string1[20] = "abcde";
char string2[20];
copy_cstring(string1,string2);
copy_cstring("fgh",string1);
copy_cstring(string1,"fgh"); // error - 2nd argument cannot
                             //             be a literal
```

A multidimensional array can be declared as a parameter but it must have all but its first dimension's size specified:

```
const int COLS = 5;

void print( int matrix[][COLS], int row )
{
   for ( int i = 0; i < row; i++ ) {
      for ( int j = 0; j < COLS; j++ )
         cout << matrix[i][j] << ' ';
      cout << endl;
   }
}
```

Here, the second dimension of matrix is fixed, but the number of rows is given at run-time. So this function will accept any two dimensional array of int with five columns. All the dimension sizes can be specified in a parameter declaration, but the first will still be ignored for type checking. The above print function can be used like this:

```
int matrix1[3][5];
int matrix2[3][6];
print(matrix1,3);   // okay - matrix has 3 rows and 5 columns
print(matrix1,4);   // okay but incorrect - matrix has 3 rows
print(matrix2,3);   // compile error - matrix has 6 columns
```

A one dimensional array can be automatically converted into a pointer to its element type, which contains the location of the first element in the array. So it is possible to declare array parameters as pointers. For example, the following is the equivalent of copy_cstring using pointers instead of subscripts:

```
void copy_string( const char* sin, char* sout )
{
   while ( *sout++ = *sin++ );
}
```

This style of manipulating arrays is more compact, but it is not as easy to understand as the subscript version. So in general, using pointers to access arrays like this is not recommended.

6.2.4 Default arguments

Default argument values can be specified for functions. However, they must be at the end of the parameter list, and they cannot be used with reference parameters. For example,

```
double percent( double val, double pcent = 1.0 )
{
    return val / 100 * pcent;
}
```

LISP
&optional (pcent 1.0)

This function can be called with:

```
amount = percent(50);        // amount is 0.5
amount = percent(50,50);     // amount is 25
```

6.3   Return values

A function is normally declared with a return type in front of its name. If a function does not return a value, it should be given a return type of `void`. Functions that do not return a value are sometimes referred to as procedures. If a function is not given a type, it is assumed to return `int`.

A function not declared as `void` must end its execution with a `return` statement containing an expression of the correct type. There can be more than one `return` statement in a function, and the function will terminate when one of these is executed:

```
int max( int a, int b )
{
    if ( a > b )
        return a;
    else
        return b;
}
```

The function `max` returns the value of its largest parameter and it can be used wherever an `int` constant is valid:

```
int biggest = max(umber1,umber2);
space = 26 * max(9,length);
cout << "biggest is " << max(length,width) << endl;
```

A `void` function is normally terminated by allowing it to execute the last statement in its body. However, it can also be terminated by a `return` statement with no expression. The following example, which calculates the

67

average of an array of numbers, shows how `return` can be used with a `void` function:

```
void mean( const float data[], it count,
           float& result, bool& okay )
{
    if (cout < 1 ) {
        okay = false;
        return;
    }
    float sum = 0.0;
    for ( int i = 0; i < count; i++ )
        sum += data[i];
    result = sum / count;
    okay = true;
}
```

The return value of a function does not have to be used. So we can write:

```
max(val1,val2);
```

This is syntactically correct, but it does nothing because the return value is discarded, and its arguments are not modified.

A function can return a reference, which allows it to be used on the left-hand side of an assignment operator. A function must not return a reference to a local variable or an input-only parameter, because these objects will not be available after the function has finished, making the reference invalid. However, an output parameter can be returned as a reference, so the following is okay:

```
int& min( int& a, int& b)
{
    if (a < b)
        return a;
    else
        return b;
}
```

This function can be used on the left or right hand side of an assignment:

```
small = min(number1,number2);
min(number1,number2) += 4;
```

In the first case, the value of the smaller of the two variables given as arguments will be assigned to `small`. In the second, 4 will be added to the smaller of the variables given as arguments. Sometimes a function returns a reference just for reasons of efficiency. To prevent such a function from being used on the lefthand side of an assignment, its return reference type should be prefixed with const.

A function can return a pointer to a variable. However, pointers to local variables or parameters should not be returned because, like references, the items pointed to will not be available after the function finishes. A function returning a pointer can be used, like an ordinary pointer, with the * and -> operators. In the following example, the function mostof takes two pointers to Stockitem objects, and returns a pointer to the Stockitem with the greater quantity member. This function is used, with the -> operator, to change the id member of the greater of two Stockitem variables. By applying the * operator to dereference the returned pointer, a copy of the greater of the two objects can be made:

```
struct Stockitem {
   int id;
   int quantity;
};

Stockitem* mostof( Stockitem* a, Stockitem* b )
{
   if ( a->quantity > b->quantity )
      return a;
   else
      return b;
}

void main()
{
   Stockitem item1 = {111,64};
   Stockitem item2 = {222,55};
   Stockitem topcopy;
   int top;
   mostof(&s1,&s2)->id = 333;
      // assign 333 to id field of max argument
   topcopy = *mostof(&s1,&s2);
      // assign pointer (to max argument) to topcopy
}
```

Notice that the parameters of mostof are not declared as const. This is because they can be modified via the returned pointer value. To prevent a function that returns a pointer being used to modify the object pointed at, the returned pointer must be declared as const.

Returning an array from a function is a syntactic problem. We are forced to use pointer notation. For example, a function that returns a C string must be declared like this:

```
char* concat( const char s1[], const char s2[], char out[] );
```

This function takes two C strings s1 and s2, that are not modified, and returns another string which is their concatenation. The returned string cannot be declared inside the function because local variables are destroyed when a function finishes. Instead, the concatenated string is built-in the input-output parameter out, which can hold the result in a permanent form. The string returned from the junction can be modified. This can be prevented by declaring the function return type as const char*.

As it is declared in the above example, the returned string can be modified. If this is not required, it can be declared as const char*.

6.4   Recursion

C++ functions can call themselves. This is called recursion. It can be a very elegant way of expressing an algorithm. For example, the factorial of an integer is given by the formula $n! = 1 \times 2 \times \ldots \times n$, and the following function calculates this value:

```
int factorial( int n )
{
   if ( n <= 0 )
      return 1;
   else
      return n * factorial(n - 1);
}
```

Here, the function repeatedly calls itself with reducing values of n to perform the calculation. The recursion stops when the function is called with n equal to zero. Recursion has a performance overhead. It takes time to call and return from a function, and each function call uses computer memory until it returns. So a recursion with many function calls can require more than the available memory, and will not be able to complete.

Used well, recursion allows algorithms to be described concisely, but only use it with problems that can be naturally expressed this way. Be careful about indirect recursion, where two or more functions form a recursive loop. Such designs can be difficult to understand and maintain.

6.5   Inline functions

Calling a function has an overhead. It takes a short time to transfer control to and from the function. As a program runs the accumulation of this time can be considerable, and it sometimes makes a program too slow to be useful. To reduce the overhead, C++ can be instructed not to generate a proper function call. This is done by declaring the function to be inline. The compiler will try to place an inline function's code in the program at the point where the call is made. A function is declared inline like this:

```
inline double max ( double a, double b)
{
    . . .
}
```

The most benefit is obtained by declaring inline only small functions that are called many times. There is a potential overhead to inline functions. The size of the executable file might increase, so more memory is needed.

An inline declaration is just a request. The compiler may not be willing to honour this if the function is very complicated. If inlining is being used, check the compiler's options. The default on some compilers is not to inline any functions. Recursive functions cannot be declared inline.

6.6   Functional polymorphism

Sometimes two functions operating on different data perform essentially the same operation. For example, these functions with different names both print details of their parameter to the output stream:

```
void printstock( Stockitem s )
{
    cout << ...
}

void printcost( Chargeitem c )
{
    cout << ...
}
```

However, it would be convenient if the same name, which captures the essential operation, could be used for both functions.

The concept of an operation that can be applied to different types of data to obtain equivalent results is called *polymorphism*. Functional polymorphism is achieved in C++ using *function overloading*. Functions are given the same name, and the compiler uses their parameters to choose the correct one for the call. The compiler creates a unique *signature* for each function from its name, and the type, number and order of its parameters. A function's return type does not contribute to its signature. The compiler

function selection more statically determined ?

Signature of function in C++ — name (T p₁ ... Tₙ pₙ) 71

in ML   Tr name(T₁ p₁ -- Tₙ pₙ)

matches signatures to choose the right function to call. So the print functions given above could be defined with the same names:

```
void print( Stockitem s )
{
    //  same as printstock
}

void print( Chargeitem c )
{
    //  same as printcost
}
```

The detailed rules for matching are very complex but the following simplified rules will do in most cases. They are applied in the given order:

1. Exact match – the type of the argument exactly matches one of the alternatives.
2. Standard conversions – the standard conversions are applied to achieve a match.
3. User defined conversions – user defined conversions (which are class constructors taking one argument) are applied to achieve a match.

When there is more than one argument, an intersection rule is applied. A set of "best" matching functions for each argument is found and the intersection of these sets is considered. A no-match error is reported if the intersection is empty. If the intersection contains more than one function, there is an ambiguity error.

6.7   Pointers to functions

A pointer to a function can be defined like this:

```
int (*p2f)(int);
```

This is a pointer, called p2f, to any function that has one int parameter and returns an int value. So the following is possible:

```
int funct1( int a ) {...}

int funct2( int a ) {...}

void main()
{
    int result;
    int (*p2f)(int);
    p2f = funct1;
    result = p2f(111);      // call funct1
    p2f = funct2;
```

```
    result = (*p2f)(222); // call funct2
}
```

There are two call notations allowed, as shown in the above example. The pointer name can be used as the function name, or an * can be used to make it clear that a pointer is being employed. A typedef can be used with a function pointer like this:

```
typedef int (*Function)(int);
. . .
Function afunctn = funct1;
. . .
afunctn(555);
```

6.8   The function main

Normally, all C++ programs have a function called main, which is automatically invoked every time a program is executed. It can have parameters and produce a return value, but it is often decared as void with no parameters. Its special role means that it cannot be explicity called like other functions.

6.8.1   Leaving main and program termination

A C++ program ends when its main function terminates. If main is declared as void, it is normally terminated by allowing it to execute the last statement in its body. However, like any other void function, it can also be terminated by a return statement with no expression.

A program can return a value to its execution environment by defining main with an int return value, and using a return statement with an expression to end the program:

```
int main()
{
    . . .
    if ( error )
        return 9;
    . . .
    return 0;
}
```

Using exit(status) is another way to immediately terminate a program, where status is an integer input argument. It does not return to its caller, and the value of the status argument is passed to the program's execution environment. This function can be called from main or any other function. The return type of main should be void if this method of ending a program is used. The status argument is typically zero if the program is terminated successfully, and non-zero otherwise. It can be set with EXIT_FAILURE to indicate abnormal termination, or EXIT_SUCCESS for a normal program termination.

A more drastic way to stop a program is to use abort(). This function immediately terminates a program with little or none of the tidying up that is performed by the other methods. Some systems will print a special error message when abort is used. The use of abort should be reserved for serious errors. The library <stdlib.h> must be included if exit or abort are used.

6.8.2   Command line arguments

Arguments can be given with the command that executes a program. For example, a program called detab, that removes tab characters from a file, might be executed with the command:

```
detab file1.dat file2.dat 3
```

A program gets its command line data by declaring main with two parameters:

```
void main( int argc, char* argv[] )
```

The first parameter gives the number of arguments. The second is an array of C strings, each of which is one of the command line arguments. The first string in the array is always the program name. For the command given above the value of argc is 4 and the elements of argv are:

```
argv[0]    "detab"
argv[1]    "file1.dat"
argv[2]    "file2.dat"
argv[3]    "3"
```

The following program shows how command line parameters can be processed:

```
#include <iostream.h>
#include <string>
#include <stdlib.h>        // for atoi and exit

const DEFSPACE = 3;

void main( int argc, char* argv[] )
{
    string in;             // input file name
```

```
    string out;             // output file name
    int spaces;             // number of spaces

    bool error = false;
    if ( argc < 3 )
        error = true;
    else {
        in = argv[1];
        out = argv[2];
        if ( argc == 3 )
            spaces = DEFSPACE;
        else
            if ( argc == 4 )
                spaces = atoi(argv[3]); // convert to int
            else
                error = true;
    }
    if ( error ) {
        cout << "Format is:" << endl
            << "DETAB <in file> <out file> [<spaces>]"
            << endl;
        exit(99);
    }
... rest of program
}
```

6.9 An example

This small program manages a list of pet dog names. The list is implemented as an array of C++ strings, where an empty string indicates a free space in the array. There are three functions for managing this array: print_dogs, add_dog and is_a_dog. The array dogs and its size MAX_DOGS are defined in main and passed to the functions as arguments. In this way, there could be more than one dog array in the program. The main program just demonstrates how the functions and array might be used.

```
#include <iostream.h>
#include <string>

int print_dogs( const string dogs[], int max )
// Print the names of all dogs
//     return the number of dogs
{
```

```
      int dcount = 0;
      for ( int i = 0; i < max; i++ )
         if ( dogs[i].length() != 0 ) {
            cout << dogs[i] << ' ';
            dcount++;
         }
      return dcount;
}

bool add_dog( string dogs[], int max, string adog )
// Add a dog
//    return false if no room, true if okay
{
   int i = 0;
   while ( dogs[i].length() != 0 && i < max )
      i++;
   if ( i < max ) {
      dogs[i] = adog;
      return true;
   }
   else
      return false;
}

int is_a_dog( const string dogs[], int max, string dog )
// Check if a dog exists
{
   if ( dog == "" )
      return false;
   else {
      int i = 0;
      while ( dog != dogs[i]  && i < max )
         i++;
      return ( i < max );
   }
}

void main()
{
   const int MAX_DOGS = 4;
   string dogs[MAX_DOGS] = {"Cleo","Penny","Brollie"};

   cout << "The dogs are ";
   int dog_count = print_dogs(dogs,MAX_DOGS);
   cout << endl << " and there are "
```

```
            << dog_count << " of them." << endl;

   if ( add_dog(dogs,MAX_DOGS,"Moss") ) {
      print_dogs(dogs,MAX_DOGS);
      cout << endl;
   }
   else
      cout << "do not expect this!!!!!" << endl;
   if ( add_dog(dogs,MAX_DOGS,"Fido") ) {
      cout << "do not expect this!!!!!" << endl;
   }
   else
      cout << "no room for dog" << endl;
   if ( is_a_dog(dogs,MAX_DOGS,"Cleo") )
      cout << "Cleo is a dog" << endl;
   else
      cout << "Cleo is not a dog !!!" << endl;
   if ( is_a_dog(dogs,MAX_DOGS,"Tigger") )
      cout << "Tigger is a dog !!!" << endl;
   else
      cout << "Tigger is not a dog" << endl;
}
```

6.10   Exercises

1. Write a function that takes an array of float numbers, and returns the smallest and largest numbers in that array.
2. Write a delete function for the example in §6.9. The function should take the name of a dog as an argument and remove it from the array of names if it is present. To remove a name replace it with an empty string.
3. Write a function that splits a file name with the format name.type into two strings containing just name and type. The string operations substr and find_first_of, which are described in Appendix B, might be useful.
4. Write a function that uses recursion to calculate the sum of the first n positive integers.
5. Write a program called addthem that takes two numbers from the command line and prints their sum. The function atof, in <stdlib.h>, will be needed to convert C strings to floating point numbers.

```
class X {
public :

        | signature


private :

        | signature


   }
```

CHAPTER 7
Classes

7.1 Classes and objects

Consider a set of functions that operates on common data. They can be written so that all operations on the data are done by calling these functions. In this way, the functions define how the data can be legitimately used. This is a useful approach to program design because it partitions a program into self contained components that can be developed independently. Unfortunately, with this informal approach, data can be accessed without using the associated functions, destroying the neat divisions between components carefully designed into the program.

In C++ we can associate functions with data, and restrict access to the data, by using a class. A class describes a group of related functions and data, and controls how they can be accessed. It has a public and a private part. Anything declared in the private part of a class can only be accessed by functions also declared in the class. Normally, functions are put in the public section of the class and the data are put into the private section, so there can be no improper use of the data. This idea is called *encapsulation* or *data hiding*. It is a very powerful programming concept.

Let us suppose that we are writing a program that manipulates information about items stored in a warehouse. We need to work with an item's code, unit cost and stock level. A class that represents this might be:

```
class Stock {
public:
    void init( int acode, double acost, int alevel );
    int code() const;
    double cost() const;
    double total_value() const;
```

```
    int level() const;
    void cost( double acost );
    void remove( int number );
    void add( int number );
private:
    int thecode;
    int thecost;
    int thelevel;
};
```

This class is called `Stock`. It is composed of function and data declarations, which are referred to as the *members* of the class. It has private and public parts. The public section follows `public:`, and the private section is between `private:` and the end of the class.

The members in the private section of a class can only be accessed by functions also declared as members of that class. (They can also be accessed by friends of the class, but we will ignore this until Ch. 9.) There is no such restriction on the public members of a class. There can be any number of private or public sections in a class, and they can be in any order. Anything at the start of the class before a named section is private, but this style is not recommended. It is best to put the public section first because this is of most interest to users of the class. Data and functions can be declared in either the public or the private sections of a class, but data is normally declared as private, to take advantage of encapsulation.

The data members of `Stock` are three integers: `thecode`, `thecost` and `thelevel`. All of these are declared in the private part of `Stock`, so they can only be accessed by member functions of the class. The functions that control how the `Stock` class can be used are declared in its public section. These functions are declared as *prototypes*, which give the function's name and its parameters. The parameter names do not have to be given, but it helps documentation if they are. A class has its own name space. The names of members declared in one class will not clash with those in another class. Member function definitions, showing how they are implemented, are given later in the program or in a separate file. They can also be defined within the class declaration. How to do this is explained later.

A class name is used as a type to define an *instance* of the class like this:

```
Stock widget;
Stock spikenard;
```

The variables `widget` and `spikenard` are class *objects*. These have the same behaviour but their state, which is stored in their data members, can be different.

After a class object is declared, it is used with a dot operator in the same way as a structure:

```
widget.init(999,2.6,100);
widget.remove(10);
if ( widget.level() < 5 )
    cout << "Order some more widgets with the code "
        << widget.code() << endl;
```

The private parts of the class are not directly available when an instance of the class is used. So the following will cause compilation errors:

```
widget.thecost = 10;                    // error
current_level = widget.thelevel;        // error
```

The `Stock` class has been designed so that these operations are not allowed. Only those operations possible with the specified public member functions can be performed on a `Stock` object. Anything else will be reported as an error.

The functions in the public part of a class define its external behaviour. To see how this works, we will look at the declaration of `Stock` in more detail. The member function `init` is used to give a `Stock` object an initial value. However, a better way of initializing objects with *constructors* is described later in this chapter. Some member functions will not change `Stock` objects, so they are declared as constant functions with the suffix `const`. For example, the functions `level` and `total_value` return information stored in a `Stock` object without changing its value. The other functions, such as `remove` and `add`, will modify the state of a `Stock` object by changing stored information. It is important to recognize that, as users of the `Stock` class, we do not care how this information is stored, only that we can obtain it when needed, and that it represents the possible valid states of a `Stock` object.

The function `cost(double acost)`, which updates unit cost, is interesting. It has the same name as `cost()`, which returns the value of unit cost. The compiler can tell the difference between these functions. This is an example of function overloading, which is explained in §6.6. Accessing the data attributes of a class object with pairs of functions like this is a useful technique. In contrast, you will notice that there are no functions for changing the value of `thecode` after initialization (apart from `init`). This correctly expresses the intended behaviour of a `Stock` object, which is that the code given to a stock item should not be changed.

There is an additional rule for the way a `Stock` object should behave that is not given by the class definition: the stock level cannot be less than zero. This would normally be stated in the class as a comment. Indeed, it is good practice to use comments in a class to describe its behaviour in more detail than can be deduced from its declaration alone.

The private parts of a class can usually be ignored when its behaviour is considered. The functions in the public section define how the private parts are used. Thus it is the public, rather than the private, section that is interesting to a user of a class. Being able to see hidden data and functions in a class is a feature of C++, but this does not mean that we need to take any notice of it. The private sections of a class are part of its implementation. They describe data and functions used to implement the public part of the class. It is a good idea to separate the ideas of definition and implementation. Implementation information is not needed to use a class. So unless we are designing and building a class we can ignore it.

A class is implemented by providing definitions for all of its functions. This can be done in the same file as the class declaration or in a separate file. The same function name can be used in different classes, so a scope operator : : is used to associate a function's definition with its class:

```
void Stock::remove( int number )
{
    thelevel -= number;
    if ( thelevel < 0 )
        thelevel = 0;
}
```

Notice that this implementation enforces the positive stock level rule for Stock objects mentioned above. Member functions have full access to the private parts of their class. So remove can reference thelevel without restriction.

A member function can be defined in its class declaration like this:

```
class Stock {
    . . .
    double total_cost()
        { return thecost * thelevel; }
    . . .
};
```

This is an example of *inline* member functions, which are discussed in §8.1. They can improve the performance of a class implementation by removing the function call overhead. However, they confuse definition and implementation, and can make class declarations difficult to read.

A class is a user defined type. It is managed by the compiler in much the same way as the fundamental types. A class can be thought of as an *abstract data type* which represents a concept in the problem domain such as a stock item, or a computer software idea such as a stack. Class objects can be composed into arrays, be data members of classes and passed as arguments to functions, just like instances of the fundamental types such as int.

In general, a class declaration is composed of data members that are normally private, and member functions that can be public or private. Public member functions are a class's interface to the rest of the program, they specify its behaviour. Private member functions are used to implement the class, and as such are not part of its interface. Enumerations and typedef statements can be used in the public or private parts of a class declaration to make its behaviour and implementation easier to express.

7.2 Constructors

A Stock class object, as described above, will not be automatically initialized. Its init member function has to be called explicitly to do this. A much better way of ensuring that objects are initialized with suitable values is to declare *constructors* for the class. These are special functions that are used by the compiler to initialize class objects. It is good practice always to declare a constructor. Constructors have the same name as their class, and do not have a return type. In Stock the init function could be replaced with:

```
Stock( int acode, double acost, int alevel );
```

This constructor will be executed when a Stock object is defined like this:

```
Stock widget(999,2.5,100);
```

The implementation of this constructor should initialize the private parts of widget, which might be done as follows:

```
Stock::Stock( int acode, double acost, int alevel )
{
    thecode = acode;
    thecost = acost;
    thelevel = alevel;
}
```

Here, the data members of the class are initialized with assignment operators. An alternative style using an initializer list is shown in §7.4.

A class can have more than one constructor provided the parameter lists are different. Function overloading is used to choose the correct version. If a class has no constructors, it cannot automatically be given an initial value. The instances of a class with constructors must be declared with initial values that match one of its constructors. In particular, if a class has constructors, and we want to declare an instance without giving any explicit initial values, there must be a constructor that takes no arguments. For example, we can declare an instance of a class with:

```
Stock widget;
```

This invokes a constructor with the following declaration:

```
Stock();
```

This is called the *default constructor* of the class, and it should supply default values for the data members of its class. In this case, a suitable implementation might be:

```
Stock::Stock()
{
    thecode = 999;
    thecost = 0.0;
    thelevel = 0;
}
```

The best default values depend on the required behaviour of the class, but they should always be chosen to initialize an object to a valid state. If suitable values cannot be identified, do not declare a default constructor. This will force a user of the class to provide initial state information using another constructor.

Constructors are called automatically when an object is created. They cannot be used like ordinary member functions, so the following will be reported as an error:

```
widget.Stock();    // error
```

It is okay to have more than one constructor for a class, but the number of constructors can sometimes be reduced by using default argument values. For example, the two Stock constructors discussed above could be replaced by one constructor with default arguments:

```
Stock( int acode = 999, double acost = 0.0, int alevel = 0 );
```

The implementation of this constructor is exactly the same as for the version without any default values. If less than the full set of arguments is given when an object is created, the default values are used. This constructor can be called with no arguments, so it can act as the class's default constructor. All the following are valid, and will be serviced by this constructor:

```
Stock widget;
Stock widget3(123), widget4(32,1.5);
Stock widget(41,3.6,9);
```

It is not necessary for all of a constructor's arguments to be given default values, but any that are must be at the end of the list.

Objects can also be declared as follows if a constructor taking a single argument of the correct type exists:

```
Stock widget = 99;
```

There is such a constructor for Stock, and the above is equivalent to:

```
Stock widget(99);
```

Sometimes we want to initialize an object to be the same value as another object of the same type. To do this we can write:

```
Stock widget2 = widget1;
```

This will look for a constructor of the form:

```
Stock( const Stock& s );
```

This is called a *copy constructor*. It is responsible for copying all of its parameter's data members to the object for which it was invoked. Its parameter must be a reference, so `Stock(Stock s)` is not allowed.

If a copy constructor is not defined, a *memberwise* copy is performed. This means that a copy operation is applied to each data member in turn. If the member is a fundamental type, a simple bitwise copy is used. Pointers are copied, but what they point to are not. Arrays are copied on an element by element basis. A copy constructor is only needed when the default memberwise copy is unsatisfactory. The most common reason for this is the use of pointers in a class.

The copy constructor should not be confused with the assignment operator. In itself the assignment operator = will not invoke a class's copy constructor. So the = symbol does not mean the same thing in the following statements:

```
Stock widget1 = widget2;    // copy constructor
widget1 = widget2;          // assignment
```

The default assignment operator performs a memberwise copy. So, if a copy constructor is needed to replace the memberwise copy, it is very likely that an assignment operator overload will be needed as well. Assignment operator overloading is explained in §9.2.2. This, together with copy constructors and destructors, is discussed in §9.4, which describes how to write safe classes.

A copy constructor is invoked at other times, in addition to class object declaration. Temporary instances of objects may be created when an object is passed to a function as an argument. For example, consider a function that combines information from the `Stock` objects `in1` and `in2`, and returns the information as another `Stock` object:

```
Stock merge( Stock in1, Stock in2 );
```

When this function is called, the arguments are passed by value. This means that temporary copies are made, and copy constructors are called to do this. The function returns a value of type `Stock`, and again a copy constructor is used to create this object. The function `merge` is used in the statement:

```
widget2 = merge(widget1,Stock(56,3.6));
```

When `merge` is called, a copy of `widget1` is created with a copy constructor, and an object is created with a constructor that matches `Stock` `(int,double)`. When the function is finished, its return value is created with a copy constructor, and the two temporary `Stock` objects holding the arguments are destroyed. The object holding the returned value is used by the assignment operator, and is then destroyed at the end of the statement.

A copy constructor is not used if the parameter is declared as a reference for input–output, or as a constant reference for input only. For example, the following will not invoke a copy constructor when it is used:

```
void convert( const Stock& in, Stock& out );
```

Constructors are used to make temporary instances of a class in order to assign a fixed value to an object:

```
widget1 = Stock(56,3.6);
widget2 = Stock();            // using default constructor
widget3 = Stock;              // error
widget4 = 9;                  // implicitly invoke Stock(9)
```

When these statements are executed, a temporary instance of a `Stock` object is created by calling a `Stock` class constructor. This temporary instance is then copied to the permanent object by the assignment operator, and then destroyed.

The implicit use of a constructor can be prevented by declaring it as `explicit` like this:

```
class Lock {
public:
   Lock();
   explicit Lock( int keynumber );
   ...
};
```

If this is done, the compiler will only allow a constructor to be used if it is named:

```
Lock door1;
door1 = Lock(9);    // okay
door1 = 9;          // error - constructor cannot be invoked
```

When an array of class objects is declared a constructor is called for each element of the array. If an initializer is given for the array, an appropriate constructor will be used with each of its values, otherwise the default constructor will be used:

```
Stock items[10];                    // Stock() used
```

```
Stock more[5] = {3,5,6,2,7};      // Stock(int) used
Stock more[2] = { Stock(), Stock(56,3.6) };
                      // Stock() and Stock(int,double) used
```

7.3   Destructors

When an object goes out of scope or is deleted, it is destroyed and cannot be used again. If the object is a class instance, a special function can be declared in the class that will be called just before this happens. This function is called a *destructor*, and it is declared in the public part of a class like this:

```
~Stock();
```

It has the same name as its class, preceded by a ~ character. It has no arguments or return type. A class can have only one destructor.

A destructor should be declared if special processing is required when an object is destroyed. This often happens when pointers are used to implement a class, in which case a destructor function is defined that uses `delete` to clean up the dynamically allocated data structures referenced by the pointers.

If a destructor is being used, it is very likely that a copy constructor and an assignment operator overload will be needed as well. These are discussed in the context of writing safe classes in §9.4. Take care, if a destructor exists for a class it will be invoked whenever an instance of that class is destroyed. This applies to more than just the explicitly defined instances of the class. It will also happen when the object is used as an input argument for a function, as a return value in a function, or when a constructor is used to provide a constant value in an expression.

When an array of class objects is destroyed a destructor, if one is declared for the class, is called for each element of the array. Destroying an instance of a class or structure will invoke its data member's destructors.

A destructor can be explicitly called like an ordinary member function, but it is unusual to do this. An object that has a destructor explicitly applied must not be used until it is initialized again. Objects with destructors cannot be members of unions. Destructors, together with constructors and assignment operator overloads, are very useful features of C++. They allow sophisticated memory management of objects, and reliable support for dynamic data structures. However, great care is required. Destructors and constructors are called automatically. If they are not designed and implemented correctly, damage can be caused that is difficult to detect and correct. Particular care is needed if destructors are used in classes with virtual functions as explained in §11.5.

87

7.4   Containment

A class can have class objects as data members. This is called *containment*. It is an obvious and useful way to use classes. We can implement a class using other classes as reusable software components. As an example, we could use a Money object to store the cost in a Stock class. The private part of Stock might look like this:

```
class Stock {
...
private:
    int thecode;
    Money thecost;
    int thelevel;
};
```

The Money object is used by the member functions of Stock to implement its behaviour. However, there is a complication. When an instance of Stock is created a Money object also has to be created, and this has to be initialized. Simply assigning a value to the Money object in Stock's constructor is possible, but a better way is to use a *member initializer list*. Assuming that Money has a suitable constructor, Stock's constructor can be written like this:

```
Stock::Stock( int acode, double acost, int alevel )
    : thecost(acost)
{
    thecode = acode;
    thelevel = alevel;
}
```

The initializer list follows the : and, in this case, it invokes the constructor Money(double) for the thecost member of Stock.

The fundamental types can also be managed with an initializer list, so the Stock constructor could be defined as follows:

```
Stock::Stock( int acode, double acost, int alevel )
    : thecost(acost), thecode(acode), thelevel(alevel)
{}
```

Here, all the data members of Stock are dealt with in the initializer list and the body of the constructor is empty.

An initializer list is processed before the body of its constructor. The order of items in the list is irrelevant. Members are initialized in the order of their declaration in the class.

A memberwise copy is used for objects that do not have a copy constructor. When this happens, the copy constructors of any contained class objects will be invoked to perform the copy operation. If a contained class object does not have a copy constructor, a memberwise copy will be used instead.

If a copy constructor does exist for a class, it must explicitly copy all of its class's data members, including those that are class objects. Using an assignment operator to copy class objects will not invoke their copy constructors. To mimic the behaviour of a memberwise copy an initializer list must be used, thus:

```
Stock::Stock( Stock& s )
    : thecost(s.thecost)
{
    thecode = s.the.code;
    thelevel = s.thelevel;
}
```

The constructors for objects are invoked in the order that the objects are declared in their containing class. All contained objects are initialized before the containing class's constructor is called. Destructors are invoked in the reverse order. First the containing class's destructor is called. Then the contained objects' destructors are applied in the opposite order to their declaration in the containing class.

7.5 An example

The following is a complete definition of a stock class with a simple example of how it might be used. The Stock class has only one constructor. This is declared with default arguments, so it can be invoked in a number of ways, including as a default constructor. There is no copy constructor or destructor defined because these are unnecessary for the chosen implementation. The declarations of the member functions have comments that briefly describe their behaviours. All the functions that modify Stock are specified to keep the class data within a limited range. The member function definitions implement this behaviour. The private function normalise is used to support the implementation. It is called from the other member functions after any update to ensure data is maintained in the correct range. It is a private function and thus part of the implementation rather than the behaviour of the class. Another implementation of Stock might not have such a function.

```
#include <iostream.h>

class Stock {
public:
```

```
    Stock( int acode = 999, double acost = 0.0,
           int alevel = 0 );
      // initial state
      //    if acost or alevel < 0, they are taken as 0
    int code() const;
      // give stock code
    double cost() const;
      // give unit cost
    double total_value() const;
      // give total value of stock
    int level() const;
      // give stock level
    void cost( double acost );
      // set new unit cost
      //    if acost < 0, set to 0
    void remove( int number );
      // remove number items from stock
      //    final level >= zero
    void add( int number );
      // add number to stock
      //    final level >= zero
private:
    int thecode;
    double thecost;
    int thelevel;
    void normalise();
};

Stock::Stock( int acode, double acost, int alevel )
      :thecode(acode), thecost(acost), thelevel(alevel)
{
    normalise();
}

int Stock::code()
{
    return thecode;
}

double Stock::cost()
{
    return thecost;
}

double Stock::total_value()
{
```

```
   return thecost * thelevel;
}
int Stock::level()
{
   return thelevel;
}
void Stock::cost( double acost )
{
   thecost = acost;
   normalise();
}
void Stock::remove( int number )
{
   thelevel -= number;
   normalise();
}
void Stock::add( int number )
{
   thelevel += number;
   normalise();
}
void Stock::normalise()
{
   if ( thecost < 0.0 )
      thecost = 0.0;
   if ( thelevel < 0.0 )
      thelevel = 0.0;
}
void main()
{
   Stock wigs(1,20);
   Stock springs(2,54.5);
   int newstock;
   cout << "How many wigs have been delivered? ";
   cin >> newstock;
   wigs.add(newstock);
   cout << "How many springs have been delivered? ";
   cin >> newstock;
   springs.add(newstock);
   cout << "Current stock is" << endl;
```

```
    cout << "wigs    " << wigs.level() << endl;
    cout << "springs " << springs.level() << endl;
}
```

7.6 Exercises

1. The example in §6.9 manages a list of pet dog names using a set of functions and a shared array of names. Write a class called Dogs to do the same thing. Provide member functions to add and remove dog's names, check if there is room for another dog, check if a dog is already stored, return the number of dogs stored, and print the dogs' names. An instance of Dogs should be able to hold up to fifteen names.

2. A stack is a first in last out data store.
   (a) Specify an integer stack by declaring a class called StackInt. The class must have member functions push and pop, for storing and retrieving data items. Some other functions will also be needed. For example, a way to check if the stack is empty, might be useful.
   (b) Show how StackInt can be used by writing a short example that inserts and removes an item from a StackInt object. Note that an implementation of StackInt is not required (see the next question for this).

3. Implement the StackInt class declared in Exercise 7.2 using a fixed length array of integers.

4. Declare and implement a class that simulates the operation of a traffic control beacon. It has two coloured lights: red and green, which go through the following sequence: red, green, red and green, and then back to red. A green light on its own indicates that a vehicle can proceed. A vehicle must stop for all other colour combinations. Call the class TLight. It should have functions that step it through its light sequence, allow the state of each light to be checked, and display its current state. Initially a TLight object should have only its red light on.

5. The following is a class that manages a pair of traffic beacons controlling a single track road:

```
class TLpair {
public:
    TLpair();
    void next();
    void display();
  private:
    // ...
  };
```

The beacons go through the sequence given in the following table:

step	beacon 1	beacon 2
1	green	red
2	red and green	red
3	red	green
4	red	red and green
5	go to step 1	go to step 1

Implement this class using the TLight class from Exercise 7.4.

6. Explore the way that constructors and destructors are called by writing a simple program. Invent a class that has some constructors and destructors that print out messages. Use this class in different situations, trying to predict the outcome.

CHAPTER 8
More about classes

8.1 Inlining

The compiler can be asked to use inline expansion rather than a conventional call for the execution of member functions. If this is done, the compiler will try to place a copy of the member function's code at the point in the program where the object is being used with that function. The use of inlining with member functions can have a significant effect on a program's speed because member functions are often used very frequently and they tend to be small. Inlining can be requested in a class declaration by providing a body for the function:

```
class Stock {
public:
    ...
    double total_value()
      // give total value of stock
      { return thecost * thelevel; }
    ...
};
```

A disadvantage of this style of inlining is that it clutters up the class declaration, and can make it difficult to read. More importantly, it has the undesirable effect of confusing specification and implementation. As an alternative, the inline keyword can be used with the function's definition:

```
inline double Stock::total_value()
{
    return thecost * thelevel;
}
```

The object oriented style of programming tends to use lots of function calls. Inlining can reduce the performance overhead caused by this approach, at the cost of possibly increasing the physical size of a program's executable image. The most benefit is obtained by only declaring inline small functions that are called many times. Inlining should always be considered for constructors and destructors because these can be called implicitly a lot of times.

A compiler may ignore an inline request if the function is too long or too complicated. Some compilers must have a special option selected before they will enforce inline requests.

8.2   Constant objects and member functions

A class can be used to define a constant in a similar way to a fundamental type:

```
const Stock rightwidget(123,100.0);
```

A constant object must be initialized, and assignment to the object is not allowed. The ordinary member functions of a constant object are assumed to modify the object, and cannot be used. However, the keyword const can be used to tell the compiler that a particular function will not change any data members, allowing it to be used with a constant object. This is done as follows:

```
class Stock {
public:
   Stock( int acode = 999, double acost = 0.0,
          int alevel = 0 );
   int code() const;
      // give stock code
   double cost() const;
      // give unit cost
   double total_value() const;
      // give total value of stock
   int level() const;
      // give stock level
   void cost( double acost );
      // set new unit cost
   void remove( int number );
      // remove number items from stock
   void add( int number );
      // add number to stock private:
   . . .
};
```

Here, all the data member functions that will not change an instance of Stock are suffixed with const. The definition of a constant function must also use the const keyword, thus:

```
double Stock::cost() const
{
    return thecost;
}
```

Constant member functions can be used with non-constant objects, but non-constant member functions cannot be invoked for a constant object:

```
Stock bluehat = 561;
const Stock STANDARD = 100;
cout << "Blue hat code is " << bluehat.code() << endl;
cout << "Standard code is " << bluehat.STANDARD() << endl;
bluehat.add(10);
STANDARD.add(10);   // error - not allowed with const object
```

Constant member functions affect the way class objects can be used as function parameters. If a parameter is declared as input-only by making it a constant reference, then it can only be used to invoke constant member functions. This restriction does not apply to input-only parameters passed by name, because in this case member functions operate on a copy of the argument that is not a constant.

A constant member function is not normally allowed to modify its class's member data. Nevertheless, it is sometimes necessary for a constant function to change member data. For example, a class might maintain statistical data that includes the number of times a constant function is used, or an implementation might periodically restructure the physical layout of private data without changing its logical constness. The constant restriction can be explicitly removed from selected member data by declaring it as mutable like this:

```
class Staff {
public:
    ...
    string name() const
        { access_count++;   // allowed because it is mutable
          return thename; }
    int accesses() const
        { return access_count; }
private:
    string thename;
    mutable int access_count;
    ...
};
```

Take care, `mutable` is a recent addition to the C++ language, and some compilers do not support it. In this case, constness is just a promise to the compiler, and a `const` function can actually modify member data without raising an error.

Member function overloading takes account of constness. If two functions with the same name and parameter list are declared, but with only one having the `const` attribute, they will be selected on the basis of the constness of the object for which they are invoked. So it is possible to have different behaviour or implementation for constant and non-constant objects. Destructors and constructors cannot be declared as `const` functions.

8.3   Compound types and classes

Pointers can, of course, be used with class objects. The member functions of an object can be accessed by dereferencing the pointer and using a dot operator, or an `->` operator can be used:

```
Stock stock1;
Stock* p2stock = &stock1;
*p2stock.cost(3.56);
p2stock->add(45);
```

The `new` operator can be used to create a class object dynamically. Specific constructors can be invoked by giving an initializer, otherwise the default constructor will be used on the object:

```
Stock* stock2 = new Stock(123,34.9);
Stock* stock3 = new Stock;
```

A dynamic class object must be explicitly destroyed with `delete` to invoke its destructor. Any dynamic objects that still exist when a program terminates will not have their destructors automatically executed.

Arrays of class objects can be declared. Constructors and destructors are applied to each element of such an array. An initializer can be used:

```
Stock item[5] = { 1,Stock(123,34.5),Stock(),2 };
```

Here, `item[0]` and `item[3]` are initialized with `Stock(int)`, `item[1]` is initialized with `Stock(int,double)`, and `item[2]` and `item[4]` are initialized with `Stock()`. An error is reported if any of the constructors specified in the list are not declared. If an initializer is not given for the array, the default constructor is used for all of its elements. When an array of class objects goes out of scope it is destroyed, and the class's destructor, if it is declared, is invoked for each element of the array.

A dynamically allocated array cannot have an initializer, but the default

constructor will be used for each class object in the array. Destructors will
be invoked when the array is destroyed by `delete[]`.

8.4 Self referencing

A normal member function has access to a hidden constant called `this`
that points to the object for which the function was invoked. It has an
appropriate pointer type that takes account of the constness of the object.
The `this` pointer can be used to access any member of the class with the
usual pointer notations. However, it is not normally used explicitly. There
is no reason to write `this->thecost` in a member function when
`thecost` is all that is needed. Occasionally the `this` pointer is invaluable.
For example, when the owning object has to be returned from a member
function:

```
Stock Stock::somefunction()
{
    ...
    return *this;
}
```

8.5 Static members

A static class member is shared by *all* the instances of its class. Unlike a
normal class member, it is not part of a particular object. Static members
are declared using the `static` keyword like this:

```
class Demo {
public:
    Demo(): moredata(0)
        { objcount++; }
    ~Demo()
        { objcount--; }
    static int count();
        { return objcount; }
    ...
private:
    static int objcount;    // class data
    int moredata;           // instance data
};
int Demo::objcount = 0;     // definition and initialization
```

Here, `count` is a static member function and `objcount` is a static data
member.

A separate definition of a static data member has to be provided outside the class. This is associated with the class by a scope operator. A static data member can and should be given an initial value, which will be assigned to the variable once at the beginning of program execution. Constructors can modify static data, but they should not be used for static initialization.

Static data can be manipulated by ordinary or static member functions, but a static function can only manipulate static data. Static member functions are used to access static data without reference to a particular object, although they can also be called like an ordinary member function. Constructor and destructor functions cannot be declared as static.

The name of a public static member is used outside its class's member functions by prefixing it with the class name and the scope operator. It can be used in this way even when there are no instances of the class defined. Alternatively, it can be used like a normal member name with the name of an object and a dot or -> operator. Private static members are accessed in exactly the same way as normal class members.

Static members are used to support class wide activities like counting the number of objects currently declared, or specialized memory management. For example, the Demo class given above uses a private static variable to count its instances. The variable objcount is initialized to zero which will always happen before any instances of Demo can be created. The Demo constructor adds one to objcount and the destructor subtracts one. Since the constructor is always called when a Demo object is created, and the destructor is called when the object is destroyed, objcount will hold the number of instances of Demo existing in the program. To find out how many instances of Demo there are, its count static member function is called like this:

```
cout << Demo::count() << endl;     // prints 0
Demo a, b;
cout << Demo::count() << endl;     // prints 2
cout << a.count() << endl;         // prints 2
```

As this shows, a public static member can be used by qualifying its name with a scope operator and its class name, even when there are no instances of the class defined. It can also be accessed like a normal class member using the name of an object and a dot operator.

Static member data are very useful for defining non-integer constants in classes. For example,

```
class Oven {
public:
    static const double MAX;
    ...
};
const double Oven::MAX = 2000.5;
```

The public constant Oven::MAX is unique, and cannot clash with constants named MAX in other classes. It will have the same value in all instances of Oven. Integer constants can also be declared in a class using an enumerated type (see §2.6).

Static functions are not related to an instance of their class, but they are part of its name space. They can be used as public support functions, or private implementation functions that do not refer to any member data. They look like non-member functions, so they can be used with software that requires a pointer to a function, where a normal member function will not be accepted.

The above example showed a static function defined inline. The static keyword is not used when a static member function is defined separately from the class declaration, although the static keyword must still appear in the class declaration. So the equivalent definition would be:

```
int Demo::count()
// This is a static function
{
    return objcount;
}
```

8.6   Constant and reference data members

Constant non-static or reference data members can be declared in a class. They have to be given a value by all the class's constructors using an initialization list (see §7.4), and cannot be changed after this.

The value of a constant data member only holds for a particular instance, and not for the class as a whole. So it is possible for different instances of a class to have different values for the same constant non-static or reference data member. Do not use this method if a named constant has the same value for all instances of a class. Use an enumeration or a constant static data member instead.

The assignment operator will not work with a class object that has a constant non-static or reference data member, unless the assignment operator is overloaded as explained in §9.2.2.

The following shows how a constant data member might be used:

```
class Vehicle {
public:
    const float MAXSPEED;
    Vehicle()
        : MAXSPEED(35.8), thelength(0) {}
    Vehicle( double speed )
```

```
      : MAXSPEED(speed), thelength(0) {}
   float length()
      {  return thelength; }
   void length( float alength )
      {  thelength = alength; }
   ...
private:
   float thelength;
   ...
};
```

Here, the constant MAXSPEED differs depending on which constructor is used to create a Vehicle object. It is constant for a particular object but not for the class. The class can be used like this:

```
Vehicle mycar1, mycar2(46.2);
cout << mycar1.MAXSPEED << endl;   // prints 35.8
cout << mycar2.MAXSPEED << endl;   // prints 46.2
mycar1.length(5.7);        // okay  - object not constant
mycar1.MAXSPEED = 10;      // error - constant data member
mycar2 = mycar1;           // error - no default assignment
Vehicle mycar3 = mycar1;   // default copy constructor okay
```

8.7   Pointers to members

A pointer to a member function or data can be declared and then used to access the member in a particular object of the correct type. The notation is similar to pointers to non-member functions described in §6.7. Consider the following trivial class:

```
class Myclass {
public:
   Myclass( int avalue ) : thevalue(avalue) {}
   int value()
       { return thevalue; }
   void value( int avalue )
       { thevalue = avalue; }
private:
   int thevalue;
};
```

We can declare and use a pointer to a member like this:

```
typedef int (Myclass::*P2mf1)();
typedef void (Myclass::*P2mf2)(int);
```

```
void main()
{
    Myclass x1(1);
    Myclass x2(2);
    Myclass* p2x2 = &x2;
    P2mf1 pointer1 = &Myclass::value;
    P2mf2 pointer2 = &Myclass::value;
    // direct access
    x1.value(99);
    cout << x1.value() << endl;
    cout << p2x2->value() << endl;
    // access via member pointer
    (x1.*pointer2)(99);
    cout << (x1.*pointer1)() << endl;
    cout << (p2x2->*pointer1)() << endl;
}
```

The typedef declarations are used to make the program a little more read-able. There are two value functions, but this does not cause a problem, because the pointer type is compared with the parameter lists to select the correct address. The .* operator is used to dereference a pointer to a member. Thus the member specified in the pointer declaration can be accessed in a particular instance of the class. The ->* operator does the same for a pointer to an instance of the class. The parentheses are needed because of operator precedence.

Pointers to members are used in programs that have to respond to dynamic inputs. For example, programs that have windows based user interfaces sometimes implement their design with pointers to member functions. The pointers support the relationship between a windows object, such as a button, and the operation that should be performed when it is pressed. However, there are better ways to do this. Virtual functions and abstract base classes, which are explained in Chapter 11, offer a much more elegant solution to this type of problem.

8.8 Nested classes

Classes (and structures) can be declared inside another class. They are called nested classes and they reduce the global name space. Nested classes are useful for implementation components. However, the overall class structure can get messy. Here is an incomplete example that uses nesting:

```
class List {
public:
    List();
```

```
    insert( int data );
    . . .
private:
    class Node {
    public:
        Node( int data, Node* node );
        void data( int somedata );
        . . .
    };
    Node* root;
};
```

The Node class is declared in the private section of List as part of a linked list implementation.

Nested class declarations can be difficult to read. A cleaner way that can sometimes be used is to employ a forward name reference:

```
class List {
public:
    List();
    insert( int data );
    . . .
private:
    class Node;   // forward reference
    Node* root;
};

class List::Node {
public:
    List::Node( int data, Node* node );
    void data( int somedata );
    . . .
};
```

Here, just the class name Node is declared in List, and the actual class is declared separately as List::Node. The name is only used before the full declaration of Node to define a pointer, which is okay because this needs very little information about the class. A definition of a Node object at this point for example would not be possible.

The definition of a Node member function needs two scope operators:

```
void List::Node::data( int somedata )
{
    thedata = somedata;
}
```

Nesting classes only affects the name space. It does not grant any access rights. The member functions of a nested class have no special access to the enclosing class. Structures can be nested in a similar way to classes.

8.9   Separate compilation

It is often convenient and sensible to separate a program into smaller components. This helps to partition the design and can make development and maintenance easier. In C++ this is done with the aid of *header* files. For each component, its *interface* is put into a header file, and its *implementation* in a *source* file.

A header file should contain all the information needed by the compiler to check that the component is being used correctly. Detail of how the various classes and functions are implemented is not provided. The source file contains this information. Header files contain constants, structure and class declarations, and function declarations. Source files contain the definitions of class member functions, static class data members, non-class function definitions and any global components private to the implementation.

To use a component, a #include directive, naming its header file, is put at the beginning of the program. When the program is compiled, a verbatim copy of the header file is copied into the program file. This ensures that all access to the component is type correct. The source file for the component must be compiled separately to produce an object file. This is *linked* to the program, with other object files, to produce an executable file that can be run on a computer. Header files are included like this:

```
#include <math.h>      // a system library
#include <iostream.h> // a system library
#include "myclass.h"  // an application component
```

Figure 8.1 shows the relationship between the parts of a program compiled as separate units. In this example, the iostream and math files are system components, and myclass is an application component. On many systems, object code for the system components is stored in special files called *libraries*, which are automatically accessed by the link program. Indeed, system components like iostream are normally referred to as the *standard libraries*. The program in §8.10 shows how separate compilation can be used in practice.

The process for compiling and linking a program, and the names of the various files, depends on the development platform. For example, on a UNIX system the following commands might be used:

```
g++ -c myclass.cxx
g++ myprog.cxx myclass.o -o myprog
```

105

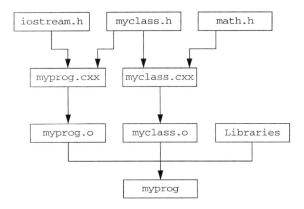

Figure 8.1 Separate compilation.

The management of a large program, with many components, can be complicated. In such cases, it is common practice to use a tool. A well known UNIX tool is make, which tracks file changes and builds programs by selectively compiling and linking components. Many compilers provide development environments that have integrated tools with similar capabilities to make. A typical approach is to collect components together as a project that can be built to form a program.

Components that use inline functions have to be managed in a slightly different way. Inline function definitions must be available at compile-time, so they have to be in a header file. This can confuse interface and implementation. A way around this is to use two header files, one for the interface part and another for the inline part. These are arranged as shown in Figure 8.2. There are now two files containing implementation code, one for inline functions which is included in the program via the normal header file, and another for non-inline functions, which is compiled and linked with the program.

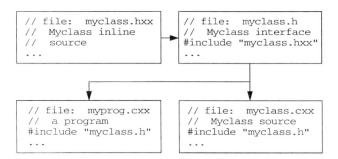

Figure 8.2 Managing inline functions.

106

8.9.1 Multiple inclusion

Useful header files are often included in other header files. This can cause multiple declaration errors when a file is included more than once in a single compilation. The solution is easy. Use preprocessing directives in each header file, like this:

```
// file : dogy.h
// Dog Management Classes
#ifndef DOGY_H
#define DOGY_H

    // The body of the header file

#endif
```

When an #include "dogy.h" is encountered by the compiler, the dogy.h file is processed. The #ifndef command in this file controls which statements are passed to the compiler. If the name DOGY_H is *not* defined, all the statements between the #ifndef line and #endif will be compiled. If it is defined, the statements will be ignored.

The name DOGY_H is not defined at the beginning of the compilation, so the first time dogy.h is included, all the statements in this file will be compiled. After this, because of the #define immediately after #ifndef, the name DOGY_H will be defined, and subsequent inclusions will not compile the statements. In effect, the file will be included only once for the compilation.

8.10 An example

This example shows how a header file can be used to support separate compilation units. It is a simple list class for storing integers, which is implemented using a linked list. A linked list is a sequence of dynamically allocated nodes connected by pointers. A private nested class is declared for the nodes used to build this list. A constructor ensures that a newly created empty List is correctly initialized. A destructor takes care of the data structure when a List is destroyed. However, this is an example of an unsafe class because doing some things, like using a List object as an input-only argument to a function, might result in unpredictable behaviour. How this class can be made safe is discussed in §9.4. There are no const functions declared because a List object cannot be sensibly used if it is declared as a constant.

Header file

```
#ifndef LIST_H
#define LIST_H

class List {
public:
    List();
        // Create a new list, empty() = true, end() = true
    void before( int data );
        // Insert new data before current item.
        //  New item becomes current item
        //      If end() true insert at end list
    void after( int data );
        // Insert new data after current item
        //  New item becomes current item
        //      If end() true insert at end list
    int current();
        // Data value of current item
    void next();
        // Make the next item current
    bool end();
        // Past last item?
        // if true current() undefined
    bool empty();
        // List empty?
        // If true, end() = true and current() undefined
    void top();
        // Goto first item if one exists
    void bottom();
        // Goto last item if one exists
    ~List();
        // Clean up
private:
    class Node;              // forward reference
    Node* theroot;
    Node* thecurrent;
    Node* theprevious;
    void clear();            // for destructor
    bool attop_empty();      // At top of list or list empty?
    bool atbottom();         // At bottom of list?
};
#endif
```

Source file

```
#include "list.h"

class List::Node {
public:
    List::Node( int data, List::Node* node = 0 )
        : thedata(data), thenext(node)
      // Initialize  a node with 'data' and connect it
      //     to 'node'.
      // If 'node' not given end of list is indicated.
      {}
    int data()
      // The data value in this node
        {  return thedata;    }
    List::Node* next()
      // The next node in the list
      //     or zero if there is not one.
        {  return thenext;    }
    List::Node* splice( List::Node* node )
      // Put 'node' into the list after this node.
      //    'node' is connected to the node this node
      //        was connected to.
      {  node->thenext = thenext;
         thenext = node;
         return node;    }
private:
    int thedata;
    List::Node* thenext;
};

List::List()
    : theroot(0), thecurrent(0), theprevious(0) {}

void List::before( int data )
{
    if ( attop_empty() )
      // insert at 'theroot'
        theroot = thecurrent = new Node(data,theroot);
    else
      // insert after 'theprevious'
        thecurrent = theprevious->splice(new Node(data));
}

void List::after( int data )
{
```

```
    if ( empty() )
      // attach to 'theroot'
        thecurrent = theroot = new Node(data);
    else
        if ( end() ) {
      // insert after the 'theprevious'
          thecurrent = theprevious->splice(new Node(data));
        }
        else {
      // insert after 'thecurrent'
          theprevious = thecurrent;
          thecurrent = thecurrent->splice(new Node(data));
        }
}

void List::next()
{
   if ( !end() ) {
      theprevious = thecurrent;
      thecurrent = thecurrent->next();
   }
}

bool List::empty()
{
   return theroot == 0;
}

bool List::end()
{
   return thecurrent == 0;
}

bool List::attop_empty()
{
   return thecurrent == theroot;
}

bool List::atbottom()
{
   return thecurrent->next() == 0;
}

void List::top()
{
   theprevious = 0;
   thecurrent = theroot;
```

```
}
void List::bottom()
{
    top();
    if ( !empty() )
       // step down list
        while ( !atbottom() )
           next();
}
int List::current()
{
    return thecurrent->data();
}
void List::clear()
{
    Node* dead;
    while ( theroot != 0 ) {
       // remove and delete top node
        dead = theroot;
        theroot = theroot->next();
        delete dead;
    }
       // set to initial state
    thecurrent = theprevious = 0;
}
List::~List()
{
    clear();
}
```

Program file

This short program uses the List class:

```
#include <iostream.h>
#include "list.h"

void main()
{
    // make a short list
    List mylist;
    mylist.after(10);
    mylist.after(11);
```

```
    mylist.after(12);

    // print list
    mylist.top();
    while ( !mylist.end() ) {
       cout << mylist.current() << endl;
       mylist.next();
    }
}
```

8.11 Exercises

1. The following class holds information about a task in a real-time system:

```
class TaskInfo {
public:
    TaskInfo( int anid, int apriority );
    void additem( long millisec );
    int id();
    int priority();
    long runtime();
private:
    ...
};
```

Write a TaskQueue class for storing objects of this type. It should have member functions for adding and retrieving TaskInfo objects on a first in first out basis. Assume the TaskInfo class is provided as a separate component, with a header file called "task.h". Implement the TaskQueue using separate header and source files.

2. Consider the following program that prints out a simple message:

```
#include <iostream.h>
void main()
{
    cout << "Hello folks" << endl;
}
```

Without changing main in any way, modify this program to print:

```
Startup
Hello folks
Shutdown
```

3. Modify the `TaskInfo` in Exercise 1 to support the definition:

```
const TaskInfo MAINTASK(0,0);
```

And implement the result.

4. Write a const correct class representing a rectangular games board, which stores markers of type:

```
enum Marker { BLACK, WHITE, NONE };
```

The dimensions of an instance of `Board` are specified when it is declared. Positions on a `Board` object are given as a pair of integers representing row and column. Users of a `Board` object must be able to place markers by giving their colour and position, and retrieve them by giving just position. If an attempt is made to access a position that is not on the board, the program should be terminated. For this exercise, include `<stdlib.h>`, and use `exit(99)` to stop the program. It must be possible to find out the dimensions of a `Board` object after it has been created. Use an inline implementation if possible. To test `const` correctness, it must be possible to use the class with the following function:

```
void print( const Board& brd )
{
    for ( int r = 0; r < brd.rows(); r++ ) {
        for ( int c = 0; c < brd.cols(); c++ )
            switch ( brd.get(r,c) ) {
                case BLACK: cout << "B "; break;
                case WHITE: cout << "A "; break;
                case NONE : cout << ". "; break;
                default   : cout << "? ";
            }
        cout << endl;
    }
}
```

Friends

```
class { _ friend f
  public .

  private :
}
```

f( )   f has NO this ptr.

CHAPTER 9

Friends and operators

9.1 Friends

Functions and classes can be declared as friends of a class. Friends have access to the private sections of a class. Friends are disliked by some programmers because they are thought to betray encapsulation. This is a mistaken point of view. Friends are part of their class as much as its member functions. They are declared in a class and must be thought of and treated as part of that class.

9.1.1 Friend functions

A function is declared as a friend like this:

```
class Stock {
    friend void transfer( Stock& s1, Stock& s2, int amt );
        // transfer amt of stock from s1 to s2
public:
    Stock( int acode, double acost, int alevel);
    ...
private:
    ...
};
```

Friends are always public, so it is convenient to declare them at the beginning of the class. The function transfer moves stock from one item to another. Its definition, based on the example in Chapter 7, is:

```
 void transfer( Stock& s1, Stock& s2, int amt )
 {
```

```
    if ( amt > s1.thelevel ) {
      s2.thelevel += s1.thelevel;
      s1.thelevel = 0;
    }
    else {
      s2.thelevel += amount
      s1.thelevel -= amount;
    }
}
```

This function is not associated with `Stock` by a scope operator because it is not a member function. Its name is global and it does not have a `this` pointer. All access to `Stock` objects must be as arguments, using qualified names. However, it can use private data in `s1` and `s2` because it is a friend of `Stock`.

Friend functions are generally a notational convenience. They allow us to have a class interface with functions of the form `f(wibble,wobble)` rather than `wibble.f(wobble)`. Sometimes, the ability to specify parts of a class in this form is useful.

9.1.2 Friend classes

A class can be declared as a friend in a similar way to a function with:

```
friend class Iterator;
```

All the member functions of `Iterator` are friends of the class that contains this declaration. As an alternative, individual member functions of one class can be declared as friends of another class with a declaration of the form:

```
friend void X::f();
```

Class friendship is asymmetric. The access permission operates in only one direction. Declaring a class as a friend does not give access to that class.

Friendship between classes implies dependency. Classes that have such a relationship cannot be considered separately. They must be treated as a single implementation entity and we can refer to them as a *compound class*. Friendship represents a behavioural relationship between the classes. The arbitrary declaration of friendship is very bad practice. Some care is needed when friend functions are used. For example, two classes with a common friend function are connected. They become friends of each other. In fact, they are a symmetrical compound class. In general, connecting classes like this should be avoided. If a compound class is wanted, explicitly declare the participating classes as friends.

Friend classes are not used very often, but they can be very useful. A common application is as *iterators* for container classes (see Exercise 9.3).

9.2 Operator overloading

Functions can be defined to overload standard C++ operators, like + or =, for class objects. When an overloaded operator is used, the compiler automatically calls the appropriate function. Almost all of the C++ operators can be overloaded, including the function call operator () and the subscript operator []. However, there are some restrictions:

- New operators cannot be invented.
- An override cannot change the precedence, associativity or arity of an operator.
- The operators . .* :: ?: and sizeof cannot be overloaded.
- The operators for standard types cannot be overloaded.

An operator function must be a non-static member function or have at least one parameter whose type is a class, reference to a class, an enumeration or a reference to an enumeration. Operator functions cannot have default arguments. The only operator that has a default definition is the assignment operator. All the other operators must be defined for a class before they can be used.

Operator overloading can greatly enhance the way class objects are used. Classes with overloaded operators can extend the standard type space in intuitively useful ways. The <iostream.h> library's use of the << and >> operators, for example, makes a complicated set of classes comparatively easy to use. Nevertheless, operator overloading can be overdone. The basic behaviour of a class should come first, with operator overloading being considered as an additional feature to make the class easier to use. It is sometimes called *syntactic sugar*. It makes the syntax of a class interface nice, but does not affect the underlying behaviour of the class.

As a simple example of how operator overloading can be used, we can declare a vector class like this:

```
class Vector {
public:
    Vector(int x, int y, int z);
    Vector& operator*=( double d );
    ...
private:
    ...
};
```

Here, the function `operator*=` is an operator overload that performs scalar multiplication. That is, its implementation multiplies every coordinate of the vector by the value d. Given a `Vector` called `top`, the function can be called with either of:

```
top.operator*=(3.4);
top *= 3.4;
```

More generally, *binary operators* can be defined as non-static member functions taking one parameter, or as non-member functions with two parameters. The expression xx◊yy is interpreted as either `xx.operator◊(yy)` or `operator◊(xx,yy)`. However, an operator function taking a basic type as its first argument cannot be a member function. So the expression aa + 2 can be `aa.operator+(2)`, but 2 + aa has to be `operator+(2,aa)`.

A *unary operator* can be a non-static member function with no parameters or a non-member function with one parameter. So the expression ◊xx is interpreted as `xx.operator◊()` or `operator◊(xx)`.

Table 9.1 gives a summary of the relationship between expressions and the equivalent function call notation.

Table 9.1   Operator overload function notation.

expression	as member function	as non-member function
◊xx	`xx.operator◊()`	`operator◊(xx)`
xx◊	`xx.operator◊(0)`	`operator◊(xx,0)`
xx ◊ yy	`xx.operator◊(yy)`	`operator◊(yy,zz)`
xx[yy]	`xx.operator[](yy)`	
xx(yy,zz)	`xx.operator()(yy,zz)`	
xx->m	`xx.operator->()`	
xx = yy	`xx.operator=(yy)`	

where ◊ is a standard operator such as +

9.2.1   Increment and decrement operators

The operators ++ and −− can be used in prefix or postfix form. As prefix operators they are the same as a normal unary operator. This means they are non-static member functions with no parameters, or non-member functions with one parameter. The expression ++xx is interpreted as `xx.operator++()` or `operator++(xx)`. Postfix operator functions are a little unusual. They must be non-static member functions with one parameter of type int, or a non-member function with two arguments the second of which must be of type int. When a postfix operator function is called the int argument always has the value zero. So the expression xx++ is interpreted as `xx.operator++(0)` or `operator++(xx,0)`. When the function is implemented, the integer parameter is ignored. This trick allows us to distinguish between prefix and postfix operators, so they can have different behaviour if required.

Some care is needed when writing these operator overloads if they are going to be compatible with the general behaviour of the standard operators. Prefix operators should return the value of the variable to which they are applied after the operation has been performed; and postfix operators should return the value of the variable before the operation is performed. The following example mimics the behaviour of the standard ++ operators for a class object:

```
class Counter {
public:
    Counter( int i = 0 )
        : data(i) {}
    int value()
        { return data; }
    Counter operator++(int)        // postfix
        { Counter pre = *this;
          data += 1;
          return pre; }
    Counter operator++()           // prefix
        { data += 1;
          return *this; }
private:
    int data;
};
```

The way this works can be understood by considering the following assignment between two Counter objects:

```
Counter c = 5, result;
result = c++;
```

Here, the postfix application of ++ to a Counter object causes the member function c.operator++(0) to be called. When this executes, a copy of the object is saved in the local variable pre using the this pointer (see §8.4). Then the object is modified, and the saved value returned from the function. Notice that the equivalent prefix operator overload does not save and return the original value.

9.2.2 Assignment operator

The assignment operator function must be a non-static member function with exactly one parameter. It overloads the = operator. Assignment operator functions are not inherited.

A default is generated if an assignment operator, with a parameter of the same type as the class, is not defined for the class. This has the form:

```
MyClass& MyClass::operator=( const MyClass& from )
{
    // copy members of from to this class
    return *this;
}
```

The default operator performs a memberwise copy. This copies each data member from the parameter to the object for which the default was invoked. If an assignment operator is defined for the member, it is used, otherwise a bitwise copy is performed. This default behaviour is an important characteristic of C++, and is discussed further in §9.4. Finally, the assignment operator returns a reference to the object for which it was invoked. A default assignment operator will not be generated if the class has a non-static data member that is a constant or a reference, or if any of its data members (or base classes) does not have an accessible assignment operator.

User defined assignment operators are easy to define:

```
MyClass& MyClass::operator=( const MyClass& from )
{
    if ( this != &from ) {
        // perform necessary processing
    }
    return *this;
}
```

As expected, this function looks very like the default version. The if statement checks for assignment to self by comparing the this pointer with the address of the function's argument.

More than one assignment operator function can be declared with parameters of different type. However, it is common practice to define only a replacement for the default assignment operator, and also to declare suitable constructors to convert other objects to the class type (see §9.2.7). In this way, the assignment overload function obtains its parameter via a constructor, which will be automatically invoked, and many different types of object can be managed by the same overload function. As a bonus, the constructors will perform a similar service whenever the class is used as a function parameter.

The compound assignment operators, like +=, do not have a default behaviour like =. They are handled as ordinary binary operators, and do not have to be member functions.

9.2.3 Function call operator

A function that overloads the call operator function must be a non-static member of its class. It overloads the ( ) of a function call, so that the expression xx(arg1,arg2,arg3) is interpreted as xx.operator()(arg1, arg2,arg3).

Function call overloads can be used to make a class object behave like a set of functions. As a trivial example we could add two member functions to the Counter class given in the last section:

```
class Counter {
    ...
public:
    ...
    void operator()( int count )
        { data = count; }
    int operator()()
        { return data; }
private:
    int data;
};

void main()
{
    Counter ticker;    // create instance
    ticker(23);        // set ticker to 23
    ticker++;          // adds one to ticker
    cout << ticker();  // print current value
}
```

9.2.4 Subscripts

A subscript operator function must be a non-static member function with one parameter. It overloads [ ], so that the expression xx[3] is interpreted as xx.operator[](3). This overload is obviously very useful for making a class object look like an array. Here is a possible member function for an IntArray class:

```
int& IntArray:operator[]( int subscript )
{
    if ( outrange(subscript) ) {
        // error processing
    }
    return privatearray[subscript];
}
```

121

The referential return type int& is significant. It allows the function to be used on either side of an assignment operator. So aa[1] = aa[2] + 3 is valid when aa is of type IntArray. In this case, the same function is called for aa[1] and aa[2], which returns a reference to be used appropriately by the assignment operator. When subscript overloads are used like this, it is not possible to differentiate between subscripts on the left- and right-hand side of an assignment operator. (Exercise 9.4 and its model solution gives a method for doing this.)

9.2.5 Pointers and address operators

We can make a class look like a pointer by overloading the -> and * operators. The class member access operator -> can be overloaded by a non-static member function with no parameters. The expression xp->m is interpreted as (xp.operator->()).m, which limits the way the function can behave. It must return one of: a pointer to a class that has the specified member, an object of a class for which operator-> is defined, or a reference to a class for which operator-> is defined.

The standard unary * operator dereferences a pointer to an object. It can be overloaded with a non-static member function with no parameters, or a non-member function with one parameter. So the expression *xp is interpreted as xp.operator*() or operator*(xp). The function can return any type that is compatible with its intended behaviour. So, in the expression (*xp).m, the function xp.operator*() must return an object with an accessible data member called m.

The address operator & is also unary, and can be overloaded by the same sort of functions as the * operator. To be consistent with the built operator, a & operator overload function must return a pointer to an object.

9.2.6 New and delete

Standard dynamic memory management for a class can be replaced by overloading the allocation and deallocation operators: new, new[], delete and delete[]. This might be done, for example, to optimize memory allocation or to implement automatic garbage collection for the class.

An overloaded allocation or deallocation operator is a static member function, even if it is not explicitly declared as static. The operator new function is always called with the amount of space requested as its first argument. The type of this argument is size_t, which is a platform dependent integer type defined in the header <stdlib.h>. Additional parameters can be declared and default arguments can be used. An allocation function should return void*. This is automatically converted to a pointer to the allocation function's class. Constructors are called, as usual, after the allocation function is finished. If any `operator new` function is declared for a class, the standard allocation function is not available for that class. The following shows how the allocation operators can be declared for a class:

```
#include <stdlib.h>
. . .
class Myclass {
public:
    Myclass();
    Myclass( string note );
    void* operator new( size_t space );               // A
    void* operator new[]( size_t space );             // B
    void* operator new( size_t space, int data );     // C
    void* operator new[]( size_t space, int data );   // D
    . . .
};
```

Here, the `space` parameter is the required allocation, and `data` is an additional user provided parameter. The functions can be called like this:

```
Myclass* aaa = new Myclass("test1");        // use version A
Myclass* bbb = new(99) Myclass("test2");    // use version C
Myclass* bbb = new Myclass[24];             // use version B
Another* ccc = new Myclass("test4");        // error - wrong
                                            // pointer type
```

In the second example above, the argument in `new(99)` is passed to the function as the `data` parameter.

A deallocation function is implicitly called by deleting an instance of an object. An `operator delete` function can have one or two parameters and must return `void`:

```
class Myclass {
public:
    . . .
    void operator delete[]( void* addr );
    void operator delete( void* addr, size_t space );
    . . .
};
```

The first parameter is of type `void*`, and is the address of the released memory block. This is the value that the `operator new` function returned when the block was allocated. The second optional parameter is the size of the released block. This is of type `size_t`, and it has the same value as the first parameter of the `operator   new` function when the block was allocated. A destructor, if is is declared for the class, will be called before the `operator delete` function. There can only be one `operator delete` and `operator delete[]` in a class.

The standard global allocation and deallocation functions can be overloaded with appropriate non-member functions, and allocation functions with extra parameters can be declared. These will be applied to all classes that do not have their own allocation and deallocation functions and to all non-class types. Take care; overloading `new` and `delete` is never simple, and the damage caused by any mistake is normally serious.

9.2.7 Type conversion

Type conversions will be performed automatically for classes if suitable constructors and conversion operators are declared. A constructor will be used if it can be invoked with a single argument that matches the type to be converted. The following shows how constructors are invoked for conversion:

```
class Puppy {
public:
    Puppy( string name );
    ...
};

class Wolf {
public:
    Wolf( string name );
    ...
};

class Dog {
public:
    Dog();
    Dog( char name[] );
    Dog( string name );
    Dog( double kilos );
    Dog( Puppy littledog );
    explicit Dog( Wolf wilddog );
};

void main()
{
    double pounds = 65;
    Dog woof;
    Puppy lick("Spot");
```

```
    Wolf bite("Big Bad");
    woof = "Fido";          // Dog(char[]) called
    woof = string("Fido"); // Dog(string) called
    woof = pounds * 0.45;  // Dog(double) called
    woof = lick;            // Dog(Puppy) called
    woof = bite;            // error - conversion not explicit
    woof = Dog(bite);       // okay - conversion explicit
}
```

Here, "Fido" is considered to be a C string so Dog(char[]) is called. To invoke Dog(string), an explicit string constant has to be used. The constructor Dog(double) is called for an arithmetic value, and a Puppy class is converted with Dog(Puppy). Implicit conversions like this can be prevented by declaring the relevant constructor with the keyword explicit, as shown with Dog(Wolf). Conversion constructors are useful, but they are limited. They can only be used for conversions to the class; they cannot be used for conversions to the fundamental types, and they must be provided by the class designer.

Conversion operators can be declared for a class. These allow conversion from a class to another type. So existing classes can be integrated without modification. They can also convert to the fundamental types. A conversion operator must be a member function with no parameters and no return type. It adopts the type given by its name. For example,

```
class Cat {
public:
    . . .
    operator Dog()
       { return Dog(thename); }
    . . .
private:
    string thename;
    . . .
};
```

The member function operator Dog in this class is a conversion operator. It is used in the following to convert a Cat to a Dog:

```
Dog woof;
Cat meaow;
. . .
woof = meaow;   // convert then assign
```

As another example, consider a Vector class. The length of a vector is called its magnitude. This is a single number and it could be returned from a conversion operator:

125

```
class Vector {
public:
   operator double() const;    // magnitude of vector
   ...
};
```

As required, the operator has no return type and no parameters. It is declared as `const` because conversion operators do not change their object's state. Its implementation returns a double value:

```
Vector::operator double() const
{
   double magnitude = ....;      // calculate magnitude
   return magnitude;
}
```

Conversion operators can be used explicitly, but they will also be implicitly called if required. So all of the following are okay:

```
Vector top(1,2,3);
double length;
length = (double)top;
length = double(top);
length = 3.6 + top / 2;
```

The built-in conversions can participate. So, for example, an `int` might be converted to a `double` before a match with a constructor is found. At most, one user defined conversion will be automatically applied to a single value. Explicit conversions can be used to overcome this limitation, as the following show:

```
class Position {
public:
   operator Vector();
   ...
};
...
Position p;
double m = p;          // error - too many conversions
double n = Vector(p);  // okay
```

Here, the automatic conversion from `Position` to `double` fails because two conversion operators are needed. The error is avoided by making one of the conversions explicit.

Almost any type can be used with a conversion operator, including pointers, classes and enumerations. However, it is not possible to convert to `void`, or to the operator's own class (or its base classes).

9.2.8 Style

Always define a operator so that it is compatible with its built-in version. *Do not surprise the user.* Notable exceptions are the << and >> operators. These are the built-in bit shift operators, but are overloaded in the standard C++ library <iostream.h> to represent input and output operations. It is this overloaded meaning that is now considered to be normal by most C++ programmers.

It is often difficult to decide how to represent an operator overload. Some guidelines are:

- Make it a member if it updates the object.
- Make it a member if it returns an lvalue (i.e. it can be on the left-hand side of an assignment).
- Make it a member if it references only the object, and declare it const if it does not update the object.
- The operators =, [], (), ->, new, delete and conversion operators must be member functions.
- A binary operator function taking a basic type as its first argument cannot be a member function.
- In general, if a binary operator function does not update its parameter objects, make it a non-member function.

It is normally acceptable to make non-member operator functions friends of their class. If this is done, all operator functions will be part of their class. This will produce a consistent interface, and allow for an optimal implementation, but take care not to couple classes inadvertently as explained in §9.1.2. However, if suitable public member functions are declared for the class, use them. This may mean that the operator does not have to be a friend or member function.

Consider the return type. If operators are going to be combined in expressions, a non-void type will be needed. Decide if the operator should return an lvalue. Return a reference if it is safe to do so. This is for efficiency with large objects. Make it a const reference if the object should not be an lvalue.

9.2.9 I/O operator overloads

The <iostream.h> operators << and >> can be overridden. They must be declared to be compatible with other I/O operators. So their form is:

```
ostream& operator<<( ostream& c, const T& t );
istream& operator>>( istream& c, T& t );
```

They are often declared as friends for efficiency and symmetry. But they do not have to be if suitable member functions already exist.

Once declared, I/O operator overloads in effect extend the standard I/O library. Their implementation must look like this:

```
ostream& operator<<( ostream& os, const Dog& adog )
{
    os << adog.name();        // print Dog data
    ...
    return os;
}

istream& operator>>( istream& is, Dog& adog )
{
    string aname;
    is >> name;               // input dog data
    adog.name(aname);
    ...
    return is;
}
```

The design of `<iostream.h>` overloads needs some care. The stream parameters os and is must be declared as references, and they should be returned from the functions, so that the overloads have the same behaviour as the standard operators. Remember to use the parameter name rather than cout or cin in these functions.

The format of data in the input and output streams is important. Output can be directed at the screen through cout. So do not inject line breaks, or << will be incompatible with the fundamental types. The << and >> operators can be used with named files. In this context they are marshalling functions that write objects to disk, and later retrieve them. Thus the >> operator must be able to read anything the << operator can produce, and such functions must be able to store and completely recover an object's state. This is not simple.

If there is no need for a class to be compatible with the standard I/O streams, do not overload << and >>. It is simpler, and will cause users of a class less confusion, to declare a specialized function, called say display, that is designed to output the relevant parts of a class to cout if this is all that is needed.

9.3   An example

The following is an example of operator overloading. It is a Money class that stores numerical values with two decimal places. It supports calculations involving addition, subtraction, multiplication and division. The result of these operations is rounded to the nearest penny (or cent), and the difference is accumulated, so the total error due to rounding can be obtained after a series of Money calculations. Member functions are provided for temporarily suspending rounding error accumulation, and for resetting the accumulator to zero. A Money object can be used with istream and ostream for input and output. The class declaration is as follows:

```
class Money {
// addition operators
 friend Money operator+( const Money& a, const Money& b );
 friend Money operator+( long double a, const Money& b );
 friend Money operator+( const Money& a, long double b );
// subtraction operators
 friend Money operator-( const Money& a, const Money& b );
 friend Money operator-( long double a, const Money& b );
 friend Money operator-( const Money& a, long double b );
// multiplication operators
 friend Money operator*( const Money& a, const Money& b );
 friend Money operator*( long double a, const Money& b );
 friend Money operator*( const Money& a, long double b );
// division operators
 friend Money operator/( const Money& a, const Money& b );
 friend Money operator/( long double a, const Money& b );
 friend Money operator/( const Money& a, long double b );
// input output operators
friend ostream& operator<<( ostream& os, const Money& om );
friend istream& operator>>( istream& is, Money& im );
 public:
   Money();
     // Initialize to zero
   Money( long double avalue );
     // Initialize to rounded 'avalue'
   operator long double() const;
     // conversion to arithmetic type
   static long double round();
     // Value of rounding accumulator
   static void clear_round();
     // Reset rounding accumulator to zero
   static void hold_round();
     // Stop accumulating rounding errors
   static void release_round();
     // Restart accumulating rounding errors
private:
   long double value;               // money value
```

```
static long double rounds;      // rounding accumulator
static bool updating;           // accumulation flag
void doupdate( long double newvalue );
    // update stored value and rounding accumulator
};
```

The interface to Money has been designed to allow mixed calculations, involving Money objects, and fundamental arithmetic variables and constants. Each operator has been declared three times, with a mixture of long double and Money parameters, which allows Money and arithmetic values to be used on either side of an operator. So the following is possible:

```
Money cash = 78.90, payment;
payment = 3.6 * cash;
payment = cash + payment;
payment = cash - 34;
double value = cash + payment; //   convert Money to double
```

An implementation for Money is not difficult. Its most complicated aspect is the calculation and accumulation of the rounding errors. The accumulator, called rounds, is declared as a static variable because it has to collect rounding errors from all the instances of Money in a program. A Boolean variable called updating controls the accumulation of rounding errors, and this is also declared as a static variable. These are defined and initialized with:

```
long double Money::rounds = 0;
bool Money::updating = true;
```

The private member function doupdate performs the rounding calculation for the constructors and friends of Money. Its definition is:

```
void Money::doupdate( long double newvalue )
{
    value = floor(( newvalue + 0.005 ) * 100) / 100;
    if ( updating )
        rounds += newvalue - value;
}
```

The rounded value is calculated by adding a half penny (or cent) to the input value, and then truncating the result after two decimal places. The rounding error is the difference between the original and rounded values. This is added to rounds only if updating is true. The value of updating is controlled by the member functions hold_round and release_round and the accumulator can be reset with clear_round. These are very simple:

```
void Money::hold_round()
{
```

```
   updating = false;
}

void Money::release_round()
{
   updating = true;
}

void Money::clear_round()
{
   rounds = 0;
}
```

The constructors look like this:

```
Money::Money() : value(0.0) {}

Money::Money( long double avalue )
{
   doupdate(avalue);
}
```

The operator overload functions for the division operator are defined as follows:

```
Money operator/( const Money& a, const Money& b )
{
   Money result;
   result.doupdate( a.value / b.value );
   return result;
}

Money operator/( long double a, const Money& b )
{
   Money result;
   result.doupdate( a / b.value );
   return result;
}

Money operator/( const Money& a, long double b )
{
   Money result;
   result.doupdate( a.value / b );
   return result;
}
```

These are very similar, the only difference being the calculation of the argument passed to doupdate. Which one is called depends on the order and type of the arguments used with the / operator.

Three `operator/` functions are declared for efficiency, as is the way they are implemented. This approach minimizes the number of function calls. However, in this case, only one function with a much simpler implementation is actually needed:

```
Money operator/( const Money& a, const Money& b )
{
    return a.value / b.value ;
}
```

If this were the only division operator, calculations like 24.7 / pay would still work. The arithmetic constant would be automatically converted to a `Money` object by a call to a constructor. The constructor will also be called to convert the result of the division calculation into a `Money` object, so that it can be returned from the function. This works as required because the relevant constructor calls `doupdate`. Thus, the `Money` class could have been written in a more concise way, but at the cost of a slightly less efficient implementation.

9.4 Safe classes

Incorrect use of constructors, destructors and assignment operators in classes that use dynamic memory allocation can result in data loss and damage. To understand why there is a potential problem, we must look at when and how objects are copied. A C++ object is automatically copied when it is used with an assignment operator; it is passed by value as an argument to a function; it is used to initialize a new instance of its type; or it is passed by value from a function with a return statement.

In all these cases a default behaviour is supplied: a member by member copy is performed. This results in a *shallow copy*. If a data member is a pointer, it is the value of the pointer that is copied, rather than the target data. This may be okay, but in most cases it will produce unfortunate results. As an extreme example, consider a class that contains a pointer to a dynamic data structure, and a destructor function that deletes the structure:

```
class Stocklist {
public:
    Stocklist( int size )
        {  codeset = new int[size];
           thesize = size;
           for ( int i = 0; i < thesize; i++ )
              codeset[i] = 1;
           ... }
    ~Stocklist()
```

```
      {  delete[] codeset; }
   ...
private:
   int* codeset;
   int thesize;
   ...
};
```

If an object of this type is passed to a function by value, a temporary copy is automatically created. This is a shallow copy, so the original and the copy are pointing to the same codeset. When the function is finished, the temporary object will be destroyed. This will invoke the class's destructor, which deletes the array using the copy of the pointer in the temporary object. In summary, we have passed a Stocklist object to a function as an input-only argument and some of its data have been destroyed. This is not what we would normally expect.

This sort of complicated situation is easily avoided by declaring a copy constructor and an assignment operator for the class:

```
class Stocklist {
public:
   Stocklist( int size )
      {  ... }
   Stocklist( const Stocklist& s )
      {  buildnew(s.codeset,s.thesize); }
   Stocklist& operator=( const Stocklist& s )
      {  if ( this != &s ) {
            delete[] codeset;
            buildnew(s.codeset,s.thesize);
         }
         return *this; }
   ~Stocklist()
      {  delete[] codeset; }
   ...
private:
   int* codeset;
   int thesize;
   ...
   void buildnew( int acodeset[], int asize )
      {  codeset = new int[asize];
         thesize = asize;
         for ( int i = 0; i < thesize; i++ )
            codeset[i] = acodeset[i];
         ... }
};
```

Now, if a `Stocklist` object is passed to a function by value, the copy constructor will be called. This will create a *deep copy* of the object. When the function finishes the destructor will be called, but this time it will be applied to a discrete copy of the object and the original will not be damaged. The assignment operator also performs a deep copy, but it checks to see if it is copying to itself before deleting the old data and doing the copy.

An alternative is to prevent the class from being used in an unsafe way. This is very easy to do, just declare the copy constructor and assignment operator as private like this:

```
class Stocklist {
public:
    Stocklist( int size )
        {  ... }
    ~Stocklist()
        {  delete[] codeset; }
    ...
private:
    Stocklist( const Stocklist& ) {}
    Stocklist& operator=( const Stocklist& ) { return *this; }
private:
    int* codeset;
    int thesize;
    ...
};
```

This will prevent the class being used in an unsafe way. The compiler will report an error if anything is done that would normally invoke the copy constructor, or assignment operator. In particular, it is not possible to pass a `Stocklist` object to a function by value. An attempt to do so will cause a compiler error. The functions do not need proper definitions, because they are never actually called. Dummy inline bodies are given for correctness, because some compilers and linkers complain if this is not done. Restricting the use of constructors and operators in this way should be considered part of a class's public behaviour, even though we are declaring private functions, because it affects the way in which the class can be used.

9.5 Exercises

1. Write a `Time` class that stores hours, minutes and seconds. It should have binary addition and subtraction operators for combining two `Time` objects, and `<iostream.h>` insertion and extraction operators. A single constructor, with default values for hours, minutes and seconds should be sufficient.

2. Make the `List` class given in §8.10 safe by:
   (a) Restricting its copy constructor and assignment operator.
   (b) Implementing a suitable copy constructor and assignment operator.

3. Write a class for storing names. It should have an iterator in the form of a friend class. The maximum number of names that can be held should be declared when a store is created. For the purpose of this exercise, the store need only have functions for adding a name, checking if a name is already in the store, and for detecting if there is room for more names to be added. The iterator should provide facilities for stepping through the names in the store, determining when all the names have been processed, and for restarting the iteration.

4. Write a class with its subscript operator overloaded in such a way that the operator has very different behaviour when used on different sides of an assignment operator. For this exercise, make the operator print a diagnostic message giving the subscript, the side of the assignment operator the `[]` is on, and if it is on the left-hand side, the value being assigned. So `x[4] = 6` will generate a message something like `subscript 4 on LHS, with 6 being assigned`. When `[]` is used on the right of an `=`, return a dummy integer value of say 99. This exercise is not easy. Consider using two classes, one being a helper class with an overloaded assignment operator.

CHAPTER 10

Inheritance

10.1   Using inheritance

Objects sometimes share common behaviour. For example, if we were to manage information about cars and buses, there might be operations that could be applied to both of these types of object. This can be achieved by having two classes with the same member functions. Alternatively, if the common behaviour can be reasonably expressed as a separate class, inheritance can be used. A Vehicle class is defined that captures the common behaviour of cars and buses. Then specializations of this class are declared using inheritance: we *derive* Car and Bus classes from Vehicle. The class Vehicle is called a *base class* of Car.

The behaviour or specification of a derived class is composed of its own public members and those in its base classes. This makes sense because there is an "is a" relationship between derived and base classes: a car is a kind of vehicle. So we would expect a Bus object to respond to the same operations as a Vehicle object. The public members of a base class must be considered as part of its derived classes. Although base and derived classes are declared separately, their public sections contribute to single derived behaviour.

A derived class has the same type as any of its base classes. Wherever the base class is used, an object derived from the base can also be used. In this way, a derived class is a subtype of its base class.

Inheritance has advantages. It encourages effective program decomposition, and it can be used to extend the standard type system of C++.

10.2 Simple inheritance

The following is a declaration for a time class:

```
class Timec {
public:
    Timec();
    Timec( long sec );
    Timec( int hr, int min, int sec );
    void forward( int sec = 1 );
    void reset();
    int pm() const;
    void showtime( ostream& c ) const;
private:
    long seconds;
    void put_seconds( int h, int m, int s );
    void get_hms( int& h, int& m, int& s ) const;
};
```

This has a few constructors, and some functions for printing, advancing, resetting, and checking the time. As well as being used to define time objects, Timec can be used as a base class like this:

```
class Tagtime : public Timec {
public:
    Tagtime( const string& atag, const Timec& time );
    void newtag( const string& atag );
    void showtag( ostream& c ) const;
private:
    string thetag;
};
```

Here, the class Tagtime, which is a time with a descriptive string, is derived from Timec.

All the public member functions of Timec can also be used with a Tagtime object. The following is an *equivalent* declaration for Tagtime that shows all the available functions:

```
class Tagtime {
public:
    Tagtime( const string& atag, const Timec& time );
    void newtag( const string& atag );
    void showtag( ostream& c ) const;
    void forward( int sec = 1 );
    void reset();
    int pm() const;
```

```
    void showtime( ostream& c ) const;
};
```

The Tagtime class is used just like the Timec class:

```
Timec time1(12,0,0);
time1.forward();
time1.reset();

Tagtime time2("Home time",Timec(17,40,0));
time2.forward();
time2.newtag("No time");
time2.reset();
```

Anything that can be done to a Timec object, can also be done to a Tagtime object, because Timec is a public base class of Tagtime. The Timec class is part of Tagtime, and its public members are also public members of Tagtime. When a Timec member function is used with a Tagtime object, the function is applied to the object's Timec part. However, Tagtime member functions cannot access the private members of Timec.

10.3 Initialization

The constructor of a derived class cannot access the private members of its base class, so the base class data cannot be initialized directly. If it exists, the default constructor for the base class will be automatically called. As an alternative, a specific constructor can be invoked by specifying it in an initializer list. For example, the constructor for Tagtime specifies Timec(t), which is the copy constructor for Timec:

```
Tagtime::Tagtime( const string& atag, const Timec& t )
        : thetag(atag), Timec(t)   {}
```

The constructors for a class object are called in a specific order. First base class constructors in declaration order, then data member constructors in declaration order, and finally the body of the specified constructor is executed. An initializer list specifies which constructors should be used. The default constructor for a class is used if one is not given in the list. Thus a constructor that takes no arguments need not appear in the list. The list can also contain constructors for member class objects. The order of constructors in the list is irrelevant. Destructors are called in reverse order to the constructors.

10.4   Copy constructors and assignment

Unlike other overloaded operators, the assignment operator is not inherited. This means that when assignment is used with instances of a derived class, the assignment operator in its base class is not directly executed.

If an assignment operator is not declared as a member function of a class, memberwise copying is used when instances of the class are assigned. This default behaviour consists of each *base class* and data member being copied from source to assignment target. If an assignment operator is declared for any of the base classes or data members, it will be invoked to perform the copy, otherwise a memberwise copy will be applied.

If an assignment operator is declared as a member function of a class, this function must take complete responsibility for the assignment of all data members and base classes. For example,

```
class Derived : public Base {
public:
    Derived& operator=( const Derived& derv )
    {   if ( this != &derv ) {
            idata = derv.idata;
            cdata = derv.cdata;
            *static_cast<Base*>(this) = derv;
        }
        return *this;
    }
    ...
private:
    int idata;
    Aclass cdata;
};
```

Here, the assignment operator function first checks to see if the source and target objects are the same. This is done by comparing the `this` pointer, which holds the address of the object for which the function was invoked, with the address of the parameter `derv`. If they are different, the = operator is used to copy the base class and each of the data members from the parameter object to the function's object.

Copying the derived class data members is simple, but the base class is a little more complicated. To apply the = operator to just the `Base` part of `Derived`, the `this` pointer is *cast* from type `Derived*` to `Base*`. This is dereferenced to be the target of the assignment. The right-hand operand of the assignment is the parameter `derv`, and this is automatically sliced so that its `Base` part fits into the `Base` part of `Derived`. The cast is performed with a `static_cast`, which is explained in §13.2.

Copy constructors are similar to assignment operators. In the absence of such a constructor, a memberwise copy is used to initialize a new class object from an existing one. The memberwise copy is applied to all base classes and data members of the class. A copy constructor will be used if it exists in the base class and data member, otherwise a memberwise copy will be applied.

If a copy constructor is declared in a class, it must manage all of the work required to initialize a new instance of the class. Using `Derived` as an example, its copy constructor might look like this:

```
Derived::Derived( Derived& derv )
    : idata(derv.idata), cdata(derv.cdata), Base(derv) {}
```

Here, an initializer list which includes the base class is used. Each of the data members is initialized with the appropriate data member from the parameter `derv`. The base class is initialized with the whole `Derived` parameter, from which the `Base` part is automatically extracted. If the base class has a copy constructor, this will be invoked, otherwise a default copy constructor will be generated to perform a memberwise copy.

10.5 Overriding inherited functions

Inherited functions can be redefined or overridden. For example, we can declare a class based on `Timec`:

```
class Daytime : public Timec {
public:
    enum Daytime( int day, int hr, int min, int sec );
    void reset();
    void forward( int seconds );
    void showday( ostream& c ) const;
private:
    int theday;
};
```

This class extends `Timec` with a day number. The `reset` and `forward` functions in `Timec` are *overridden* because they have to handle the day number. As an alternative, specially named functions such as `day-forward` could be declared, leaving the original `Timec` member functions visible. However, overriding base class functions is a good way of maintaining a consistent interface in a derived class.

The overridden functions are members of `Daytime` and their definitions are:

```
void Daytime::reset()
{
```

```
    theday = 0;
    Timec::reset();
}
void Daytime::forward( int seconds )
{
    int prevpm = pm();
    Timec::forward(seconds);
    if ( prevpm && !pm() )
        theday++;
}
```

Both of these functions combine processing for the Daytime part of the class with the compatible processing for Timec. The derived class has no access to the private parts of Timec, so the work is delegated to the overridden functions in Timec. These are called with a scope operator to prevent a recursive loop. The Daytime::forward function uses the pm function in Timec to identify a transition from one day to the next. The pm function does not need a scope operator because its name is unique within Daytime and Timec.

The constructor for Daytime is simple to implement using an initializer list:

```
Daytime::Daytime( int day, int hr, int min, int sec )
    : Timec(hr,min,sec), theday(day) {}
```

Overriding does not remove a function from the base class, it just replaces it in the derived class, hiding the original. Under some circumstances the original can still be used. For example, if an instance of a derived class is accessed through a pointer to its base, any overriding functions present in the derived class will be ignored.

10.6 Restriction

The behaviour of an inherited class can be restricted by overriding its member functions. We could have decided that Tagtime objects should not be reset, even though this operation is available for its base class Timec. The reset function in Timec can be disabled by declaring it as private in Tagtime:

```
class Tagtime : public Timec {
public:
    Tagtime( const string& atag, const Timec& time );
    void newtag( const string& atag );
    void showtag( ostream& c ) const;
```

```
private:
   void reset() {};   // hides inherited reset
   string thetag;
};
```

It does not have to do anything, so it is defined inline with an empty body. Now, if reset is used with a Tagtime object, the compiler will report an error:

```
Tagtime time2("Home time",Timec(17,40,0));
time2.forward();
time2.newtag("Tea time");
time2.reset();          // error - private in derived class
```

Restriction does not remove a function from the base class, it just hides it in the derived class. Under some circumstances it can still be used. For example, if an instance of a derived class is accessed through a pointer or reference to its base, any restrictions present in the derived class will not be enforced.

10.7 Multiple inheritance

A class can have more than one base class. This is called *multiple inheritance*. As a simple example, we will declare two classes, Time and Date:

```
class Time {
public:
   Time() : mins(0), hours(0) {}
   void set( int h, int m )
      { mins = m; hours = h; }
   void get( int& h, int& m ) const
      { m = mins; h = hours; }
private:
   int mins;
   int hours;
};

class Date {
public:
   Date() : day(0), month(0), year(0) {}
   void set( int d, int m, int y )
      { day = d; month = m; year = y;}
   void get( int& d, int& m, int& y ) const
      { d = day; m = month; y = year; }
private:
```

143

```
    int day;
    int month;
    int year;
};
```

These are used to form another class called `Appointment`. There is an "is a" relationship between the classes: `Appointment` is a `Time`, and `Appointment` is a `Date`. The new class looks like this:

```
class Appointment : public Time, public Date {
public:
    Appointment();
    void set( const string& c );
    string get() const;
    void display( ostream& c ) const;
private:
    string comment;
};
```

It has two base classes, `Time` and `Date`. Its behaviour combines its public section with the public parts of both these classes.

The member function names in the base classes are unfortunately similar, so a lot of scope operators have to be used. For example the `display` function has to access information in both of the base classes using their `get` functions:

```
void Appointment::display( ostream& c )
{
    int day, month, year, hour, min;
    Date::get(day,month,year);
    Time::get(hour,min);
    c << day << '/' << month << '/' << year;
    c << " @ " << hour << '.' << min;
    c << " | " << comment;
}
```

The scope operator is also needed, when the `Appointment` class is used, to distinguish between three different `set` functions:

```
Appointment urgent;
urgent.Time::set(1,30);
urgent.Date::set(1,2,1992);
urgent.set("go to shops");
urgent.display();
```

When `set` is called without a scope operator, the function in `Appointment` is used. There is no initializer list for `Appointment`, which means the default constructors `Timem()` and `Date()` are invoked.

144

10.8   Virtual base classes

There is a particular problem associated with multiple inheritance. When a base class is accessed via two different inheritance routes, the base class may not be unique. This situation is easier to understand with an example.

(**a**) Without virtual base class   (**b**) With virtual base classes

Figure 10.1   Arrangement of classes with multiple inheritance.

Consider two classes `ShiftReg` and `BitReg`, both derived from `Reg`, and another class called `ShiftBit` derived from `ShiftReg` and `BitReg`. Figure 10.1a shows the normal relationship between these classes. Here, there are two distinct instances of `Reg`: one accessed through `ShiftReg` and the other through `BitReg`. Sometimes this is exactly the relationship required, but in this case we want `ShiftReg` and `BitReg` operations to be applied to the same data value. Thus separate instances of `Reg` are inappropriate. A single shared instance of `Reg` is obtained by making `Reg` a *virtual base class* of `BitReg` and `ShiftReg`, as shown in Figure 10.1b.

The following example demonstrates how virtual base classes are declared:

```
class Reg {
public:
    Reg()
        : thevalue(0) {}
    Reg( int avalue )
        : thevalue(avalue) {}
    int value()
        { return thevalue; }
    void value( int avalue )
        { thevalue = avalue; }
private:
    int thevalue;
};
```

145

```
class ShiftReg : public virtual Reg {
public:
    ShiftReg( int n = 0 ) : Reg(n) {}
    void shiftleft();
       // shift register value left one bit
    void shiftright();
       // shift register value right one bit
};

class BitReg : public virtual Reg {
public:
    BitReg( int n = 0 ) : Reg(n) {}
    void setbit( int mask );
       // Set bits in register to one, depending on mask.
       // If mask bit is one, equivalent bit in register
       // is modified, otherwise bit is unaffected
    void clearbit( int mask );
       // Set bits in register to zero depending on mask.
       // If mask bit is one, equivalent bit in register
       // is modified, otherwise bit is unaffected
};

class ShiftBitReg : public ShiftReg, public BitReg {
public:
    ShiftBitReg( int n ) : Reg(n) {}
};
```

Here, the virtual keyword is used when declaring Reg as a base class. The member functions of ShiftReg and BitReg both use Reg:

```
void ShiftReg::shiftleft()
{
    value(value() * 2);
}

void BitReg::setbit( int mask )
{
    value(value() | mask);
}
```

Notice that the derived class requiring the behaviour of multiple inheritance is not the one that asks for it. This has to be done by the classes immediately derived from the virtual base class.

The declaration of a virtual base class in the example above ensures that here is one copy of Reg in an instance of ShiftBitReg. So the following, which calls member functions from the base and derived classes, works as expected, with all operations being applied to the same data:

```
ShiftBitReg register1(24);   // from ShiftBitReg
register1.value(16);         // from Reg
register1.shiftleft();       // from ShiftReg
register1.setbit(2);         // from BitReg
```

There are restrictions on the way constructors can be used with virtual base classes. A constructor for a virtual base class will only be invoked from the derived class that actually creates the object. Base class constructors specified in the initializer lists of intermediate classes will not be called. However the initializer lists must still be correctly formed and the constructors must be defined in the relevant base classes. In the above example, when the instance of ShiftBitReg called register1 is created, the constructor Reg(int) is executed once with an argument of 24. It is not invoked again when the constructors for ShiftReg and BitReg are executed as part of the object's construction, despite its specification in their initializer lists. If the creating class does not explicitly specify a constructor for a virtual base class, the default base class constructor is used.

10.9   Class access

There are three levels of access to a member of a class: *public*, *private* and *protected*. Public members are available to users of an instance of the class. Private members can only be used by the friends and member functions of their class. Protected members are not available to users of an instance of the class, but they can be used by the friends and member functions of a derived class. The following example demonstrates the rules of access for the protected section of a class:

```
class Base {
public:
   void pub();
protected:
   void prot();
private:
   void priv(); // can only be used in pub() and prot()
};

class Derived : public Base {
public:
   void test()
      {  pub();         // okay
         prot();        // okay
         priv();        // error - cannot access private member
      }
};
```

```
void main()
{
    Base bb;
    bb.pub();        // okay
    bb.prot();       // error - cannot access protected member
    bb.priv();       // error - cannot access private member
    Derived dd;
    dd.test();       // okay
    dd.pub();        // okay
    dd.prot();       // error - cannot access protected member
    dd.priv();       // error - cannot access private member
}
```

In summary, if the declaration is:

private   The data or function can only be used by member functions and friends of the class in which they are declared.

protected   The data or function can only be used by member functions and friends, *plus* member functions and friends of derived classes.

public   The data or function can be used by member functions and friends of the class, and non-member functions.

The public and protected sections of a class allow two interfaces to exist at the same time: one that specifies the behaviour of objects of that class, and another that assists the implementation of derived classes. The approach used for the design of the protected part of a class should be the same as that used for its public parts. They are both interfaces that define the behaviour of the class. The data members of a base class can be declared as protected, but this is not a recommended approach. Allowing access to data means that the implementation of the base class cannot be altered without disrupting derived classes. It is much better to provide protected access functions that mask the implementation of the base class.

10.10   Methods of inheritance

A base class can be declared as public, private or protected when it is inherited, as the following shows:

```
class Derived : public Base    {...};
class Derived : protected Base {...};
class Derived : private Base   {...};
class Derived : Base {...};  // private by default
```

The kind of inheritance used affects the visibility of the base class members, as shown in Figure 10.2. A derived class can always access the public and protected sections of its base class, but cannot access the base class's private section. When *public inheritance* is used the public members of the base class become part of the public section of a derived class, and in a similar way, the base class's protected section is merged with a derived class's protected section. If *protected inheritance* is used, the public and protected sections of the base class become part of the derived class's protected section. Thus the public members of the base class are not available to normal users of a derived class. If *private inheritance* is used, the public and protected sections of the base class both become private, and are not visible to normal users of a derived class.

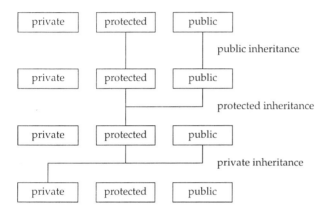

Figure 10.2   Access after inheritance.

When private or protected inheritance is used, access to the members of the base class can be adjusted at most back to its original form, as the following example shows:

```
class Base {
public:
    int pub1();
    int pub2();
    int pub3();
private:
    int priv1();
    ...
};

class Derived : private Base {
public:
    Base::pub1;
    int pub2();          // function overriding
```

```
    Base::priv1; // not allowed
private:
    ...
};

void main()
{
    Derived dd;
    cout << dd.pub1() << endl;    // Base::pub1 executed
    cout << dd.pub2() << endl;    // Derived::pub2 executed
    cout << dd.pub3() << endl;    // Base::pub3 not accessible
}
```

Here, the function `pub`, declared public in `Base`, would normally be private in `Derived` because private inheritance is used. However, in this example, it has been changed to have public access by naming it in the public section of `Derived`. The name must be given in its full form with a scope operator, in this case, `Base::pub`. Any attempt to give a member more access than its original, as with `priv1`, will be rejected.

We can call this process *exposure*. Do not confuse this method with function overriding, which is also demonstrated in the above example. An overridden function replaces the original, whereas an exposed function allows use of the original. In a sense, exposure is the reverse of restriction, discussed in §10.6, where a function in a publicly inherited class is overridden as a private member function.

10.11   Access through a base class

Classes and inheritance can be used to create programmer defined data type hierarchies. We have already seen, in Chapter 7, that classes are treated as data types. Public inheritance extends this idea to allow *subtypes.* This means that wherever instances of a base class are allowed by the type system, an instance of a class derived from the base can be used. This has a significant restriction: derived class members cannot be used. Only those members defined in the base class and publicly inherited are available.

There can be permanent loss of information. Consider the assignment of a derived object to a base class object. This will be allowed because the derived class is a subtype of its base. However, the base class object is not big enough to hold all the information stored in the derived object. The consequence is simple: the derived part of the object is discarded and only the base class's portion of the object is copied to the assignment target. This process is called *slicing*. The following generalized example illustrates the slicing mechanism:

```
class Base {
public:
   Base( int data ) : basedata(data) {}
   int basef()
      { return basedata; }
private:
   int basedata;
};
class Derived : public Base {
public:
   Derived ( int data )
      : dervdata(data), Base(-data) {}
   int dervf()
      { return dervdata; }
private:
   int dervdata;
};
class Derived2 : public Base {
public:
   Derived2 ( int data )
      : Base(-data) {}
};
void main()
{
   Base b1(1);
   Derived d1(2), d2(3);
   Derived2 d3(4);
   d1 = d2;      // simple copy
   b1 = d2;      // slice off base class part
   d2 = b1;      // error: Derived not subtype of Base
   d3 = d2;      // error: Derived2 not subtype of Derived
   cout << b1.basef() << endl;   // okay -3 printed
   cout << b1.dervf() << endl;   // error: dervf not in Base
}
```

Derived is a sub-type of Base

Here, when d2 is assigned to d1 a full copy is performed, and d2 is exactly equal to d1. When d2 is assigned to b1, an instance of its base class, it is sliced. Thus object b1 does not hold the value of dervdata from d1. The basef function can be used with b1, but the dervf function cannot. The assignment of b1 to d2 fails because a base class is not a subtype of its derived class. And d3 = d2 fails because two classes derived from the same base class are not subtypes of each other.

A pointer to an instance of a derived class can be copied to a pointer to an instance of its base class. No slicing is applied to the object, but access to it through the pointer is restricted. Only the base class portion of the object is available. Thus:

```
Base* pb;
Derived d1(5);
pb = &d1;
d1.dervf();      // okay
bp->derv();      // error
```

References to base and derived objects behave in a similar way:

```
void myfunction( Base bin, Base& bout, Derived& dout )
{
   bin.dervf();       // bin is sliced
                      // error: not a member of base class
   bout.basef();      // okay
   bout.dervf();      // bin is not sliced
                      // error: not a member of base class
   dout.basef();      // okay
   dout.dervf();      // okay
}

void main()
{
   Base b2(30);
   Derived d5(3);
   Derived2 d6(20);
   myfunction(b2,b2,d5);     // okay
   myfunction(d5,d6,d5);     // okay
   myfunction(b2,b2,b2);     // error - 3rd arg is of base
type
}
```

In this example, myfunction has three parameters of type Base, Base& and Derived&. Obviously, instances of Base can be used for the first two parameters. But these parameters can also have arguments that are instances of Derived or Derived2. For the first parameter, of type Base, any instance of a derived class will be sliced and the remaining value passed into the function for input only. The second parameter is a reference, so it can be used for input and output. A derived object can be used as its argument. It will not be sliced, but only its base part can be used in the function.

Subtyping is only available with public inheritance. If private or protected inheritance is used, there is no subtype relationship between base and derived classes.

10.12 Design style

Deciding how best to use inheritance in a program design can be difficult. The choice of base and derived classes is not always obvious. In the absence of a more organized object oriented design method, there are two complementary ways of identifying possibilities for inheritance in a program design. Look for "is a" relationships between objects. If Aaa is a Bbb, make Bbb a base class of Aaa. In addition, look for common behaviour in a group of classes. Move this behaviour into a separate class and derive the other classes from this new class.

If a base class is well designed, it can be used during systems maintenance and evolution without modifying its implementation. Its public and protected sections define a stable interface for the use of derived classes. In this way, inheritance promotes code reuse because existing classes can be exploited to develop new derived classes. However, the key feature for reuse is the encapsulation provided by the public and protected interfaces rather than inheritance itself. Base classes should be identified by behavioural decomposition without reference to code reuse. Conceptually it is behaviour that is being reused and shared, not implementation.

Code reuse is an important side effect of inheritance, but it must not be allowed to dominate design decisions. Two classes might both have operations that could share code, but that does not mean that they should be linked by a common base class. For example, a Car and a Vegetable class might both have member functions that calculate weight. An approach that is preoccupied with code reuse might lead to a common base class called say Weighablething. In contrast, a behavioural approach would most likely identify these as completely separate objects, because cars and vegetables do not usually have much in common. So a shared base class would not be used. A behavioural approach to class decompositions is preferred because it reflects the relationship between objects rather than their implementations. Of course, the implementations of Car and Vegetable may use classes and functions that are the same, but inheritance will not be employed just to achieve code reuse.

The different forms of C++ inheritance can cause confusion. Only public inheritance supports a behavioural "is a" relationship and subtyping. The other forms, protected and private, are really forms of containment. Their effect on users of the derived class is exactly the same as if the base class had been declared as a private data member instead of being inherited. They do not make a derived class a subtype of its base class, and they do not support the "is a" relationship. Generally, private and protected inheritance should be avoided and containment used instead. Nevertheless, they are used by some programmers as a notational convenience. For example, naming functions, to expose them in a privately derived class, is easier than writing complete functions that delegate operations to a contained class object.

10.13 Exercises

1. The following `Account` class stores money values. Money can be deposited or withdrawn, and the current balance can be obtained. Objects of this type are initialized with a money value of zero:

```
class Account {
public:
    Account() : amount(0) {}
    void deposit( float money )
        { amount += money;   }
    void withdraw( float money )
        { amount -= money;   }
    float balance() const
        { return amount;      }
private:
    float amount;
};
```

Define another class called `Interest`. This new class should have the same behaviour as `Account`, but should also have member functions for storing and retrieving an interest rate, calculating its value, and adding or removing interest from the account.

2. Write a charity project class called `Cproj` that has start and finish dates and a money account. The start and finish dates should be set in the class's constructor, and only read access allowed after this. Withdrawals should not be allowed for the money account. For simplicity store the dates as strings. Use the `Account` class from Exercise 10.1 as a private base class. Consider if the use of private inheritance would be suitable for an alternative `Cproj` class that had more than one money account.

3. Given the `Account` and `Interest` classes from Exercise 10.1:
   (a) Write a `Named` class that has all the properties of `Account`, plus an account name and code. It should be impossible to change the code after an instance of this class has been created.
   (b) Write a class called `Inamed` that has all the properties of `Named` and `Interest`. Clearly, there should only be one instance of the `Account` base class present. The `Interest` class, as it is designed for Exercise 10.1, is not suitable. How should it be changed to work in this new context?

CHAPTER 11
Virtual functions

11.1 Polymorphism

In general, the concept of polymorphism is concerned with the capability a programming language has for describing the behaviour of a function without depending on its parameters. In an object oriented language this extends to a program's ability to treat many forms of a class as though they were one. In C++ polymorphism is supported in a number of ways:

Adhoc Function overloading provides a kind of polymorphism, where the same operation, in the form of a function name, can be applied to different objects. Adhoc polymorphism is also present when different class objects have functions with the same name and purpose. So, for example, a number of classes might have a function called `print` that displays a value on a computer's screen. Adhoc polymorphism can happen by accident, but it is normally planned.

Parameterized A class can have type parameters that are supplied at compile-time to create a distinct version of the class. All instances of such a class will have the same behaviour and will respond to the same operations. This facility is provided by *templates* which are explained in Chapter 12.

Structural inheritance provides a form of polymorphism. Structural, or inclusive, polymorphism can be static or dynamic. Static polymorphism is present in all class inheritance hierarchies. It is supported by normal inheritance, as discussed in Chapter 10, and it is resolved at compile-time. Dynamic structural polymorphism is resolved at run-time. It uses pointers and references to class objects, and it has to be designed into a class hierarchy using *virtual function*. This chapter concentrates on this kind of polymorphism.

155

A classic example of the use of polymorphism is a graphical interface. Different shaped objects such as `Circle` and `Square` must respond to the same operations, such as `display` and `rotate`. So a list of `Shape` objects can be displayed by performing a `display` operation on all the objects in the list. It is unnecessary to know exactly what shapes are in the list because all objects of this type respond in an appropriate way to a `display` operation.

11.2   Using virtual functions

The mechanism for providing dynamic polymorphism involves common base classes, virtual functions, function overriding, and pointers or references to class objects. Polymorphic operations are defined as virtual functions in a base class that is publicly inherited by all the classes that will respond to the operation. The virtual functions are overridden in the derived class to provide suitable responses. When derived objects are accessed through pointers, or references, to their base class, a call to a virtual function will be directed to the appropriate overridden function in the derived class. The selection of the actual function is performed at run-time. This is called *dynamic* or *late binding*.

A virtual function is declared in a class like this:

```
virtual void display();
```

It has almost the same format as an ordinary member function, and it can be defined in the same way. If a separate definition is used, it should not repeat the `virtual` keyword. The definition provided in the base class will be used if the virtual function is not overridden in a derived class.

The whole mechanism may be complicated to understand but it is easy to use in practice. The rules are:

1. Declare a base class that defines a common interface. The common features are given as virtual functions.
2. Declare derived classes with member functions that override the virtual functions in the base class.
3. Create instances of the derived classes.
4. Access the derived class instances with pointers or references to the base class.

As an example, the following is a simplified graphic interface that draws shapes:

```
class Shape {
public:
    ...
    virtual void display();
```

```
   virtual void rotate();
private:
   . . .
};
class Circle : public Shape {
public:
   . . .
   void rotate();
   void display();
private:
   . . .
};
class Square : public Shape {
public:
   . . .
   void rotate();
   void display();
private:
   . . .
};
```

The Square and Circle classes inherit Shape and override its virtual
functions. Suitable definitions for the overridden functions must be
provided. The Shape class hierarchy is used in the following incomplete
program, which stores and displays a number of different shapes:

```
void main()
{
   . . .
   Square square1, square2;
   Circle circle1;
   . . .
   Shape* shape[MAX_SHAPES]
         = { &square1, &square2, &circle1 };
   . . .
   for ( int i = 0; i < MAX_SHAPES; i++ ) {
      if ( shape[i] != 0 )
         shape[i]->display();
   }
   . . .
}
```

This has an array of pointers to Shape, which is loaded by an initializer
with the addresses of objects derived from Shape. The array is processed

with a for loop that applies a display function to all the objects pointed at by the array. The unused elements in the array are automatically set to zero by the initializer, so the for loop can check if an element of the array is empty, and ignore it. The function display is virtual, so the version executed in each case is not the one defined in Shape, but the one that is in Circle or Square, as appropriate.

Virtual functions can also work in the absence of pointers or references to a base class if they are called from within the base class. Consider the following:

```
class Base {
public:
    void do_it()
        {  action(); }
    virtual void action();
    . . .
};
class Derived : public Base {
public:
    void action();
    . . .
};
void main()
{
    Base b;
    Derived d;
    b.do_it();   // Base::action() called
    d.do_it();   // Derived::action() called
}
```

Here, the function action is declared in Base, and overridden in Derived. The Base member function do_it calls action. If do_it is called for an instance of Base, then action in Base is called, as expected. However, if do_it is called for an instance of Derived, the virtual nature of action has an effect. It is still do_it in Base that is invoked, but when this calls action, it is the overriding function in Derived that is invoked, not the version in Base.

11.3   The behaviour of virtual functions

The behaviour of virtual and non-virtual functions is different. Consider the following classes, where Derived inherits Base, and overrides one of its virtual functions and one of its non-virtual functions:

```
class Base {
public:
   virtual void virt_one();
   virtual void virt_two();
   void norm_one();
   void norm_two();
};
class Derived : public Base {
public:
   void virt_two();   // override Base function
   void norm_two();   // override Base function
   void newfunct();
};
```

When an instance Base is used, either directly or through a pointer, the presence of the virtual functions has no effect. They are treated as normal functions and the outcome is the same for both forms of access. Virtual and non-virtual functions are also treated the same when an instance of Derived is used directly, or through a pointer to Derived, or when it is accessed directly. So, if the overridden functions norm_two and virt_two are used, the versions declared in Derived are invoked.

Virtual functions affect the outcome when an instance of Derived is accessed through a pointer or reference to Base. Then the virtual declarations determine which functions are actually used. For example,

```
Derived d;            // derived from Base
Base* pb = &d;
pb->virt_one();       // in Base
pb->virt_two();       // in Derived - overridden in Derived
pb->norm_one();       // in Base
pb->norm_two();       // in Base - overridden in Derived
pb->newfunct();       // error - not a member of Base
```

Here, an instance of Derived is accessed through a pointer to Base. Only functions declared in Base can be used with this pointer, so an attempt to use newfunct is an error. Functions in the derived class can only be used if they override a virtual function in the base class. Thus, when pb->virt_two() is executed, it is virt_two in Derived that is invoked rather than the function of the same name in Base. Access with the pointer to the other functions of Base will not invoke a Derived function: virt_one is virtual but is not overridden; norm_two is overridden but is not virtual.

The significant effect of the mechanism supporting this behaviour is that calls to virtual functions are resolved at run-time (late or dynamic binding), while calls to non-virtual functions are resolved at compile-time (early or static binding). With the help of virtual functions and pointers, a function in a derived class can be invoked without knowing exactly what type of object is being accessed.

A function that overrides a virtual function is itself a virtual function, even if it is not declared as such. If a virtual function is overridden repeatedly, in a series of derived classes, the last override is the one used when the function is called for an instance of the most derived class. A friend function cannot be declared as a virtual function because it is not a member function and cannot be overridden in a derived class.

11.4   Virtual function return types

A function override is identified by the name of the function and its parameter list. The return type can be different for non-virtual functions, but apart from a specific exception, this is not so for virtual functions. In most cases it is illegal to override a virtual function in a base class with a function returning a different type.

The return type can only be different if the overridden function returns a pointer or a reference to a base class, and the overriding function returns a pointer or reference, respectively, to a class derived from this base class. The derived class being returned must be accessible from the overriding function, and the override must not violate the constness of the overridden return type. This access restriction means that the derived class being returned must be either the same as the overriding function's class, or it must be a friend of that function's class. The returned object is converted to the return type of the overridden function.

The following generalized example shows how this works:

```
class B {
public:
    void bbb();
    ...
};

class D : private B {
    friend class Derived;
public:
    void ddd();
    ...
};

class Base {
public:
    virtual void vf1();
    virtual B* vf2();
```

```
    virtual Base* vf3();
    ...
};

class Derived : public Base {
public:
    char vf1();          // error - char is not void
    D* vf2()             // okay
        {  ...
            return &d; }
    Derived* vf3()       // okay
        {  ...
            return this; }
private:
    D d;
};
```

Here, the class Derived attempts to override three virtual functions in its
base class, changing their return types. The first override to vf1(), is
illegal because the return types are incompatible. The second, to vf2(), is
okay because class D is derived from B, and Derived is a friend of D.
Finally, the vf3() override is in order because it returns a pointer to its own
class, which is derived from Base.

11.5   Constructors and virtual destructors

Constructors cannot be virtual. The exact type of an object must always be
known when it is created, so virtual constructors do not make sense and are
illegal. However, destructors can, and in some cases must, be virtual.

Virtual destructors are needed when new and delete are used with
objects that are accessed through pointers or references to their base class.
For example, if we declare the following classes:

```
class Base {
public:
    Base();      // default constructor
    ...
    ~Base();     // destructor
};

class Derived : public Base {
public:
    Derived();   // default constructor
    ...
    ~Derived();  // destructor
```

```
   ~Derived();
};
```

An instance of `Derived` can be created with something like this:

```
Derived derv;
```

This works without any surprises. Default constructors are called for `Base` and `Derived`. Eventually, the destructors `~Derived()` and `~Base()` are called when `derv` goes out of scope and is destroyed.

An instance of `Derived` can also be created using new with a pointer to its base class:

```
Base* pbase = new Derived;
```

Again, default constructors for both classes are called. Unfortunately, all is not well when the object is destroyed with:

```
delete pbase;
```

Only the destructor for `Base` is executed. The destructor for `Derived` is not invoked, because `pbase` is a pointer to `Base`. This problem is easy to resolve by making the base class's destructor a virtual function, like this:

```
class Base {
public:
   ...
   virtual ~Base();
};
```

With this in place, the virtual function mechanism will ensure that all destructors are invoked as expected.

Base classes with virtual functions that have a destructor should *always* declare it as virtual. Furthermore, it is good practice to provide a virtual destructor in any base class that has virtual functions. This will ensure correct execution of destructors in any derived classes. If the base class's implementation does not need a destructor, an empty definition can be defined. This has very little overhead when the class is used, and it makes the base class much safer to use.

Classes without virtual functions do not normally need a virtual destructor, because it is unlikely that such a class will be dynamically allocated, and then deleted using a base pointer.

Virtual functions can be used in constructors and destructors. However, any overriding functions are ignored. The function called is the one in the constructor's or destructor's own class, or its bases. This ensures that non-constructed parts of an object are not accessed. This restriction does not apply to other member functions. In these, calling a virtual function will invoke the overriding function in the derived class.

162

11.6 Abstract base classes

Sometimes a class is only used to derive other classes. It is never used to create an instance of itself. Such a class is called an *Abstract Base Class.*

An abstract base class is a specification of a common interface for a collection of derived classes. It is usual to specify the functions needed in the derived classes as virtual functions. In this way, the abstract base class forms the type base for a class hierarchy that supports polymorphism.

It is often impossible to give useful definitions for virtual functions declared in an abstract base class, because they should always be overridden in a derived class. An error response can be provided:

```
virtual void display()
   { cout << "Shape::display() should be overridden"
          << endl; }
```

However, a better alternative is available:

```
virtual void display() = 0;
```

This is called a *pure virtual function.* It has no definition, and it must be overridden in a derived class. A class containing a pure virtual function cannot be declared an object on its own. It can only be used as an abstract base class. Pure virtual functions cannot be used in their class's constructors or destructor. A derived class must override all pure virtual functions in its base class.

Abstract base classes can be used to design a package that operates on pointers or references to class objects. Users of the package derive classes from the abstract base class, and then use objects of these types with the package. The abstract base class ensures that the derived classes have the polymorphic behaviour needed by the package's components. As an example of an abstract base class, there is part of a very simplified and simulated object oriented windows based graphic user interface:

```
class Window {
public:
   virtual void testpress() = 0;
   virtual ~Window(){}
};

class Callback {
public:
   virtual void doit() = 0;
   virtual ~Callback(){}
};

class Button {
public:
```

```
    Button( Window* window, Callback* acallback )
        : thewindow(window), thecallback(acallback){}
    void dummypress()
        { click(); }
private:
  Window* thewindow;
  Callback* thecallback;
  void click()
     { thecallback->doit(); }
};
```

This example illustrates the use of *callback objects* to respond to window's events. (This approach is much superior to the use of pointers to member functions.) The general idea is to pass the address of a callback object, derived from an abstract base class, to the windows object. This callback object can respond to a function call issued by the window object when the event occurs. The virtual function mechanism ensures that the correct function is called. In effect, we have created a callback type that can be used to make callback objects to be used by the windows interface.

Looking at the actual example in detail, the class Button manages a visual button in a window. We will assume that, in normal operation, a mouse button is clicked with the cursor in the visual button that executes the click function. This in turn executes the doit function in a Callback object given to the button when it was created. The Window class represents an interface feature that can hold buttons.

To complicate the example, there are a few extra functions to simulate the interface in the absence of any real windows, and button events. The virtual function testpress in Window is provided so that a dummy button press can be generated in an application defined window, and dummypress in Button provides the actual mechanism to do this, by calling click. The following shows how all of this can be used:

```
class OKcallback : public Callback{
public:
    OKcallback() : count(0) {}
    void doit()
       { cout << "PRESSED " << count++ << endl; }
private:
    int count;
};

class MyWindow : public Window {
public:
    MyWindow() : okay(this,&okcallback) {}
    void testpress()
```

164

```
      { okay.dummypress(); }
private:
   Button okay;
   OKcallback okcallback;
};

void main()
{
   Window* mainwindow = new MyWindow;
   mainwindow->testpress();
   mainwindow->testpress();
   mainwindow->testpress();
   delete mainwindow;
}
```

The class OKcallback is derived from the Callback abstract base class. The doit function is overridden. It counts the number of times the callback is used and prints a simple message. The class MyWindow is derived from Window. It contains an instance of Button called okay. This object is initialized by passing it the address of the MyWindow using this, and the address of a callback object of type OKcallback. For the sake of the simulation the testpress function is overridden to call dummypress in okay.

In main, an instance of MyWindow is created, and accessed through a pointer to Window, named mainwindow. The function testpress is called. This is a virtual function in Window, so the overridden function in MyWindow is executed. This, in turn, calls the Button member function dummypress. This initiates the normal behaviour of the button, which is to call the doit function in its callback object, though a pointer to its base class. The function is virtual, so the overridden function in the user supplied OKcallback object is called as required.

11.7 Exercises

1. Write a *simple* version of the Shape classes discussed in §11.2. Provide support for a square and a rectangle. Do not bother about screen location. (This simplification allows the exercise to be performed on any terminal, without knowledge of its graphic or control interface.) Implement display and rotate functions. For the display function print the shapes as character patterns. Since this simplified version of Shape ignores location, just start printing at the start of the current line, and let the screen scroll. The rotate function should rotate its object clockwise through 90 degrees.

2. Experiment with virtual, pure virtual and non-virtual functions, with

and without pointers. Explore the various combinations and their effects. Try to derive the same results as those discussed earlier in §11.3. *There is no model solution for this exercise.*

3. Write a `Circle` class that has a member function to modify its radius, and a `Rectangle` class that can have its width and height modified. They should both be able to supply area and circumference information. It must be possible to maintain some form of mixed list of `Circle` and `Rectangle` objects, and to use this list to print the areas of the objects. Use an abstract base class.

CHAPTER 12
Templates

12.1 Introduction

A template is a common definition for a set of classes and functions. Templates are parameterized, and instances are generated using a supplied set of arguments. Templates offer a direct way of supporting code reuse. For example, separate implementations of a list of integers and a list of strings are not needed. A template list, parameterized on the type of its contained object, will do for both. Indeed, template classes are most useful for defining container classes such as lists and queues.

There are some problems associated with designing and implementing templates. A compiler can often detect mistakes in a template definition, but some faults will only be reported when an instance of the template is created. Thus some errors are not detected until the template is used. These late error messages can be confusing. Do not assume that a template works until it has been fully tested with a comprehensive set of arguments.

The syntax of a set of related templates can get very complicated. One way of approaching the design and implementation of templates is to use a non-parameterized prototype. Use an ordinary class or function, with no parameters, to model a specific instance of the template. When this is implemented correctly, convert it to a fully operational template by substituting parameters. Development and testing of the template can then continue with some confidence that the underlying algorithms and data structures work.

Templates are a currently evolving part of C++. This chapter covers the features that can be found in some, if not most, compilers at the moment. These generally comply with the draft ANSI standard, but there are some template features, defined in the draft standard, that are not discussed in this chapter.

12.2 Class templates

A class template is a parameterized type. Parameters in the template's definition are replaced at compile-time to generate instances of the template.
Parameters can be type names or scalar values, but we will start by concen-
trating on type parameters.

An array class is a good example of how templates can be used:

```
template< class Type >
class Array {
public:
    Array( int low, int high );
        // subscript in range low to high
        // initialize to default constructor of Type
    void put( int loc, const Type& value );
        // store value in element at loc.
    Type get( int loc ) const;
        // recover value from element at loc.
    bool inbound( int loc ) const;
        // check loc is within bounds for this array
    ~Array();
private:
    Array( Array& ) {}
        // restrict copy
    Array& operator=( Array& ) { return *this; }
        // restrict assignment
    Type* store;
    int lowbound;
    int highbound;
};
```

Classes that have array-like behaviour often overload the [] operator,
but in this case operator overloading has not been used. The Array class
has put and get functions to store and retrieve values from locations in
Array. The number of locations in an instance of an Array are given as a
range. The bound member function can be used to check if a location is
within bounds before it is used with put or get. The copy constructor and
assignment operator are restricted to prevent problems with the pointer to
Type used in the implementation. (See exercises for an alternative.)

The type of values held in Array is parameterized as Type, so an
instance of this class can be generated to hold almost any type of object,
provided the type supports all the operations performed on it by the array.
The parameter is named at the start of the template with:

```
template< class Type >
```

The class keyword indicates that the parameter Type is a type name. Any valid C++ identifier can be used as a parameter name, and there can be more than one parameter.

Instances of Array are created by giving an actual value:

```
Array<double> costs(3,10);
Array<Stock> bins(1,1000);
...
if ( costs.inbound(item) )
   costs.put(item,newcost);
```

Here, two objects are created from the Array template. The definitions give the name of the template, followed by an argument list between < and >. In this case, there is only one argument, which is the type of the objects stored in that instance of Array. This combination of class name and argument list is the type of the template object. The instance name and constructor arguments follow as usual. Once defined, a template class object is used like any other class object.

A template with class parameters is polymorphic, but instances of the template are not. When an instance of a template is defined, the types of object it can work with are fixed. So the two Array objects in the above example have different types: Array<double> is not the same type as Array<Stock>. Thus the following function will accept costs but not bins as an argument:

```
void print( const Array<double>& array );
```

The member functions of a template class are defined in a similar way to ordinary class member functions. For example, the put function in the Array template is defined as follows:

```
template< class Type >
void Array<Type>::put( int loc, const Type& value )
{
    store[loc - lowbound] = value;
}
```

The function definition is preceded with template< class Type >, so that its parameters are the same as Array. The function is associated with its class, like any member function, using the scope operator. The class is a template in this case so Array<Type>:: prefixes the function name. When an instance of the Array template is declared and used, the correct version of the function is generated. Thus, if we have an instance of type Array<double>, the function will be:

```
void Array<double>::put( int loc, const double& value )
```

The rest of the Array template's implementation is written in the same way, and looks like this:

```
template< class Type >
Array<Type>::Array( int low, int high )
    : lowbound(low), highbound(high)
{
    store = new Type[highbound - lowbound + 1];
}
template< class Type >
Type Array<Type>::get( int loc ) const
{
    return store[loc - lowbound];
}
template< class Type >
bool Array<Type>::inbound( int loc ) const
{
    if ( loc >= lowbound && loc <= highbound )
        return true;
    else
        return false;
}
template< class Type >
Array<Type>::~Array()
{
    delete[] store;
}
```

Apart from the complication of the template, this is a comparatively simple implementation. A dynamically allocated array is used to store the class's data, which is created in the constructor as an array of the type given as the template's parameter. The array will be automatically initialized using the default constructor for Type.

We do not know what sort of object will be used with Array, but we are assuming that it has *standard copy semantics*. This means it behaves like a fundamental type, such as double, when it is declared, used as a function argument or assigned. Such an object will have a default constructor. It will also have a copy constructor, a destructor and a standard assignment operator overload if the memberwise defaults are inappropriate. It should look like this example:

```
class Probe {
public:
    Probe();
```

```
    Probe( const Probe& );
    Probe& operator=( const Probe& p);
    ~Probe()
        ...
private:
        ...
};
```

The member functions and friends of a template class are the same as those in a normal class, and can be defined in similar ways. For example, they can be inline:

```
template< class Type >
class Array {
public:
    void put( int loc, const Type& value )
        // store value in element at loc.
        { store[loc - lowbound] = value; }
    ...
private:
    ...
};
```

12.3   Function templates

Templates can be used for functions as well as for classes. They are very simple to define. For example, the following function swaps two variables of the same type:

```
template<class Type>
void swap( Type& a, Type& b )
{
    Type temp = a;
    a = b;
    b = temp;
}
```

Here, the template parameter Type is used to declare the function parameters and a local variable.

A template function is generic, and it will be automatically used by the compiler when it is appropriate.The compiler does all the work and the function can be used without effort. So wherever a function called swap with two arguments of the same type is encountered, the template defined above is used to generate a suitable function:

```
Stock i,j;
double x,y
swap(i,j);
swap(x,y);
swap(i,x);      // error - does not match template
```

The selection of function templates is based on their template parameters. The match is performed on a name basis, and the actual behaviour of the objects involved is not considered. Thus it is possible to generate a template function that will not work with the actual objects in its argument list. The swap template will work with any object that has standard copy semantics, but consider the following:

```
template<class Type>
void inquotes( ostream& os, const Type printable )
{
    os << '"' << printable << '"' << endl;
}
```

This template matches all of the following function calls:

```
inquotes(cout,6);            // okay
inquotes(cout,"hello");      // okay
inquotes(cout,Noprint());    // possible error
```

However, there may be a problem with the last call. This has a class object as its second argument, and many classes do not have an operator<< overload. If this is the case for Noprint, then the generated template function cannot work.

Template functions can be overloaded with normal functions. The following is a slightly different version of the function defined in the inquotes template:

```
void inquotes( ostream& os, const double printable )
{
    os << '^' << printable << '^' << endl;
}
```

It will be used instead of the template only when the function is called with a floating point number as its second argument.

The errors reported for template functions can be confusing. Faults are only detected in generated functions. Just because a template function works with a particular set of arguments does not mean it will work with others. Some compilers even report a fault in a template without indicating where the generating function call is in the program.

12.4 Template arguments

Template arguments do not have to be type names. Character strings, function names and constant expressions can all be used. The `Array` example discussed above can be recast using template arguments to define its bounds:

```
template< class Type, int LOW, int HIGH  >
class Array {
public:
    void put( int loc, const Type& value );
      // store value in element at loc.
    Type get( int loc ) const;
      // recover value from element at loc.
    bool inbound( int loc ) const;
      // check loc is within bounds for this array
private:
    Type store[HIGH - LOW + 1];
};
```

The `store` array is now statically allocated. Its size can be calculated from template parameters, so there is no need to use a pointer to `Type` and the `new` operator in a constructor. A copy constructor and assignment operator are not needed because the default memberwise copy semantics are okay. In use, only object definition is different:

```
Array<double,3,10> costs;
const int FIRST = -4;
const int LAST = 6;
Array<Stock,FIRST,LAST> bins;
...
if ( costs.inbound(item) )
    costs.put(newcost);
```

The member functions of this `Array` use its integer template parameters as follows:

```
template< class Type, int LOW, int HIGH >
void Array<Type,LOW,HIGH>::put( int loc, const Type& value )
{
    store[loc - LOW] = value;
}

template< class Type, int LOW, int HIGH >
Type Array<Type,LOW,HIGH>::get( int loc ) const
{
```

```
      return store[loc - LOW];
}

template< class Type, int LOW, int HIGH >
bool Array<Type,LOW,HIGH>::inbound( int loc ) const
{
    if ( loc >= LOW && loc <= HIGH )
        return true;
    else
        return false;
}
```

Using template parameters for the bounds of `Array` means that the class can be implemented without using dynamic data structures allocated from free store. However, now the bounds must be known at compile-time, and cannot be calculated at run-time. The bounds also become part of an `Array` instance's type, restricting some operations:

```
Array<Stock,1,30> trialstock;
Array<Stock,1,100> finalstock;
Array<Stock,1,30> localstock;

trialstock = localstock;    // okay
finalstock = trialstock;    // error - not the same type
```

The design of a template class can often employ either non-type parameters or a constructor to supply initial conditions for an instance of the class. The choice depends on the required behaviour of the class. Use template parameters if the values are constant for the life of an object, and it is acceptable for them to be part of the object's type name.

Other sorts of non-type parameter are possible. Function names can be used with a template like this:

```
template< void (*F1)() >
class Demo1 {
public:
    void use_it();
};

template< void (*F1)() >
void Demo1<F1>::use_it()
{
    F1();  // call template argument
}
```

Given the function `void myfunction()`, creating an instance of the above template that uses it is simple:

```
Demo1<myfunction> test1;
test1.use_it();            // this calls myfunction
```

Arrays are a little more troublesome. They are specified using pointer notation:

```
template< const char* MESSAGE >
class Demo2 {
public:
   void report();
//    ...
};

template< const char* MESSAGE >
void Demo2<MESSAGE>::report()
{
   cout << "Message is " << MESSAGE << endl;
}
```

Creating an instance of this template is done as follows:

```
const char message[] = "A short note";
Demo2<message> test2;
test2.report(); // use message array
```

Some compilers insist that an array used as a template argument has global scope.

12.5 Exercises

1. Modify the `Array` template in §12.2 so that assignment and copy constructors are not restricted.
2. Write an array template that is parameterized by type and size. Give it a `[]` subscript operator and bounds checking. It must support multi-dimensional arrays.
3. Create an array template with bound parameters that is derived from an abstract base class so that arrays with different bounds can be used polymorphically.
4. Write a list class template that can store any kind of object. Base it on the integer `List` class given in §8.10.

CHAPTER 13
Advanced features

13.1 Exception handling

Managing errors can complicate the way we use software components, such as functions and objects, in a program. Some commonly used approaches for ordinary functions are to return a special value indicating failure of the operation, or to have an extra status parameter that can be checked to see if the function worked. These techniques can also be used for the member functions of a class. However, a better way to manage errors in a class is to have a status that can be checked with special member functions after an operation is complete. The `<iostream.h>` library uses this approach. It has a number of error flags and associated member functions that can be used to check for errors while inputting and outputting data. These are discussed in §14.6. We do not expect errors to occur very often, but it is often best to check for them every time we do something. This overhead can complicate the structure of our programs, making them difficult to understand and maintain. But if the checks are not made, and an error does occur, the program may produce invalid results.

Exceptions offer an alternative way to manage fault capture and recovery. The mechanism is simple. Any function can *throw* an exception when it discovers an error that prevents further execution. For example, the following function throws an integer exception with the value zero if it finds an error in its parameter:

```
Stock lookup( const string& binname )
{
   Stock item;
   if ( !Bin::valid(binname) )
      throw 0;
```

```
   // use binname to find item ...
   return item;
}
```

A function immediately terminates when throw is executed. The exception is *caught* by putting the function in a try block, which is followed by one or more *handlers*. These are catch blocks that have a single parameter defining what type of exception they can handle:

```
try {
  newstock = lookup("Widgets");
}
catch ( int ecode ) {
   cout << "Look up failed with error code "
        << ecode << '.' << endl;
   cout << "Processing will continue." << endl;

}
catch( ... ) {
   cout << "Unexpected exception encountered."
        << endl;
   throw;              // rethrow exception
}
// rest of the program
```

When there is more than one handler, they are tried in order. The first catch block that has a parameter that matches the thrown exception is executed. When this handler is finished the program continues with the first statement after the last catch block. If a match for the exception is not found, the search continues with the next most recently activated try block. If no match is found in any of the active try blocks, the program is terminated. In the example above, the first catch handles all integer exceptions thrown in the try block. The second handler has . . . as its exception declaration. This special notation indicates that the handler will look after *any* type of exception. Some care is needed with a list of handlers. It can be specified in such a way that a particular handler will never be executed, because the ordering prevents it from being reached. In particular, if a . . . handler is present, it must be last.

If a handler or one of the functions called while it is executing throws an exception, this will not be managed by the try block that owns the handler. That try block is finished as soon as the handler is started. Sometimes a handler finds it cannot manage the exception for which it was invoked. In this case, it can explicitly reactivate the exception using a throw with no value, as shown in the last catch block of the example above. Such a reactivated exception is treated like any other exception, so it is thrown out of the try block.

13.1.1 Exception objects

The previous example used an integer, but an object of almost any type can be thrown as an exception. Class objects make very good exceptions. They can contain detailed information about the particular problem that caused the exception. In addition, inheritance can be used to create a hierarchy of related exceptions that can be managed polymorphically. This approach is used in the draft ANSI standard, which uses classes to provide exceptions for things like bad memory allocation and the standard libraries. When such a standard exists, it is nice to make application program code compatible with it. So the standard's exception classes can be used as a base for families of application specific exceptions.

The standard exception base class looks something like this:

```
class Exception {
public:
   Exception( const char message[] )
      {  strncpy(themessage,message,MAXMESS);
         themessage[MAXMESS-1] = 0;   }
   virtual const char* what()
      {  return themessage;   }
   virtual ~Exception() {}
protected:
   enum { MAXMESS = 100 };
private:
   char themessage[MAXMESS];
};
```

This uses C strings. There is a proposal in the draft C++ standard for a string class, and it is very likely this will be used instead of a C string in the standard exception class. Nevertheless, the way that our class can be used is much the same.

As an example, Exception can be the base class for a family of exceptions associated with a Stock class library:

```
class Xstock : public Exception {
public:
   Xstock()
      : Exception("Non-specific stock error") {}
protected:
   Xstock( const char message[] )
      : Exception(message) {}
};

class Xinvalbin : public Xstock {
public:
```

```
    Xinvalbin( const char abin[] )
       : Xstock("Invalid bin name")
       {  strncpy(thebin,abin,MAXBIN);
          thebin[MAXBIN-1] = 0;   }
    const char* bin()
       {  return thebin;  }
private:
    enum { MAXBIN = 32 };
    char thebin[MAXBIN];
};

class Xunlist : public Xstock {
public:
    Xunlist( int anitem )
       : Xstock("Unlisted item"), theitem(anitem)
       {  char temp[20];
          strcpy(fullmess,Xstock::what());
          strcat(fullmess," ");
          strcat(fullmess,itoa(theitem,temp,10));   }
    const char* what()
       {  return fullmess;   }
    int item() const
       {  return theitem;    }
private:
    int theitem;
    char fullmess[Exception::MAXMESS + 10];
};
```

The Xstock class is a general exception. It is used to build more specific
Stock exceptions like Xinvalbin and Xunlist. The Xstock constructor, which allows the what message to be modified, is only available to
derived classes. An Xstock exception can be thrown in its own right, and
a constructor is provided for this purpose. This constructor does not allow
the what message to be modified. Instead, it defines a standard message.

These Xstock exceptions are designed to be used by the member, friend
and supporting functions of a class called Stock. In use, an actual instance
of a class exception must be thrown. This is normally done by specifying a
fixed value with the throw to create a temporary instance of the exception.
For example,

```
throw Xinvalbin(binname);
throw Xstock();
```

These invoke a constructor to create a temporary instance of the exception,
which is passed to its handler. This temporary instance is destroyed when
the handler that processes it has finished.

Handling these exceptions is easy. A suitable try block might look like
this:

```
try{
   // some stock processing
}
catch ( Xinvalbin xcptn ){
   cout << xcptn.what()
        << " error with bin called "
        << xcptn.bin() << endl;
}
catch ( Xstock& xcptn ){
   cout << xcptn.what() << endl;
}
```

Here, if an Xinvalbin is thrown, it will be picked up by its specific handler. Any other stock exception will be caught by the Xstock& handler. This is able to print out the particular details because what is a virtual function, and the exception is passed as a reference. In contrast, if the handler were able to accept a non-referential Xstock, the what function in the base would be used, but this would give less information. In both cases item cannot be used because it is not a virtual function.

If the value of an exception is not used, a name does not have to be given:

```
try {
   // do some Stock things
}
catch ( Xstock ) {
    cout << "Unexpected error in stock processing" << endl;
    exit(3);
}
```

13.1.2   Exception management

The availability of exception handlers is dynamic. At any time there may be a number of active try blocks. These are arranged in a hierarchy with the most recently entered try block at the lowest level. The search for a handler that matches an exception travels up this hierarchy. This will cause the program prematurely to leave active loops, functions and try blocks as it looks for a suitable handler. Any local declarations that go out of scope during the search will be cleaned-up.

If a destructor invoked during the search for a handler throws an exception, the search is abandoned and the program is ended. It is generally a good idea to avoid throwing an exception from a destructor, because this can disrupt the smooth operation of exception management. Exceptions can be used by destructors, but they should all be caught and handled within the destructor function.

The function `terminate` is called if a match is not found, or if the search is abandoned. This in turn calls `abort`, which actually stops the program. Sometimes this simple default behaviour is not suitable, so the terminate function can be replaced with one of our own design. For example:

```
#include <except.h>
#include <stdlib.h>    // for exit and abort

void managecrash()
{
    // termination activities
    ...
    abort();   // or exit(0);
}

void main()
{
    terminate_handler oldterm = set_terminate(managecrash);
    // managecrash() will be used
    ...
    set_terminate(oldterm); // restore old terminate function
    ...
}
```

Here, the replacement for `terminate` is called `managecrash`. This is a function with no parameters that does not return a value. It must not throw an exception, and it must not return to its caller. It finishes by calling `abort`, but `exit` can be used instead for a nearer to normal program termination. The `managecrash` function is installed with `set_terminate`, which returns the address of the existing terminate function. This address can be stored in a variable of type `terminate_handler`, to be restored later by another call to `set_terminate`. In practice, `managecrash` might close down the program's file system, set off an alarm, or just print out a special warning message.

13.1.3   Restricting exceptions

The type of exceptions that a function is allowed to throw can be controlled by giving it an *exception specification* that lists valid exceptions. If this list is violated, the program is immediately terminated. The list of exceptions is given at the end of a function declaration like this:

```
void printitem( char binname[], int item )
        throw(Xinvalbin,Xunlist)
{
```

```
   . . .
}
```

While this function is executing the only exceptions that can be thrown
are Xinvalbin and Xunlist. Any other exception type will cause the
program to terminate.

When sets of exceptions are derived from a common base class, they can
all be specified by using the base class like this:

```
void printitem( char binname[], int item ) throw(Xstock)
{
   . . .
}
```

This is similar to the previous example because Xinvalbin and Xunlist
are derived from Xstock.

If necessary, all exceptions can be prevented with an empty list:

```
void afunction( int parm ) throw()
```

When a program is terminated because a function's exception specification is violated, the function unexpected is called. This calls terminate,
which then calls abort to actually terminate the program. Sometimes
this simple default behaviour is not suitable, so the default functions can
be replaced. How to replace terminate is described in §13.1.2. The
unexpected function can be replaced in a similar way:

```
#include <except.h>
#include <stdlib.h>    // for exit and abort

void manageunexp()
{
   // termination activities
   . . .
   abort();
}

void main()
{
   set_unexpected(manageunexp);
   // manageunexp() in effect
   . . .
}
```

Like a terminate replacement function, an unexpected function
should not return to its caller. However, it can throw or rethrow an exception. Handlers for this exception will be looked for starting at the call of the
function whose exception specification was violated. So an unexpected
function can be used to bypass an exception specification.

13.2 Casting

C++ is a typed language. All objects have type, and this information is used at compile-time to check that everything fits together. The compiler will complain about an operation that is incorrect for an object of a particular type. This is called *static type checking*.

The compiler will implicitly convert the type of objects when appropriate. For example, this happens when a `double` is assigned to an `int`. The types of the objects involved ensure that a suitable conversion is used. Conversion operations can also be invoked explicitly by the programmer when the default behaviour is inappropriate. The standard types, such as `char`, `int` or `float`, have built-in conversions. Classes are user defined types, and the compiler includes them in its static type checking system. If suitable constructors and conversion operators are defined, they will be implicitly invoked just like the standard type conversions. Inheritance can be used to create subtypes, which can be polymorphic if virtual functions are declared in the base class. Virtual functions involve *dynamic type checking*. This allows a C++ program to decide on the type of a class object at run-time.

Type checking is a very important feature of C++. In its static form, it helps prevent faults that can be very difficult to find at run-time. Some programmers find statically typed languages restrictive, but many others find the type warning and error messages generated by strongly typed languages extremely useful. Nevertheless, the basic type checking system can sometimes get in the way, and programmers need a method of modifying or overriding its operation. Casts are the way to do this in C++.

Casting should be treated with great care. It can be very useful in specific cases, but it always carries some risk. If we bypass the strict type rules, we must accept responsibility for the consequences. Casts can be used for a number of things, some safer than others. They can perform conversions, navigate a class hierarchy (statically or dynamically), modify constness, manipulate pointers, and reinterpret storage formats. C++ offers four different sorts of cast to manage all of this:

- `static_cast`   A reasonably well behaved cast. Used for conversions and static class navigation.

- `dynamic_cast`   Used for dynamic class navigation.
- `const_cast`   Used for casting away constness (and volatility). This can be dangerous.
- `reinterpret_cast`   Used for values that must be cast back to be used safely. This cast can seriously damage the health of your programs.

All of these casts have a similar syntax. For example, if the object being cast is `anobject` and the required type is `Atype`, we might use:

```
static_cast<Atype>(anobject)
```

The resulting object has the type Atype, and the whole cast expression can be used wherever an object of that type can be used.

C++ cast operations are complicated. Any programmer intending to use them must understand how they work. So the following sections explain their operation in detail.

13.2.1 Static casts

Anything that can be converted can be statically cast. So one way to get a floating point result from an integer divide is:

```
int a, b;
...
double x = a / static_cast<double>(b);
```

This is okay because there is a standard conversion between int and double. However, there is no conversion between a pointer to int and a pointer to double, so:

```
double x;
int a, b;
int* pint = &b;
...
x = a / *static_cast<double*>(pint);   // is an error
x = a / static_cast<double>(*pint);    // but this is okay
```

Preventing casts between pointers to unrelated types is sensible. Casting such a pointer would not convert the format of the target object. So it would be possible, for example, to treat the bit pattern of an int as a double. This is not safe, and static_cast prevents it.

There is no need to cast explicitly from an enumerated type to an integer. However, assigning an int to an enumerated type can cause a warning or error message. Enumerated types can be statically cast, but there is no bound checking. For example,

```
enum Colour { RED, BLUE, GREEN };
Colour paint = RED;
...
int a = paint;                       // okay
paint = 1;                           // warning or error
paint = static_cast<Colour>(1);      // okay
paint = static_cast<Colour>(33);     // okay but whoops!!
```

Of course, in all the above examples, static_cast can be replaced with suitable conversions:

```
double x = a / double(b);
Colour paint = Colour(1);
```

It is a matter of style. Use the notation you like best.

A more powerful use of static_cast is class navigation. We can cast between pointers or references to instances of classes that are directly or indirectly related by inheritance. So a pointer to a base class can be converted into a pointer to one of its derived classes. Conversion can be in either direction: from base to derived, or from derived to base, and it can skip levels in the inheritance hierarchy. Consider the following simple classes:

```
class Vehicle {
public:
    float enginesize();
    ...
};

class Car : public Vehicle {
public:
    int colourcode();
    ...
};
```

The class Car is derived from Vehicle, but Vehicle has no virtual functions. So if a Car object is accessed though a pointer to Vehicle, its colourcode member function cannot be used. This problem can be bypassed with a cast, which is allowed because Car is derived from Vehicle:

```
Car  acar;
Vehicle* vhclpntr = &acar;
...
vhclpntr->enginesize(); //  okay
vhclpntr->colour();     //  error - not virtual
static_cast<Car*>(vhclpntr)->colourcode(); // okay
```

There are some general restrictions: the classes involved must be completely defined, a conversion from the derived class to the base class must be possible, and the base class must not be virtual. Casts between pointers and references cannot be mixed. A reference cast is the only cast that can be used on the left-hand side of an assignment statement.

We can also cast from a pointer (or reference) to a base class into a pointer (or reference) to a derived class, but only if the base class is accessible from the derived class. This is the same as the automatic conversion that occurs when a pointer to a derived class is assigned to a pointer to a related base class.

Do not confuse casting pointers and references to classes, with casting actual class objects. A derived class object can be cast to one of its base classes. This is just a standard conversion that extracts the base class sub-object from the derived class. A base class normally cannot be cast to a derived class. This can only be done if a suitable constructor or conversion operator has been defined.

Static casting is not entirely safe, it can be fooled. A cast from a pointer to a base class into a pointer to a derived class is allowed if the inheritance relationship between the classes is correct. This is true, regardless of the actual objects involved. As an example, consider the following class which, like `Car`, is derived from `Vehicle`:

```
class Bus : public Vehicle {
public:
    int seats();
    ...
};
```

Instances of `Bus` and `Car` can both be accessed with a pointer to `Vehicle`. So the following is possible:

```
Bus bus;
Vehicle* p2Vehicle = &bus;

// This is okay
Bus* p2Bus = static_cast<Bus*>(p2Vehicle);

// The compiler lets this through but it's an error!!
Car* p2Car = static_cast<Car*>(p2Vehicle);
```

The pointer `p2Bus` in this example can be used safely, but any use of `p2Car` will produce undefined results because it is not really pointing at an instance of `Car`. It is clear that a static cast should only be used if we are absolutely sure of an object's type. However, this particular problem can be overcome by using a dynamic cast, which is discussed later in this chapter.

13.2.2 Const casts

The C++ type checking system maintains the integrity of constant objects. This is important, because changing the value of a constant will normally have disastrous consequences. The other C++ casts cannot change the constness of an object. It would be too easy to make a mistake if this were possible. However, since casting away constness is sometimes necessary, C++ has `const_cast`. This can be used to add or remove the `const` (or `volatile`) modifier from a type. But the effect of writing to a constant object that has its constness cast away is undefined. So we can cast away constness from an object but we must still treat it as a constant. If we accidently write to such an object, it will not be reported as an error because we have overridden type checking.

A const_cast can only be applied to pointers and references, and the type being cast to must be identical to the original apart from constness. The notation is simple:

```
const int MAXWHEELS = 4;
...
int& iref = const_cast<int&>(MAXWHEELS);
int* ipnt = const_cast<int*>(&MAXWHEELS);
int  ival = const_cast<int>(MAXWHEELS);
        // error - can only cast pointers or references
```

A const_cast can also be used to add constness, although in most cases this will not make any difference:

```
const int* cipnt1 = const_cast<const int*>(&age);
const int* cipnt2 = &age;    // same as above
```

Constant casts can be useful with legacy systems. C typing rules are more easy-going than C++ rules. So using a C function from C++ can cause problems. For example:

```
extern "C" char* strchr( char* p, char c );

inline const char* strchr(const char* p, char c )
{
    return strchr(const_cast<char*>(p),c);
}
```

The first line tells the compiler there is a C function called strchr that is in an external library. The inline C++ function, of the same name, is a wrapper for this, giving stronger C++ type behaviour. The constness of the C++ argument has to be cast away to pass it to the C function. This is safe because we know the behaviour of the C function.

Much thought is needed before the constant nature of an object is ignored with a cast. Casts should never be used casually, but there must be a specially good reason for using const_cast.

13.2.3 Reinterpret casts

The reinterpret_cast is the most dangerous C++ cast. It basically instructs the compiler to ignore the internal storage format of an object. It does not perform any conversions. The result of a reinterpret_cast is machine and compiler dependent. The only safe thing to do with a reinterpret_cast object is to cast it back to its original type. This cast can only be applied to pointers and references. The notation is similar to `const_cast`:

```
double real = 12.34, *p2real = &real;
...
int& iref = reinterpret_cast<int&>(real);
int* ipnt = reinterpret_cast<int*>(p2real);
```

Pointers can be converted to and from integers:

```
double* absptr = reinterpret_cast<double*>(24);
int pointervalue = reinterpret_cast<int>(p2real);
```

There are a few limitations. For example the following will generate errors:

```
int ival = reinterpret_cast<int>(real);
            // error - cannot cast double to int
double* dpntr = reinterpret_cast<double*>(2.4);
            // error - cannot cast double to pointer
double dval = reinterpret_cast<double>(p2real);
            // error - cannot cast pointer to double
```

As an example of how a `reinterpret_cast` might be legitimately used, consider the following function designed for use with C:

```
void setcallback( Widget* w, void (*cbfunct)(void*),
                  void* cbdata );
```

This sort of function might be found in a graphical user interface such as Xwindows. Its purpose is to register a function as a callback for a component in a window. For example, if the `Widget` is a button, the function `cbfunct` will be called with `cbdata` as its parameter when the button is clicked by the mouse pointer. A `void*` type is used for `cbdata` so that anything can be specified as callback data. This is clumsy, but it is the kind of thing that is often done.

The `setcallback` function can be used as follows where the callback function `cbokay` is attached to `okaybutton`:

```
const int OKAY = 1;
const int CANCEL = 2;

void cbokay( void* cbdata )
{
    switch ( *reinterpret_cast<int*>(cbdata) ) {
    case OKAY :
       // Do okay button pressed processing
       break;
    case CANCEL :
```

```
        // Do cancel button pressed processing
        break;
    }
}

void main()
{
    Widget okaybutton;
    ...
    setcallback(&okaybutton,cbokay,
        reinterpret_cast<void*>(const_cast<int*>(&OKAY)));
    ...
}
```

The callback data cause some problems. We cannot pass a constant integer directly to a void* parameter. First the address of OKAY has its constness cast away. Then it is cast to void*, which can be used for setcallback without complaint. In the callback function cbokay, the argument is cast back to int*, and the result is dereferenced to access the actual value. This is complicated, but it works. The cbokay function must be carefully written. It must cast back its parameter to int*, and it must respect the parameter's actual constness.

13.2.4 Dynamic casts

Dynamic casts are used to navigate a class hierarchy. In this, they are similar to static casts. However, dynamic_cast checks if the cast is correct at run-time. It does not rely on static type information. Dynamic casts only work with pointers and references to class types.

The following function uses dynamic_cast to make sure its processing is being applied to the correct type of Vehicle:

```
void statistics( const Vehicle* p2vhcl )
{
    Bus* p2bus = dynamic_cast<Bus*>(p2vhcl);
    if ( p2bus != 0 ) {  // zero if cast fails
        // do Bus processing with valid pointer value
        ...
    }
    ...
}
```

The dynamic_cast in this function cannot be fooled in the same way as a static_cast. The function can be called with a Car or a Bus object, and it will handle both correctly:

```
Car acar;
Bus abus;
...
statistics(&abus);
statistics(&acar);    // NO Bus processing
```

If statistics is called with a Car argument, the cast to Bus * fails. When this happens the cast returns a null pointer, so the failure can be detected and appropriate action taken. Some dynamic cast errors are reported at compile time by some compilers, but this should not be relied on. Always check the return from the cast, and do not use it if zero.

The above example casts from base to derived pointer. It is also possible to dynamically cast pointers and references in the other direction. So a pointer to a derived class can be dynamically cast to a pointer to one of its base classes. A pointer or reference to the unique base class sub-object will be returned.

It is normally much neater to use reference parameters for functions. These can be managed in a similar way to pointers, but detecting a bad dynamic cast is different:

```
#include <typeinfo.h>
...
void update( Vehicle& vhcl )
{
    Bus abus;
    try {
        abus = dynamic_cast<Bus&>(vhcl);
        // cast worked - okay to use abus.
        ...
    }
    catch( bad_cast ) {
        // handle cast failure.
        ...
    }
}
```

A dynamic reference cast throws a bad_cast exception when it fails. If this exception is not caught, the program will be terminated.

There are a few requirements for dynamic_cast to work. As described above, it can only be used with pointers and references, to cast between classes related by inheritance. Furthermore, if the cast is from base class to derived class, the base class must contain at least one virtual function. A virtual function is not needed if the cast is from derived to base class. A dummy virtual function can be defined in a base class to enable dynamic casting:

```
class Vehicle {
   ...
private:
   virtual void vf(){} // dummy does nothing
   ...
};
```

Dynamic casts are safer than the equivalent static casts provided that, for pointer casts, the returned pointer is checked. However, dynamic casts need base classes with virtual functions, and there is some run-time overhead.

13.2.5 C casts

C style casts are supported by C++ for compatibility. They look like this, with the target type in braces:

```
(double)anint;
(int*)pntr2double;
```

Their behaviour is a combination of static and reinterpret casting. They are entirely unsafe and should be avoided. If a cast has to be used, always use a C++ cast.

13.3 Run-time type information

C++ supports limited run-time type information. This facility is normally referred to as RTTI. The mechanism is simple. There is a typeid operator that can be applied to any object or type. It returns a constant type_info object that contains type information. The type_info class looks like this:

```
class type_info {
public:
   const char* name() const;
      // name of type
   int operator==( const type_info& ) const;
   int operator!=( const type_info& ) const;
      // comparison
   int before( const type_info& ) const;
      // ordering
   virtual ~type_info();
      // it's polymorphic
private:
   // cannot be used.
```

```
type_info(const type_info& ){};
type_info& operator=( const type_info& ){return *this;};
};
```

The following prints the type of the object addressed by a pointer to a polymorphic base class:

```
Vehicle* p2vhcl;
...
cout << typeid(*p2vhcl).name();
```

The base class `Vehicle` and its derived classes, `Car` and `Bus`, are defined earlier in this chapter. The pointer `p2vhcl` can point to a `Car`, `Bus` or `Vehicle` object. The type of the one it actually points to is printed when the `typeid` operation is performed.

If the `typeid` argument is a reference or a dereferenced pointer to a polymorphic type, the dynamic type of the actual object referenced or pointed to is returned. A polymorphic type is any class that has at least one virtual function. If the argument is non-polymorphic, `typeid` returns a `type_info` object that represents the static type. If a dereferenced pointer is used as the argument, and it is zero, a `bad_typeid` exception is thrown. The `typeid` operator works with the standard data types as well as user-defined types.

Other member functions of `type_info` are the operators `==` and `!=`, which can be used to compare two `type_info` objects. The function `before` orders `type_info` objects, but the ordering is implementation dependent. The copy constructor and assignment operator are private, so a copy of a `type_info` object cannot be made.

Here is a simple example of RTTI being used with dynamic casting. Notice `typeid` is used, with both object and class arguments, to check the type of an object before the dynamic cast is applied:

```
#include <typeinfo.h>
...
void update( Vehicle& vhcl )
{
    Bus abus;

    if ( typeid(vhcl) == typeid(Bus) ) {
       abus = dynamic_cast<Bus&>(vhcl);
       // do Bus processing
    }
    else {
       // non-Bus processing
    }
    ...
}
```

In general, designs based on explicit RTTI should be avoided. If functions need to respond to run-time type information, this can be supported by designing a polymorphic class hierarchy using virtual functions. If RTTI is going to be used for building a generic class or function, use a template instead. Program designs based on polymorphic classes and templates cope with program evolution much better than those based on RTTI. The use of RTTI can encourage a poor *switch on type* style that ignores some of the more powerful and resilient features of C++. It can appeal to inexperienced C++ programmers because it avoids some initially complicated parts of the language.

On the positive side, designs that incorporate legacy systems can often benefit from RTTI. Sometimes it is difficult to extend or modify the design of an existing library to make it polymorphic. In such cases RTTI can be used to create effective wrappers for the old software. The C++ RTTI method provides a common standard for library developers who need to incorporate some form of run-time type information facility in their products. RTTI can be useful for debugging instrumentation, with messages that contain run-time correct type information.

13.4 Namespaces

Namespaces are a way of preventing name clashes in larger programs composed from a number of components. Named items such as functions, classes and objects are put into distinct namespaces. The name of the namespace is used to qualify the name of the item to make it unique in the program. A namespace definition looks like this:

```
namespace Release1 {
    class Vehicle {
        . . .
    };
    . . .
    void print( Vehicle& vhcl );
}
```

The names in a namespace will not collide with global names or names in any other namespaces. Names within a namespace behave like global names, but their scope is restricted to the namespace.

The members of a namespace can be defined within the name space:

```
namespace Release1 {
    . . .
    void print( Vehicle& vhcl )
        { cout << vhcl; }
}
```

Or, they can be defined outside their namespace by explicit qualification:

```
void Release1::print( Vehicle& vhcl )
{
    cout << vhcl;
}
```

The definition and its associated namespace must both be in the same enclosing name space, which in the above case is the global namespace.

There are three ways of accessing names in namespaces. A *qualified name* can be used to access an item in a namespace:

```
Release1::Vehicle rented;
Release1::print(rented);
```

Or a *using declaration* can be used to allow a single name to be used unqualified:

```
using Release1::Vehicle;
Vehicle rented;
Release1::print(rented);
```

Or a *using directive* can be used to make all of the names in a namespace available for unqualified access:

```
using namespace Release1;
Vehicle rented;
print(rented);
```

The result of employing using declarations and directives is slightly different. A using declaration introduces a synonym for the qualified name into the local scope. This means that the semantics of a using declaration are the same as for a local declaration. It hides any global declarations with the same name, and an error will be reported if its name conflicts with another local declaration.

A using directive makes all the namespace names accessible. They behave like global names. They are hidden by local names, and an error is reported if they are the same as any global names. Where there are name clashes, a qualifier can be used to remove ambiguity. Global is, in effect, just another namespace. So ::x means x in the global namespace. The following example shows these differences in action:

```
namespace A {
    int a, b, c;
}

int c;          // c is in global namespace

void demo1()
```

```
{
   int a = 0;
   using namespace A;

   a = 3;          // local a
   b = 4;          // b in A
   c = 5;          // error - ambiguity, is c global or in A?
   ::c = 5;        // global c
   A::c = 5;       // c in A
}

void demo2()
{
   int a = 0;
   using A::a;  // error - clash with local a
   using A::b;
   using A::c;  // hides global c

   a = 3;
   b = 4;          // b in A
   c = 5;          // c in A
}
```

Alternative names can be declared for a namespace, or a class. These are called aliases. For example,

```
namespace University_of_Northumbria_at_Newcastle {
   ...
}
namespace UNN = University_of_Northumbria_at_Newcastle;
// duplication is allowed ...
namespace UNN = University_of_Northumbria_at_Newcastle;
namespace UNN = UNN;
```

Nested namespaces are allowed. The scope rules are illustrated in the following example:

```
namespace Outer {
   int a;
   namespace Inner {
      void f1( int i )
         { a = i; // Outer::a }
      int a;
      void f1( int i )
         { a = i; // Inner::a }
   }
}
```

The usual function overloading rules apply to namespaces, and over-loading can occur across namespaces. Namespaces are open, so they can be distributed over several header and source files. For example, the name-space A is in two parts:

```
// in header file a.h
namespace A {
   void f( int i );
}

...

// in source file a.cxx
#include "a.h"
namespace A {
   void f( int i )
   {
       ...
   }
}
```

Classes are a kind of namespace, and using declarations can be employed to remove ambiguity caused by name clashes with base class members.

```
class Base {
public:
   void fa( int i );
   void fb( int i );
};

class Derived : public Base {
public:
   using Base::fa;
   void fa( int i )
      { fa(i); }      // calls Base::fa(int)
   void fb( int i )
      { fb(i); }      // recursively calls Derived::fb(int)
};
```

Unnamed namespaces can be used to restrict the visibility of items to a particular compilation unit, which can be a header or a source file. An unnamed namespace is just like any other namespace except its name does not have to be used:

```
namespace { ... }
```

This is equivalent to:

```
namespace uniquename { ... }
using namespace uniquename;
```

Every unnamed namespace in a single scope shares the same unique but hidden name. In particular, all the global unnamed namespaces in a compilation unit are part of the same namespace, and this is different from unnamed namespaces in other compilation units.

The method of restricting visibility in C is to declare specific items as `static`. Although this is still possible, unnamed namespaces should be used instead. In C++ the `static` keyword should only be used to mean static allocation (see §8.5).

13.5 Exercises

1. Write a template for a bound array class. It should throw an exception if an array instance is accessed with a subscript that is out of range. This can be based on the solution to Exercise 12.2, which is an array template parameterized by type and size.

2. The class `Store` holds pointers to objects derived from `Storable`:

```
class Store {
public:
   Store();
   add( Storable* s )
      // add pointer to Store
   void top()
      // set current to first Storable item
   Storable* current()
      // return pointer to current Storable item
   void next()
      // set current to next
   bool end()
      // no more Storable items
   ...
private:
   ...
};
```

The definition of `Storable` allows the price of an object derived from this class to be accessed polymorphically:

```
class Storable {
public:
   virtual double price() = 0;
};
```

However, the other parts of an object derived from `Storable` cannot be accessed by a pointer returned from an instance of `Store`. Show how casting can be used to do this as safely as possible.

3. Casting can seriously damage the health of a program. Show how the misuse of casting can produce incorrect results.

CHAPTER 14

More input and output

14.1 The standard streams

There are four standard stream objects: cin, cout, cerr and clog. Extracting from cin reads from the standard input stream, and inserting to cout writes to the standard output stream. Inserting to cerr or clog writes to the standard error stream. The cerr stream should be used for debugging and error messages, and the clog stream is better for large amounts of data such as trace information. These stream objects are supported by the header file <iostream.h>, which defines three important classes: istream, ostream and ios. The istream class is for input and ostream is for output. The ios class defines lots of constants that are used to configure input and output operations.

The << operator inserts data into an output stream, and >> extracts data from an input stream. Versions of these, for the fundamental types, are supplied with <iostream.h>. These can be overloaded to provide a similar service for any class (see §9.2.9). Here is an example of how they can be used with cin and cout:

```
#include <iostream.h>
#include <string>
#include <ctype.h>  // for toupper

void main()
{
    char choice;
    string code;
    int amount;

    do {
```

```
    cout << "Options:" << endl
          << " a - Add" << endl
          << " b - Delete" << endl
          << "Choose: ";
    cin >> choice;
  choice = toupper(choice);    // convert to uppercase
  } while ( choice != 'A' && choice != 'B' );

  bool okay = false;
  switch ( choice ) {
  case 'A':
    cout << "Give new stock code: ";
    cin >> code;
    cout << "Give new amount: ";
    while ( !okay ) {
      cin >> amount;
      if ( amount < 0 )
        cout << "Amount cannot be negative" << endl
              << "Please reenter: ";
      else
        okay = true;
    }
    break;
  case 'B':
    cout << "Give stock code to delete: ";
    cin >> code;
    amount = 0;
    break;
  }
... rest of program
}
```

This program prompts the user for information from the keyboard. It displays a simple menu and waits for a response. The reply is stored in choice. It is converted to upper case by the function toupper from <ctype.h>, before being used to control the rest of the input operation. Some checking is performed to ensure the input data are valid. The results are stored in the variables choice, code and amount.

The streams cin and cout are *tied*, so the output buffer is flushed to the screen before input begins. This ensures that the prompt message appears before the program waits for the answer.

14.2 Setting flags and parameters

A number of functions are provided in <iostream.h> for modifying the flags and parameters that control the behaviour of input and output streams. Parameters are managed with the following functions:

- width (int w)   For output this sets the width of the print field. When inputting strings this sets the maximum number of characters read to width –1. This is transient and only applies to the next I/O operation.
- fill (char c)   Specifies the pad character.
- precision (int p)   If the ios::scientific or ios::fixed flags are set, this specifies the number of digits to the right of the point. Otherwise, it specifies the total number of digits displayed. It only affects the format of floating-point numbers.

These are stream member functions, and they are easy to use. For example, the following will print 00123.46:

```
cout.fill('0');
cout.width(8);
cout.precision(2);
cout << 123.456;
```

The use of width affects only the next insertion or extraction operation. After this, the width reverts to the default value.

Other attributes of a stream can be modified by setting ios flags with the flag function. This is a little more complicated than setting a parameter. Table 14.1 gives a list of some of the most useful flags. A flag argument is built by ORing these flags, so if we wanted to print in hexadecimal, aligned to the left, we would use the argument ios::hex|ios::left. Some examples are:

```
cout.flags(ios::hex | ios::left);
cout.flags(ios::dec);
const long my_options = ios::left | ios::fixed;
long old_options = cout.flags(my_options);
```

The flags function sets the specified flags and clears all the others. The functions setf() and unsetf() can be used instead of flags(). They only modify the flags specified in their argument. The setf() function sets flags and unsetf() clears them. There is a two argument version of setf() for setting flags in named bit fields:

```
cout.setf(ios::hex, ios::basefield);
```

Table 14.1 Format state flags.

Field	Flag	Use
ios::adjustfield		*field adjustment bit field*
	ios::left	pad after value
	ios::right	pad before value
	ios::internal	pad between sign and value
ios::basefield		*integer base bit field*
	ios::dec	decimal
	ios::oct	octal
	ios::hex	hexadecimal
ios::floatfield		*floating point notation bitfield*
	ios::scientific	d.dddd Edd
	ios::fixed	ddd.dd
	ios::boolalpha	insert and extract bool type in alphabetic format
	ios::showbase	show integer base
	ios::showpos	explicit + for positive integers
	ios::unitbuf	flush output after each output operation
	ios::uppercase	E and X rather than e and x, and uppercase hex characters
	ios::skipws	skip white space on input

In each of the named bit fields only one flag can be set.
Default is ios::skipws and ios::dec set with all the other flags clear.

This sets the ios::hex flag and clears all the other flags in ios::basefield. All the flags not in ios::basefield are unchanged. Table 14.1 gives the bit fields and their related flags. If the first argument is zero, all the flags in the field are cleared. So to reset output to its default state we would use:

```
cout.setf(0,ios::floatfield);
```

All these parameter and flag setting functions return the relevant state before it is changed. The flag, setf and unsetf return the complete state of all the flags. The following function calls get their relevant states without modification:

```
char c = cout.fill();
int  p = cout.precision();
int  w = cout.width();
long f = cout.flag();
```

The stored values can be used to restore the state later by specifying them as arguments in the relevant function.

14.3 Manipulators

Manipulators can be used with << and >> operators to modify a stream's flags, parameters and state. The most commonly used manipulator is endl, which inserts a line break:

```
cout << "this is one line" << endl;
```

There are many other useful manipulators. Table 14.2 shows some manipulators with no arguments, like endl, and Table 14.3 shows some single argument manipulators. The header file <iomanip.h> must be included when manipulators with arguments are used. Manipulators do not return the current state of the flags or parameters they modify. They are used like this:

```
#include <iomanip.h>
...
cout << setwidth(10) << 13 << endl;
cout << hex << setw(10) << 13 << endl;
cout << dec << setiosflags(ios::left) << 13 << endl;
cout << setw(10) << hex << 13 << endl;
```

Table 14.2 Manipulators with no arguments.

Manipulator	Use	Stream
dec	use decimal notation	input or output
hex	use hexadecimal notation	input or output
oct	use octal notation	input or output
boolalpha	use alphabetic format for bool type	input or output
noboolalpha	do not use alphabetic format for bool type	input or output
endl	add \n and flush	output only
ends	add \0 and flush	output only
flush	flush output steam	output only
ws	eat white space	input only

These manipulators do not need <iomanip.h>.

Table 14.3 Manipulators with one argument.

Manipulator	Equivalent member function
setiosflags(ios::fmtflags)	setf(ios::fmtflags)
resetiosflags(ios::fmtflags)	unsetf(ios::fmtflags)
setfill(char)	fill(char)
setw(int)	width(int)
setprecision(int)	precision(int)

The header file <iomanip.h> must be included for these manipulators.

As a more comprehensive example, the following program uses a combination of parameters, flags and manipulators to print out a formatted table of information:

```
#include <iostream.h>
#include <iomanip.h>
#include <math.h>

const int MAXSTEPS = 8;
const double START = 0.0;
const double STEP = 1.25;

void main()
{
   const int COLw1 = 4;
   const int COLw2 = 10;
   const int COLw3 = 13;
   const int COLw4 = 13;
   const int COLw5 = 10;
   double seed = START;

   cout << setw(COLw1) << "seed"
        << setw(COLw2) << "seconds"
        << setw(COLw3) << "minutes"
        << "   " << setw(COLw4) << "hours"
        << setw(COLw5) << "days" << endl;

   for ( int steps = 0; steps < MAXSTEPS; steps++ ) {
      double secs = pow(10,seed);
      double mins = secs / 60;
      double hours = mins / 60;
      double days = hours / 24;

      long fsave = cout.flags();
      cout << setw(COLw1) << seed;
      cout.setf(ios::scientific);
      cout.precision(1);
      cout << setw(COLw2) << secs;
      cout.setf(ios::fixed);
      cout.precision(2);
      cout << setw(COLw3) << mins;
      cout.fill('0');
      cout << "   " << setw(COLw4) << hours;
      cout.fill(' ');
      cout << setw(COLw5) << days;
      cout << endl;
      cout.flags(fsave);
```

```
        seed += STEP;
    }
}
```

This program produces the following output:

```
SEED    SECONDS     MINUTES           HOURS      DAYS
   0    1.0e+00        0.02  0000000000.00      0.00
 1.2    1.8e+01        0.30  0000000000.00      0.00
 2.5    3.2e+02        5.27  0000000000.09      0.00
 3.8    5.6e+03       93.72  0000000001.56      0.07
   5    1.0e+05     1666.67  0000000027.78      1.16
 6.2    1.8e+06    29637.99  0000000493.97     20.58
 7.5    3.2e+07   527046.28  0000008784.10    366.00
 8.8    5.6e+08  9372355.42  0000156205.92   6508.58
```

14.4   Unformatted input and output

Unformatted input is possible using `get` functions:

- `int get()`   Returns one character from an input stream as value of function, or `EOF` on end of file. The return type of `int` is needed to accommodate the end of file indicator.

- `istream& get( char& c )`   Extracts a single character from the input stream and stores it in `c`.

- `istream& getline( char p[], int n, char t = '\n' )`
  Gets a line of at most n - 1 characters from the input stream and places them in the buffer p. The end of line character is not put in the buffer. The character \0 is added to the end of the input to form a C string. By default, as given by t = '\n', input stops at end of line, but another character can be used to delimit input. The stream `failbit` is set if the buffer fills before delimiter is read, or if the buffer ends up empty.

These are used with an input stream like this:

```
char c;
cin.get(c);
c = cin.get();
char buff[100];
cin.getline(buff,100);
```

Unformatted output is performed with the `put` member function:

- `int put( char c )`   Inserts the single character in c into the output stream, and returns `EOF` if the insertion fails for any reason.

This might be used, with `get` as follows:

```
int c;
while ( (c = cin.get()) != EOF )
   cout.put(c);
```

Here, characters are extracted from cin in the condition part of the while statement and stored in the variable c. The characters are then written to cout in the body of the loop. At end of file, get will return the value EOF, and this is used to control loop termination.

14.5   Other useful functions

There is an ignore function, which is useful when an error occurs:

- istream& ignore(int n = 1, int delim = EOF)   Stops after discarding n characters, or on a character that matches delim. If n is set to INT_MAX, which is defined in <limits.h>, it is effectively infinite.

An example of how this function can be used is given in §14.6.

There is also a member function called putback that returns a character to the input stream, which can sometimes help when interpreting, or parsing, complicated input:

```
// do nothing !!
cin.get(c);
cin.putback(c);
```

However, this can only be done once after a character is extracted.

The header file <ctype.h> contains some functions that are useful for processing input. For example, the function isprint takes a single character as its input argument, and returns true if it is printable:

```
char ans;
...
if ( isprint(ans) )
   cout << "The answer is " << ans << endl;
```

Table 14.4   End of file and error detection functions.

Function	Returns true to indicate
bool good();	The last operation succeeded. The next operation might succeed.
bool eof();	An input operation reached the end of an input sequence.
bool fail();	Some kind of formatting error occured, and the next operation will fail unless the error is corrected. Or, the stream is corrupted.
bool bad();	The stream is corrupted. Data might be lost.

Table 14.5 Error states.

Function returning true	eof	State fail	bad
good()	no	no	no
eof()	yes	–	–
fail()	–	yes	no
	–	no	yes
	–	yes	yes
bad()	–	–	yes

14.6 Detecting end of file and errors

The error state of a stream can be examined with the functions given in Table 14.4. If good() is true, the previous operation was successful and we can expect the next operation to succeed. The function eof returns true when an input operation reaches the end of an input sequence. For an input file this happens when its end is reached. If fail() is true, then either the stream is corrupted, or there has been some sort of format error on input or output. The function bad can be used to distinguish between these two possibilities. If it returns true, then the stream is corrupt. This may appear complicated, but in practice it is very simple. Table 14.5 shows the possible error states when these functions return true, and the following summarizes some possible tests and responses:

```
cin.get(c);
while ( cin.good() ) {
    // process c
   cin.get(c);
}
if ( cin.eof() ) {
    // Normal termination
}
else
   if ( cin.bad() ) {
     // Fatal error message
   }
   else {
     // Attempt to recover
   }
```

Stream failure is commonly caused by a user entering the wrong type of data during formatted input. For example, entering abc when the following is executed will cause a stream failure:

```
int ivalue;
cin >> ivalue;
```

After a failure occurs the stream is unusable. The behaviour of a program attempting to extract more data from such a stream is unpredictable. To correct the failure, so that the stream can be used again, the stream error state must be reset, and the offending data must be removed from the stream's buffer. Calling the function `clear()` with no arguments resets the error state. This function can also be used to individually clear the bits `ios::eofbit, ios::failbit` and `ios::badbit,` like this:

```
cin.clear(ios::badbit|ios::fail);
```

The buffer is cleared to the next end of line with:

```
cin.ignore(INT_MAX,'\n');
```

The following program, which get four integers from the keyboard, shows how input stream failure can be handled:

```
#include <iostream.h>
#include <limits.h>

void main()
{
    const int NUMVALS = 4;
    int value[NUMVALS];
    int count;

    cout << "enter " << NUMVALS << " integers: ";
    bool done;
    do {
        done = true;
        for ( count = 0; count < NUMVALS; count++ ) {
            cin >> value[count];
            if ( cin.fail() ) {
                cin.clear();
                cin.ignore(INT_MAX,'\n');
                cout << "Invalid data," << endl
                     << "please try again: ";
                done = false;
                break;
            }
        }
    } while ( !done );
... rest of the program
}
```

After each integer is extracted, the fail state is checked. If an error occurs, the state is reset and the stream cleared. An error message is printed, and the inner data entry loop is immediately stopped with a `break` statement. Input processing stops when `done` is true, which is only the case when all four integers are successfully extracted from `cin` without error, otherwise all four values have to be input again.

Table 14.6   File modes.

Flag	Purpose
`ios::in`	open for input
`ios::out`	open for output
`ios::app`	seek to end of file before each write
`ios::ate`	open and immediately seek to end of file
`ios::trunc`	truncate an existing file when opening it
`ios::binary`	open file in binary mode

14.7   Named files

Named files can be used as well as the standard streams. The classes that support this are defined in the header file `<fstream.h>`. There are three important classes `ifstream`, `ofstream` and `fstream`. The `ios` class contains some constants that are relevant to files. When `<fstream.h>` is included we get `<iostream.h>` as well.

To use a named file, an instance of a file object must be defined, and it must be opened with a valid name. To open a file we provide a name and a file mode. Possible file modes are given in Table 14.6. Files opened in modes `ios::out` and `ios::app` will be created if they do not exist. Modes can be combined using the bitwise OR operator. For example, `ios::out | ios::in | ios::ate` specifies an input output file that should retain existing data.

A file can be opened in binary mode as opposed to text mode. In text mode a file is assumed to be composed of lines of text terminated by newline characters. It is possible that the way the file is physically stored on disk is different from this. For example, end of line is sometimes stored as two characters. Automatic translation is performed for a text mode file on input and output to resolve these differences. This translation is not performed for a file opened in binary mode.

A file can be opened when it is defined:

```
fstream infile("report.doc",ios:in);
fstream list("result.txt",ios::out);
fstream master("main.dta",ios::in|ios:out);
```

The ifstream defaults to input and ofstream defaults to output. So we can write:

```
ifstream infile("memo.doc");
ofstream list("result.txt");
```

The function fail can be used to check if a file has been opened without error, or the file object's name can be used on its own:

```
ifstream data("input.txt");
if ( data.fail() )
   cout << "open failed for input" << endl";
ofstream list("result.txt");
if ( list )
   cout << "open okay for output" << endl;
```

Here, list is equivalent to !list.fail() as the condition of an if statement. A *not* operator can be used with a file object name, so !list is the same as list.fail().

The definition of a file object can be separated from its opening, and files can be repeatedly opened and closed:

```
fstream file;
...
file.open("myfile.dat",ios::out);
...
file.close();
file.open("myfile.dat",ios::in);
...
file.close();
```

The close member function shuts down an open file in an orderly manner. A file does not have to be closed explicitly. A stream's destructor is called when a file object goes out of scope, and this will close the file if it is open. Thus a normally terminated program will have all of its files correctly closed. However, if a program crashes with open files, they may be left in an undefined state.

To bring these ideas together, consider a program that copies one file to another. The following example illustrates how this can be done. The file names are hard-wired into this version of the program. A method of getting the file names from the command line is shown in §6.8.2.

```
#include <fstream.h>
#include <stdlib.h>

void main()
{
```

```
cout << "file copy beginning" << endl;

ifstream in;
in.open("test.in");
if ( in.fail() ) {
  cout << "Unable to open input file" << endl;
  exit(99);
}

ofstream out("test.out");
if ( !out ) {
  cout << "Unable to open output file" << endl;
  exit(99);
}

char c;
in.get(c);                    // read ahead
while ( in.good() ) {
  out.put(c);
  in.get(c);
}

cout << "file copy complete" << endl;
}
```

Here, the copying is done by a while loop that stops at the end of the input file. The file is read just before the loop is entered and in the last statement of the loop. This technique is called *read ahead,* and it ensures the correct management of data when end of file is encountered, and when the input file is empty.

14.8   Redirection

The standard streams can be redirected to named files. Some versions of C++ allow stream object assignment for this purpose, but this approach is non-standard. The preferred method is to replace the standard stream buffer with one that is connected to a named file. This is easy:

```
#include<fstream.h>
...
filebuf fb;
fb.open("log.dat",ios::out);
cout.rdbuf(&fb);
```

Here, a file buffer is created, and connected to a file called log.dat. The `cout` buffer is then replaced using the `rdbuf` member function. Older versions of C++ might not allow `rdbuf` to be used in this way, and an implementation dependent method for redirecting the standard streams will have to be used instead.

It is generally bad practice to redirect `cerr` as important error messages may be lost.

14.9   Persistent classes

Class objects that remain in existence after a program has finished are often called *persistent*. A simple way to achieve persistence is to save and restore objects at appropriate times. The following example shows how an object can be written to and read from a named file using *marshalling* functions:

```
#include <fstream.h>
#include <string>

class Stock {
public:
    Stock( int acode = 999, double acost = 0.0,
           int alevel = 0, const string& adescription = "" );
    // ...
    void write( ostream& out ) const;
    void read( istream& in );
private:
    int thecode;
    string thedescription;
    double thecost;
    int thelevel;
};

Stock::Stock( int acode, double acost,
              int alevel, const string& adescription )
    : thecode(acode), thecost(acost), thelevel(alevel),
      thedescription(adescription) {}

void Stock::write( ostream& out ) const
{
    out << thecode << endl;
    out << thedescription << endl;
    out << thecost << endl;
    out << thelevel << endl;
}

void Stock::read( istream& in )
```

```
{
   in >> thecode;
   getline(in,thedescription);
   in >> thecost;
   in >> thelevel;
}

void main()
{
   cout << "persistence test" << endl;
   fstream file;
   Stock item1(111,2.5,25,"Left-handed widgets");
   Stock item2(222,5.6,200,"Right-handed widgets");
   Stock item3(333,8.1,12,"Blue widgets");
   Stock buff;
   file.open("stock.dat",ios::out);
   if ( file.fail() ) {
       cout << "Unable to open stock file for output"
            << endl;
      exit(99);
   }
   item1.write(file);
   item2.write(file);
   item3.write(file);
   file.close();
   file.open("stock.dat",ios::in);
   if ( file.fail() ) {
      cout << "Unable to open stock file for input" << endl;
      exit(99);
   }
   buff.read(file);
   while ( !file.eof() ) {
      buff.write(cout);
      cout << "---------------" << endl;
      buff.read(file);
   }
   file.close();
}
```

The marshalling functions in Stock are called read and write. They are not completely symmetric because the read function cannot simply reverse the insertions in the write function. In this case, the write function is also suitable for direct screen output, and it is used to list the Stock objects recovered from the file.

14.10 Exercises

1. Write a program that converts all the `tab` characters in a text file to a specified number of space characters. It should work as a command with the following format: `detab filein fileout [space]` where `filein` is the input file and `fileout` is the resulting file with all of its `tab` characters replaced. The last parameter is optional. It is the number of spaces that replace a `tab` character. If it is not given, it defaults to 3.

2. A file contains names and addresses in the following *comma delimited* format: `name,addr1,addr2,addr3` where each field is separated by a comma and each name and address record is on its own line. Some fields might be blank, but the commas will still be present in the record. Write a program that prints this file. Each field should start on a new line, and the address lines should be indented by three spaces.

3. Take the `List` class given in §8.10, and add marshalling functions. This class uses a linked list implementation, so the solution to this is not trivial.

APPENDIX A

Model solutions

Index

Exercise 2.2 Write a program that asks for your first name and then prints a hello message with your name in it.

```
#include <iostream.h>
#include <string>

void main()
{
    string name;
    cout << "Please give your first name: ";
    cin >> name;
    cout << endl;
```

217

```
    cout << "Hello " << name
          << ". It is nice to know you." << endl;
}
```

Exercise 2.3 **Write a program that asks for two numbers and prints out their sum.**

```
#include <iostream.h>

void main()
{
    float a, b;
    cout << "Please give two numbers: ";
    cin >> a >> b;
    cout << "The sum of " << a << " and " << b
          << " is " << (a + b) <<  endl;
}
```

Exercise 3.1 **Value added tax (VAT) is 17.5%. Write a program that asks for a value, then prints out the value, the VAT amount and the total cost.**

```
#include <iostream.h>

const float VAT = 17.5;

void main()
{
    float value;
    float vatamount;
    float total;

    cout << "VAT Calculation Program" << endl;
    cout << "Please enter value: ";
    cin  >> value;
    vatamount = value * VAT / 100;
    total = value + vatamount;
    cout << "value        " << value << endl;
    cout << "VAT amount " << vatamount << endl;
    cout << "total        " << total << endl;
}
```

Exercise 3.2 **Write a program to calculate the area and circumference of a circle.**

```
#include <iostream.h>

const double PI = 3.1416;
```

```
void main()
{
    double radius;

    cout << "Circle Program" << endl;
    cout << "Please enter radius: " << endl;
    cin >> radius;
    cout << "Area is "
        << PI * radius * radius << endl;
    cout << "Circumference is "
        << 2 * PI * radius << endl;
}
```

Exercise 3.3   Calculate the value of various C++ expressions.

Part	Calculation	Result	Comments
a	b = c * 6	56	Operator * calculated first.
c	c % b	1	Remainder is 1.
c	c / b + 4	8	The expression c/b is calculated as integer.
d	c / b + 4.0	8	The same as part c. The double 4.0 makes no difference.
	c / double(b) + 4.0	8.5	The expression c/double(b) is calculated as floating point
e	a - 4 != 3	1	This is true.
f	c / (a - 3 * b)	?	Error caused by divide by zero.
g	a == 6 && b == 3	0	This is false.

Note that if (e) or (g) are written explicitly in a cout statement they must be enclosed in brackets like this:

```
cout << ( a - 4 != 3 ) << endl;
```

The << operator has a higher priority than the logical operators such as !=. This causes an error because the expression does not group correctly about the << and logical operators.

Exercise 3.4   Experiment with ++ and -- operators.

Statement	Value of i
i = j++ - --k;	−4
i = k * -i;	20
i = j * i++;	undefined

The undefined value produced by i = j * i++; was actually 41 with a test program compiled with Borland's C++ v4.0. But it might be different with another compiler. Expressions like this are unreliable. Never use them.

Exercise 3.5   Write some expressions that modify individual bits in an integer value.

```
motor = ~0x3;              // (a) initialize
motor |= 0x03;             // (b) set both bits on
motor &= 0xFFFFFFFD;       // (c) motor off
motor |= 0x02;             // (d) motor on
motor ^= 0x01;             // (e) toggle direction
```

This is a crude solution. It is unsatisfactory for a number of reasons. Understanding the bit patterns is difficult, and calculating them is error prone. Statement (c) is particularly poor because it makes the assumption that motor is 16 bits long. Here is a better solution:

```
enum MotorBits { MBdIR = 1, MBoNoFF= 2 };

motor = ~(MBdIR | MBoNoFF);    // (a')
motor |= MBdIR | MBoNoFF;      // (b')
motor &= ~MBoNoFF;             // (c')
motor |= MBoNoFF;              // (d')
motor ^= MBdIR;                // (e')
```

This method gives the control bits names, and then uses them to build the bit patterns, which is much safer and easier to understand than the first attempt. The value of each bit represents its position in motor. If a bit's position is n, its name's value is 2^n where the low order bit is $n = 0$.

Exercise 4.1   Write a program to calculate the sum of the integers between two values input at the terminal.

There is a formula for calculating the sum of the integers between two values:

$$sum = \frac{(end - start + 1)(end + start)}{2}$$

But in the spirit of this chapter, here is a solution that uses a loop:

```
#include <iostream.h>

void main()
{
    int start, end;
    cout << "Give two integers please: ";
    cin >> start >> end;
    int sum = 0;
    for ( int i = start; i <= end; i++ )
        sum +- i;
```

```
   cout << "The sum of the integers between "
        << start << " and " << end
        << " is " << sum << endl;
}
```

Exercise 4.2   Calculate the factorial of a value input at the terminal.

```
#include <iostream.h>

void main()
{
   int number;
   cout << "Factorial Calculator" << endl
        << "--------------------" << endl;
   cout << "Give integer: ";
   cin >> number;
   long factorial = 1;
   for ( int i = 1; i <= number; i++ )
      factorial *= i;
   cout << "Factorial " << number << " is "
        << factorial << endl;
}
```

Exercise 4.3   Write a short program to print out a character's binary code.

This is a technically difficult problem. This solution exploits the fact that a character is an integral type, and that the senior, or right most, bit of a negative number is 1. After each senior bit is tested it is removed with a left shift operation:

```
#include <iostream.h>

void main()
{
   char thechar;
   cout << "Character to Binary Converter" << endl
        << "-----------------------------" << endl;
   cout << "Give a character: ";
   cin >> thechar;
   cout << "the binary code for this is ";
   int i = 1;
   while ( i++ <= 8 ) {
      if ( thechar < 0 )
         cout << 1;
      else
```

```
        cout << 0;
      thechar <<= 1;   // shift left one bit
  }
  cout << endl;
}
```

Exercise 4.4   Write a program that finds a root of a particular quadratic using Newton's method. (Formula given in question.)

```
#include <iostream.h>
#include <math.h>

const float MINdIFF = 0.001;
const float START   = 1.0;

void main()
{
   float xold;
   float xnew = START;
   do {
      xold = xnew;
      xnew = xold - ( xold*xold*xold - xold - 1 ) /
                    ( 3*xold*xold -1 );
      cout << "approximation is " << xnew << endl;
   } while ( fabs(xnew - xold) >= MINdIFF );
   cout << "Root is " << xnew << endl;
}
```

Exercise 4.5   Write a program that prints a multiplication matrix.

```
#include <iostream.h>
#include <iomanip.h>

const int START = 1;
const int END = 12;
const int FwIDTH = 4;
const int TiDENT = 15;

void main()
{
   cout << setw(TiDENT) << "";
   cout << "Multiplication Matrix" << endl;
   cout << setw(TiDENT) << "";
   cout << "---------------------" << endl << endl;
   for ( int row = START; row <= END; row++) {
```

```
    for ( int col = START; col <= END; col++ )
       cout << setw(FwIDTH) << col * row;
    cout << endl;
  }
}
```

Exercise 5.1 Write a program that inputs five floating point numbers and stores them in an array. After they are all input, the program should print them out. Then calculate and print the average of the values stored in that array.

```
#include <iostream.h>

const int NUMS = 5;

void main()
{
    float number[NUMS];
    int i;
    float sum = 0;

    for ( i = 0 ; i < NUMS; i ++ ) {
       cout << "Number please: ";
       cin >> number[i];
    }
    cout << "The numbers are ";
    for ( i = 0 ; i < NUMS; i ++ ) {
       cout << ' ' << number[i];
    }
    cout << endl;
    for ( i = 0 ; i < NUMS; i ++ )
       sum += number[i];
    cout << "The average of these numbers is "
          << sum / NUMS << endl;
}
```

Exercise 5.2 Write a program that inputs a word and checks if it is a palindrome, using C strings.

```
#include <iostream.h>
#include <string.h>

void main()
{
    const int MAXsTRLEN = 128;
```

```
    char word[MAXsTRLEN];
    cout << "Give a word: ";
    cin >> word;
    char revs[MAXsTRLEN];
    int wordpos = strlen(word) - 1;
    int revpos = 0;
    while ( wordpos >= 0 )
      revs[revpos++] = word[wordpos--];
    revs[strlen(word)] = '\0';
    if ( strcmp(word,revs) == 0 )
       cout << word << " is a ";
    else
       cout << word << " is not a ";
    cout << "palindrome" << endl;
}
```

A C++ string version can be written using almost the same algorithm. It is actually slightly simpler because a string termination character does not have to be considered, and a maximum string length does not have to be specified. It looks like this:

```
#include <iostream.h>
#include <string>

void main()
{
    string word;
    cout << "Give a word: ";
    cin >> word;
    string revs(' ',word.length());
    int wordpos = word.length() - 1;
    int revpos = 0;
    while ( wordpos >= 0 )
      revs[revpos++] = word[wordpos--];
    if ( word == revs )
       cout << word << " is a ";
    else
       cout << word << " is not a ";
    cout << "palindrome" << endl;
}
```

Exercise 5.3 **(a)** Write an algorithm to printout all of the data items stored in the stack example given in §5.8.

```
Node* ppntr = stack;
while ( ppntr != 0 ) {
   cout << ppntr->data << endl;
   ppntr = ppntr->next;
}
```

(b) Write an algorithm to destroy the whole of the above stack.

```
Node* dpntr = stack;
while ( dpntr != 0 ) {
   Node* next = dpntr->next;
   delete dpntr;
   dpntr = next;
}
```

Exercise 5.4 Write an algorithm that creates an independent copy of a linked list (details given in question). The new list should be in the same order as the original, and the location of its first node should be stored in a pointer called **duplicate**.

```
Node* in = accountlist;
if ( in == 0 )
   duplicate = 0;   // list empty
else {
                     // process first node
   Node* out = duplicate = new Node;
   out->name = in->name;
   out->account = in->account;
   out->next = 0;
   in = in->next;
                     // process rest of list
   while ( in != 0 ) {
      out = out->next = new Node;
      out->name = in->name;
      out->account = in->account;
      out->next = 0;
      in = in->next;
   }
}
```

Exercise 5.5   Write an algorithm that will double the size of a dynamically allocated array without losing any of the stored numbers.

```
float* temp = new float[20];
for ( int i = 0; i < 20; i++ ) {
   if ( i < 10 )
      temp[i] = height[i];
   else
      temp[i] = 0.0;
}
delete[] height;
height = temp;
```

Exercise 6.1   Write a function that takes an array of **float** numbers and returns the smallest and largest numbers in that array.

```
void limits( const float data[], int dsize,
             float& min, float& max )
{
   min = max = data[0];
   for ( int i = 1; i < dsize; i++ ) {
      if ( min < data[i] )
         min = data[i];
      if ( max > data[i] )
         max = data[i];
   }
}
```

Exercise 6.2   Write a delete function for the example in §6.9. The function should take the name of a dog as an argument and, if it is present, remove it from the array of names. To remove a name replace it with an empty string.

If the add_dog function in §6.9 is considered, it can be seen that there can be duplicate names in the array. This function removes the first occurrence of the target string:

```
void delete_dog( string dogs[], int max, string adog )
{
   int i = 0;
   bool done = false;
   while ( !done && i < max ) {
      if ( dogs[i] == adog ) {
         dogs[i] = "";
         done = true;
```

```
        }
        i++;
    }
}
```

Exercise 6.3 Write a function that splits a file name with the format name.type into two strings containing just name and type.

```
void namesplit( string full, string& name, string& type )
{
    int dotloc = full.find_first_of('.');
    name = full.substr(0,dotloc);
    if ( dotloc == NPOS ) // dot not found
        type = "";
    else
        type = full.substr(dotloc+1,NPOS);
}
```

Exercise 6.4 Write a function that uses recursion to calculate the sum of the first *n* positive integers.

The function sum calls itself with decreasing values of n, until n is equal to zero. The test actually checks for n less than or equal to zero. This ensures that the function handles negative numbers in a reasonable way, by returning zero.

```
int sum( int n )
{
    if ( n <= 0 )
        return 0;
    else
        return n + sum(n-1);
}
```

Exercise 6.5 Write a program that takes two numbers from the command line and prints their sum.

```
#include <iostream.h>
#include <stdlib.h>

void main( int argc, char* argv[] )
{
    double num1, num2;
    if ( argc != 3 ) {
        cout << "Format is:" << endl
```

```
                << "addthem <number> <number>"
                << endl;
        exit(99);
    }
    num1 = atof(argv[1]);
    num2 = atof(argv[2]);
    cout <<  num1 + num2;
}
```

Exercise 7.1   The example in §6.9 manages a list of pet dog names using a set of functions and a shared array of names. Write a class called Dogs to do the same thing.

This solution uses the standard C string function strncpy.This version of the copy function limits the number of characters processed. It is used in the member function add to safely copy names into an array of strings. At most NSIZE characters are copied, so a Dogs object cannot be damaged by adding a name that is too long.

```
#include <iostream.h>
#include <string>

class Dogs {
// maintain a list of dogs
public:
    Dogs();
    bool room();
       // True if room for another dog.
    void add( string name );
       // Add 'name' to list of dogs
       // If 'name' is blank it is ignored.
       // Do nothing if no room.
    void remove( string name );
       // Remove 'name' from list of dogs.
       // If 'name' is blank it is ignored.
       // Do nothing if 'name' not found.
    int count();
       // The number of dogs in list.
    bool is( string name );
       // True if 'name' is in list.
    void print();
       // Print the list of dogs.
    enum { NSIZE = 10 };
       // Maximum length of a name
private:
```

```
    int thecount;
    enum { MAXnAMES = 15 };
    string names[MAXnAMES];
    bool find( string target, int& loc );
};

Dogs::Dogs() : thecount(0) {}

void Dogs::add( string name )
{
    int loc;
    if ( name.length() != 0 )
        if ( thecount != MAXnAMES ) {
            find("",loc);
            names[loc] = name;
            thecount++;
        }
}

void Dogs::remove( string name )
{
    int loc;
    if ( name.length() != 0 )
        if ( find(name,loc) ) {
            names[loc]= "";
            thecount--;
        }
}

bool Dogs::find( string target, int& loc )
{
    loc = 0;
    while ( target != names[loc] && loc < MAXnAMES )
        loc++;
    if ( loc < MAXnAMES )
        return true;
    else {
        loc = 0;
        return false;
    }
}

int Dogs::count()
{
    return thecount;
}
```

```
bool Dogs::is( string name )
{
   int ignore = 0;
   return find(name,ignore);
}

void Dogs::print()
{
   for ( int loc = 0; loc < MAXnAMES; loc++ )
      if ( names[loc].length() != 0 )
         cout << names[loc] << ' ';
}

bool Dogs::room()
{
   return bool(thecount < MAXnAMES);
}

void main()
{
   Dogs dogs;
   dogs.add("Cleo");
   if ( dogs.room() ) {
      dogs.add("Penny");
   }
   else
      cout << "no room for more dogs" << endl;
   cout << "The dogs are ";
   dogs.print();
   cout << endl << " and there are "
        << dogs.count() << " of them." << endl;
   if ( dogs.is("Ann") )
      cout << "Ann is a dog" << endl;
   else
      cout << "Ann is not a dog" << endl;
   dogs.remove("Cleo");
   cout << "The dogs are now ";
   dogs.print(); cout << endl;
}
```

Exercise 7.2 (a) Specify an integer stack by writing a class declaration.

```
class StackInt {
public:
   StackInt();
```

```
    int pop();
        // Remove the top item on stack
        // returning its value;
        // Return value undefined if stack is empty.
    void push( int item );
        // Put 'item' onto the top of stack.
        // Ignore if stack full.
    bool empty();
        // True if no items in stack.
    bool full();
        // True if no room for another push.
private:
    enum { SIZE = 20 };    // implementation
    int data[SIZE];
    int stacktop;
};
```

(b) Show how the above class can be used by writing a short example that inserts and removes an item from a stack object.

```
StackInt mystack;
if ( !mystack.full() )
    mystack.push(99);
if ( !mystack.empty() ) {
    int item = mystack.pop();
    cout << "item from stack is " << item << endl;
}
```

Exercise 7.3 **Implement the class declared in the previous exercise using a fixed length array of integers.**

```
StackInt::StackInt() : stacktop(0) {}

int StackInt::pop()
{
    if ( stacktop > 0 )
        return data[--stacktop];
}

void StackInt::push( int item )
{
    if ( stacktop < SIZE )
        data[stacktop++] = item;
}

bool StackInt::empty()
```

```
{
    return stacktop == 0;
}

bool StackInt::full()
{
    return stacktop > SIZE;
}
```

Exercise 7.4 Declare and implement a class that simulates the operation of a traffic control beacon. (Brief specification given in question.)

```
class TLight {
public:
    TLight();
    void next();
    bool red();
    bool green();
    void display();
private:
    bool redlight;
    bool greenlight;
};

TLight::TLight() : redlight(true), greenlight(false){}

void TLight::next()
{
    if ( redlight && !greenlight ) {
        redlight = false;
        greenlight = true;
    }
    else
        if ( !redlight && greenlight ) {
            redlight = true;
            greenlight = true;
        }
        else
            if ( redlight && greenlight ) {
                redlight = true;
                greenlight = false;
            }
}

bool TLight::red()
{
```

```
    return redlight;
}

bool TLight::green()
{
    return greenlight;
}

void TLight::display()
{
    if ( redlight )
        cout << "RED ";
    else
        cout << "--- ";
    if ( greenlight )
        cout << "GREEN";
    else
        cout << "-----";
}
```

Exercise 7.5 **Implement a class that manages a pair of traffic beacons controlling a single track road. (Class declaration and brief specification given in question.)**

```
class TLpair {
public:
    TLpair();
    void next();
    void display();
private:
    TLight beacon1;
    TLight beacon2;
};

TLpair::TLpair()
{
    beacon1.next();
}

void TLpair::next()
{
    if ( !beacon1.red() && beacon1.green() &&
         beacon2.red() && !beacon2.green() ) {
        beacon1.next();
    }
    else
```

```
        if ( beacon1.red() && beacon1.green() &&
             beacon2.red() && !beacon2.green() ) {
           beacon1.next();
           beacon2.next();
        }
        else
           if ( beacon1.red() && !beacon1.green() &&
                !beacon2.red() && beacon2.green() ) {
                beacon2.next();
           }
           else
              if ( beacon1.red() && !beacon1.green() &&
                   beacon2.red() && beacon2.green() ) {
                beacon1.next();
                beacon2.next();
              }
}

void TLpair::display()
{
   cout << "( ";
   beacon1.display();
   cout << " )( ";
   beacon2.display();
   cout << " )";
}
```

Exercise 7.6 Explore the way that constructors and destructors are called by writing a simple program.

A suitable program might look something like the following. An assignment operator overload has been included in this solution because it makes the output even more informative. Details of assignment operator overloading can be found in §9.2.2.

```
#include <iostream.h>

class Test {
public:
   Test()
      { cout << "Test()" << endl; }
   Test( Test& )
      { cout << "Test(Test&)" << endl; }
   Test( int )
      { cout << "Test(int)" << endl; }
   ~Test()
```

```
      { cout << "~Test()" << endl; }
   Test& operator=( const Test& xx )
      { cout << "Test& operator=(const T&)" << endl;
        return *this; }
};

Test f( Test t1, Test t2 )
{
   cout << "in function" << endl;
   return t1;
}

void main()
{
   Test tt1, tt2;
   cout << "statement starting" << endl;
   tt2 = f(tt1,Test(1));
   cout << "statement over" << endl;
}
```

Exercise 8.1 Write a **TaskQueue** class for storing **TaskInfo** objects (definition given in question). Assume the **TaskInfo** is provided as a separate component, with a header file called **"task.h"**. Implement the **TaskQueue** using separate header and source files.

The header file for the TaskInfo queue should look something like this:

```
#ifndef TASKQ_H
#define TASKQ_H
#include "task.h"

enum bool {false,true};

class TaskQueue {
public:
   TaskQueue();
   void add( TaskInfo task );
   TaskInfo get();
   bool empty();
   ~TaskQueue();
private:
   class Node;
   Node* first;
   Node* last;
};
#endif
```

The source code file for the `TaskQueue` is given below. This uses a similar method to that used in the `List` class given in §8.10.

```cpp
#include "taskq.h"

class TaskQueue::Node{
public:
    TaskQueue::Node( TaskInfo task, TaskQueue::Node* node = 0
)
        : thetask(task), thenext(node) {}
    TaskInfo task()
        {   return thetask; }
    TaskQueue::Node* next()
        {   return thenext; }
    TaskQueue::Node* splice( TaskQueue::Node* node )
        {   node->thenext = thenext;
            thenext = node;
            return node; }
private:
    TaskInfo thetask;
    TaskQueue::Node* thenext;
};

TaskQueue::TaskQueue()
    : first(0), last(0) {}

void TaskQueue::add( TaskInfo task )
{
    if ( first == 0 )
        first = last = new Node(task);
    else
        last = last->splice(new Node(task));
}

TaskInfo TaskQueue::get()
{
    TaskInfo temp = first->task();
    Node* dead = first;
    first = first->next();
    delete dead;
    if ( first == 0 )
        last = 0;
    return temp;
}

bool TaskQueue::empty()
{
```

```
      return bool(first == 0);
}

TaskQueue::~TaskQueue()
{
   while ( first != 0 ) {
      Node* dead = first;
      first = first->next();
      delete dead;
   }
}
```

Exercise 8.2   Write a program that performs startup and shutdown processing without explicitly invoking it from main. (Consult the question for full details of the particular problem.)
There are at least two solutions. The simplest is to declare a global class object with a constructor and destructor that do the required processing:

```
class StartEnd{
public:
   StartEnd()
      { cout << "Startup" << endl; }
   ~StartEnd()
      { cout << "Shutdown" << endl; }
};
StartEnd globobj;
```

This works because global variables are always initialized before `main` begins, and are destroyed after `main` finishes.

An alternative is to use a global declaration of a private static class variable to invoke a private nested class's constructor and destructor:

```
class StartEnd{
private:
   StartEnd(); // prevent declaration
   class Message {
   public:
      Message()
         { cout << "Startup" << endl; }
      ~Message()
         { cout << "Shutdown" << endl; }
   };
   static Message mess;
};
StartEnd::Message StartEnd::mess;
```

237

The declaration of a private constructor for StartEnd ensures than an actual instance of this class can never be declared.

Exercise 8.3   Modify the `TaskInfo` in Exercise 8.1 to support constant instances of the class, and implement the result.

The TaskInfo class should be modified by the addition of const qualifiers, to look like the following declaration. An inline implementation has been used for simplicity.

```
class TaskInfo {
public:
   TaskInfo( int anid, int apriority )
      : theruntime(0), theid(anid), thepriority(apriority)
{}
   void addtime( long millisec )
      { theruntime += millisec; }
   int id() const
      { return theid; }
   int priority() const
      { return thepriority; }
   long runtime() const
      { return theruntime; }
private:
   long theruntime;
   int thepriority;
   int theid;
};
```

Exercise 8.4   Write a const correct class representing a rectangular games board which has its dimensions supplied at run-time. Use an inline implementation if possible. (Details of required member functions are given in the question.)

Inline definitions are used for most of the member functions in this implementation of the Board class. This has not been done for clear() because it contains a for loop, which prevents it from being expanded inline on some C++ compilers. The public member functions get, rows and cols are declared as const so instances of this class can be used as constants.

An obvious approach to this problem uses a two dimensional array to represent the board. However, it is not possible to allocate dynamically a two dimensional array when both of its dimensions are variables. So a one dimensional array is used instead, with a private member function called map that converts a pair of two dimensional subscripts into an offset for a one dimensional array. This function also performs the required bounds checking.

```
enum Marker { BLACK, WHITE, NONE };

class Board {
public:
    Board( int rows, int cols )
        : rowsize(rows), colsize(cols)
        {  square = new Marker[rowsize*colsize];
           clear(); }
    ~Board()
        {  delete[] square; }
    void put( Marker piece, int row, int col )
        {  square[map(row,col)] = piece; }
    Marker get(int row, int col) const
        {  return square[map(row,col)]; }
    int cols() const
        {  return colsize; }
    int rows() const
        {  return rowsize; }
    void clear();
private:
    int map( int row, int col ) const
        {  if ( row < 0 || row >= rowsize ||
                col < 0 || col >= colsize ) {
               cerr << "Board bound error" << endl;
               exit(99);
            }
            return row * rowsize + col;
        }
    int rowsize, colsize;
    Marker* square;
};

void Board::clear()
{
    for ( int i = 0; i < rowsize * colsize; i++ )
        square[i] = NONE;
}
```

Exercise 9.1   Write a Time class that stores hours, minutes and seconds.
This solution is given with its member functions defined in line. The actual
time is stored as a long integer because this makes the calculations much
easier. A conversion to hours, minutes and seconds is made when time values are being input and output. Two private member functions are used
to handle these calculations. The insertion and extraction operators are
designed so that any value written with << can be read with >>.

```
class Time {
  friend Time operator+( const Time& t1, const Time& t2 )
    { Time temp;
      temp.inseconds = t1.inseconds + t2.inseconds;
      return temp; }
  friend Time operator-( const Time& t1, const Time& t2 )
    { Time temp;
      temp.inseconds = t1.inseconds - t2.inseconds;
      return temp; }
  friend ostream& operator<<( ostream& c, const Time& t )
    { long h, m, s;
      t.hms(h,m,s);
      c << h << '.' << m << '.' << s;
      return c;   }
  friend istream& operator>>( istream& c, Time& t )
    { int h, m, s;
      char ignore;
      cin >> h >> ignore >> m >> ignore >> s;
      t.upsecs(h,m,s);
      return c;   }
public:
  Time( int hours = 0, int minutes = 0, int seconds = 0 )
    { upsecs(hours,minutes,seconds); }
  Time operator-() const
    { Time temp;
      temp.inseconds = -inseconds;
      return temp;  }
  long secs() const
    { return inseconds; }
private:
  long inseconds;  // data store
  void upsecs( int h, int m, int s )
    { inseconds = (( h * 60 ) + m ) * 60 + s; }
  void hms( long &h, long &m, long &s ) const
    { long tempsecs;
      int sign;
      if ( inseconds < 0 ) {
        tempsecs = -inseconds;
        sign = -1;
      }
      else {
        tempsecs = inseconds;
        sign = 1;
      }
```

240

```
    s = tempsecs % 60;
    m = tempsecs / 60;
    h = m /60 * sign;
    m %= 60; }
};
```

Exercise 9.2   (a) Make the `List` class given in §8.10 safe by restricting its copy constructor and assignment operator.

To prevent the assignment operator and the copy constructor from being used add the following to the `List` class:

```
private:
    List( const List& ){}
    List& operator=( const List& ){ return *this; }
```

(b) Make the List class given in 8.10 safe by implementing a suitable copy constructor and assignment operator.

To support assignment and initialization add the following to the public section of `List`:

```
List( const List& alist );
List& operator=( const List& alist );
```

And this to its private section:

```
void deepcopy( const List& alist);
```

This `deepcopy` function is used in the assignment operator and copy constructor to copy all of the nodes to a new linked list. The `List` class already has a `clear` private member function that can be used in the assignment operator function to dispose of any existing data prior to the copy.

The new member functions are as follows:

```
void List::deepcopy( const List& from )
{
    theroot = 0;
    Node* cfrom = from.theroot;
    while ( cfrom != 0 )  {
        insert(cfrom->data());
        cfrom = cfrom->next();
    }
}

List::List( const List& from )
    : theroot(0), thecurrent(0)
{
```

```
      deepcopy(from);
}

List& List::operator=( const List& from )
{
   if ( this != &from ) {
      clear();
      deepcopy(from);
   }
   return *this;
}
```

Exercise 9.3 Write a class for storing names. It should have an iterator in the form of a friend class.

To keep this solution short the classes have been declared with inline member functions. An array implementation has been chosen for simplicity. The container class is called `Names`. The private nested class `Nstring` provides basic string class support, making the rest of the classes easier to implement. If an alternative string class is available, it could be used instead. The iterator is called `NameIter`. Its `getname` function gives the current name, in the form of a constant C string, and moves on to the next. If `endofnames()` returns `true`, `getname` should not be used.

```
#include <string>

class Names {
friend class NameIter;
public:
   Names( int maxnames ) : max(maxnames), free(0)
      {  array = new string[max];   }
   void insert( const string& aname )
      {  array[free++] = aname; }
   bool contains( const string& aname )
      {  bool found = false;
         int current = 0;
         while ( current < free && !found )
            found = bool(array[current++] == aname);
         return found;   }
   bool room()
      {  return bool(free < max);   }
   ~Names()
      {  delete[] array;   }
private:
   int max;
   int free;
```

```
   string* array;
};

class NameIter {
public:
   NameIter( Names& namestore )
       : store(namestore), current(0) {}
   string getname()
       {   return store.array[current++]; }
   bool endofnames()
       {   return bool(current > store.max - 1); }
   void restart()
       {   current = 0; }
private:
   Names& store;
   int current;
};
```

Assuming an instance of Name called roads the iterator could be used as follows to print all the names in road:

```
NameIter iter(roads);
while ( !iter.endofnames() ) {
   cout << iter.name() << endl;
}
```

Exercise 9.4 Write a class with its subscript operator overloaded in such a way that the operator has very different behaviour when used on different sides of an assignment operator.

```
class HelpStore {
   friend class Store;
public:
   double operator=( double d );
   double operator=( HelpStore& t );
   operator double();
private:
   HelpStore( Store* a, int s )
       : thestore(a), subscript(s) {}
   Store* thestore;
   int subscript;
};

class Store {
   friend class HelpStore;
public:
   HelpStore operator[]( int subscript );
```

```
private:
    void asLvalue( int subscript, double value );
    int asRvalue( int subscript );
    double data[20];
};

double HelpStore::operator=( double d )
{
    thestore->asLvalue(subscript,d);
    return d;
}


double HelpStore::operator=( HelpStore& t )
{
    double d = t.thestore->asRvalue(t.subscript);
    thestore->asLvalue(subscript,d);
    return d;
}

HelpStore::operator double()
{
    return thestore->asRvalue(subscript);
}

HelpStore Store::operator[]( int subscript )
{
    return HelpStore(this,subscript);
}

void Store::asLvalue( int subscript, double value )
{
    cout << "subscript " << subscript << " on LHS, with "
         << value << " being assigned" << endl;
    data[subscript] = value;
}

int Store::asRvalue( int subscript )
{
    cout << "subscript " << subscript << " on RHS" << endl;
    return data[subscript];
}
```

Exercise 10.1 Given a class called **Account** (definition given in question), define another class called **Interest**. This new class should have the same behaviour as **Account**, but should also have member functions for storing and retrieving an interest rate, calculating its value, and

244

adding or removing interest from the account.

```
class Interest : public Account {
public:
   Interest() : percent(10){};
   void rate( float rate )
      { percent = rate; }
   float rate() const
      { return percent; }
   float interest() const
      { return balance() * percent / 100; }
   void add_interest()
      { deposit(interest()); }
   void remove_interest()
      { withdraw(interest()); }
private:
   float percent;
};
```

Exercise 10.2 Write a charity project class called **Cproj** that has start and finish dates and a money account. Use the **Account** class from Exercise 10.1 as a private base class. Consider if the use of private inheritance would be suitable for an alternative **Cproj** class that had more than one money account.

```
class Cproj : private Account {
public:
   Cproj( string start = "no date", string finish = "no
date" )
      : startdate(start), enddate(finish) {}
   string start() const
      { return startdate; }
   string finish() const
      { return enddate; }
   Account::balance;
   Account::deposit;
private:
   string startdate;
   string enddate;
};
```

Private inheritance is not an appropriate method when more than one money account is needed in Cproj. Containment has to be used as the following shows:

APPENDIX A

```
class CprojX {
public:
   CprojX( string start = "no date", string finish = "no
date" )
      : startdate(start), enddate(finish) {}
   string start()
      { return startdate; }
   string finish()
      { return enddate; }
   void deposit1( float money )
      { account1.deposit(money);  }
   void deposit2( float money )
      { account2.deposit(money);  }
   float balance1() const
      { return account1.balance(); }
   float balance2() const
      { return account2.balance(); }
private:
   string startdate;
   string enddate;
   Account account1;
   Account account2;
};
```

Exercise 10.3   (a) Write a Named class that has all the properties of Account (from Exercise 10.1) plus an account name and code. It should be impossible to change the code after an instance of this class has been created.

```
class Named : public virtual Account {
public:
   Named( string aname, int acode )
      : thename(aname), thecode(acode) {}
   string name() const
      { return thename; }
   int code() const
      { return thecode; }
private:
   string thename;
   int thecode;
};
```

(b) Write a class called Inamed that has all the properties of Named and Interest (from Exercise 10.1). How should the Interest class, designed for Exercise 10.1, be modified to work in this context?

```
class Inamed : public Interest, public Named {
public:
    Inamed( string aname, int acode )
        : Named(aname,acode) {}
};
```

The class `Interest`, as it is given in the solution for Exercise 10.1, will not work with the above. Its `Account` base class has to be declared as virtual to ensure that there is only one instance of it under multiple inheritance. This is easy, the first line of the `Interest` is changed to look like this:

```
class Interest : public virtual Account {
```

This will not affect the direct use of `Interest`. The common base class `Account` has to be declared as virtual in `Named` as well.

Exercise 11.1   Implement the virtual display and rotate functions of a shape class. Display the shapes as character patterns. Implement for a square and a rectangle.
The `Shape` class might look like this:

```
class Shape {
public:
    Shape( int colr, int x = 0, int y = 0 )
        : colour(colr), x_loc(x), y_loc(y) {}
    virtual void display() = 0;
    virtual void rotate() = 0;
// ...
protected:
    void print() // print a colour mark
        {  cout << colour; }
    void nprint()      // print a blank mark
        {  cout << ' '; }
private:
    int x_loc;         // not used
    int y_loc;         // not used
    char colour;
};
```

This is used to derive a `Rectangle` class:

```
class Rectangle : public Shape {
public:
    Rectangle( int aheight, int awidth, char colr = 'r' )
```

```
        : height(aheight), width(awidth), Shape(colr) {}
    void rotate()
        {   int t = height;
            height = width;
            width = t;   }
    void display()
        {   for ( int h = 0; h < height; h++ ) {
                for ( int w = 0; w < width; w++ )
                    print();
                cout << endl;
            }
            cout << endl;   }
private:
    int height;
    int width;
};
```

The Square class can be derived from Rectangle, with its height and width the same. The rotate function is overridden to do nothing because a square rotated through 90° is not changed:

```
class Square : public Rectangle {
public:
    Square( int side, char colr = 's' )
        : Rectangle(side,side,colr) {}
    void rotate()
        { /* do nothing */ }
};
```

Exercise 11.3 Write a **Circle** class that has a member function to modify its radius, and a **Rect** (rectangle) class that can have its width and height modified. They should both be able to supply area and circumference information. It must be possible to maintain some form of mixed list of **Circle** and **Rect** objects, and to use this list to print the areas of the objects.

The abstract base class should look something like this:

```
class Geometric {
public:
    virtual double area() const = 0;
    virtual double circumference() const = 0;
};
```

The classes Circle and Rect are derived from this base class. They are declared as follows:

```
class Circle : public Geometric {
public:
   Circle( double aradius = 1 )
      : theradius(aradius) {}
   void radius( double aradius )
      { theradius = aradius; }
   double radius()
      { return theradius; }
   double area() const
      { return PI * theradius * theradius; }
   double circumference() const
      { return 2 * PI * theradius; }
private:
   static double PI;
   double theradius;
};
double Circle::PI = 3.14159;

class Rect : public Geometric {
public:
   Rect( double aheight = 1, double awidth = 1 )
      : theheight(aheight), thewidth(awidth) {}
   void height( double aheight )
      { theheight = aheight; }
   double height()
      { return theheight; }
   void width( double awidth )
      { thewidth = awidth; }
   double width()
      { return thewidth; }
   double area() const
      { return theheight * thewidth; }
   double circumference() const
      { return 2 * ( theheight + thewidth ); }
private:
   double theheight;
   double thewidth;
};
```

Exercise 12.1   Modify the `Array` template in §12.2 so that assignment and copy constructors are not restricted.

The example forming the basis of this exercise has its subscript bounds specified in its constructors. The main difficulty with this problem is deciding on sensible copy semantics when the bounds of the two arrays are different. For copying, the target array is given the same bounds and element values as the source array. For assignment, the target bounds are not changed. The source is copied to the target an element at a time, starting from the lowest bound, until either the target array is full or all the elements in the source array are used. The template is:

```
template< class Type >
class Array {
public:
    Array( int low, int high );
        // subscript in range low to high
        // initialize to default constructor of Type
    Array( const Array& a );
        // support copy semantics
    Array& operator=( const Array& a );
        // support assignment semantics
    void put( int loc, const Type& value );
        // store value in element at loc.
    Type get( int loc ) const;
        // recover value from element at loc.
    bool inbound( int loc ) const;
        // check loc is within bounds for this array
    ~Array();
private:
    Type* store;
    int lowbound;
    int highbound;
    void copyin( const Array& a );     // elementwise copy
};
```

This is much the same as the example in §12.2, but there are now full implementations for the copy constructor and assignment operator. These both use the private copyin member function:

```
template< class Type >
void Array<Type>::copyin( const Array& a )
{
    int target = lowbound;
    int source = a.lowbound;
    while ( target <= highbound && source <= a.highbound )
        put(target++,a.get(source++));
}

template< class Type >
Array<Type>::Array( const Array& a )
    : lowbound(a.lowbound), highbound(a.highbound)
```

```
{
   store = new Type[highbound - lowbound + 1];
   copyin(a);
}

template< class Type >
Array<Type>& Array<Type>::operator=( const Array& a )
{
   if ( this != &a )
      copyin(a);
   return *this;
}
```

Exercise 12.2 Write an array template parameterized by type and size. Give it a subscript operator and bounds checking. It must support multidimensional arrays.

The member functions in the following solution have been declared inline for brevity:

```
template< class Type, int SIZE >
class Array {
public:
   Type& operator[]( int subscrpt )
      {  abortcheck(subscrpt);
         return data[subscrpt]; }
   const Type& operator[]( int subscrpt ) const
      {  abortcheck(subscrpt);
         return data[subscrpt]; }
   int topbound() const
      {  return SIZE - 1; }
   bool inbounds( int subscrpt ) const
      {  return bool( subscrpt >=0 && subscrpt < SIZE ); }
private:
   Type data[SIZE];
   void abortcheck( int subscrpt ) const
      {  if ( !inbounds(subscrpt) ) {
            cerr << "Array subscript out of bounds." << endl
               << "Program abnormally terminated." <<
endl;
            abort(); // from <stdlib.h>
         } }
};
```

In `Array`, the subscript operator is overloaded for both constant and non-constant objects. This supports the use of constant references such as:

```
double sum( const Array<double,50>& marks )
{
    double sum = 0;
    for ( int i = 0; i <= marks.topbound(); i++ )
        sum += marks[i];
    return sum;
}
```

The Array template can be used to create multidimensional arrays. The following defines a 5 by 3 matrix of integers, assigns a value to one of its elements, and prints out the matrix:

```
Array<Array<int,3>,5> matrix1;
matrix1[4][2] = 8;
for ( int j = 0; j <= matrix1.topbound(); j++ ) {
    for ( int k = 0; k <= matrix1[0].topbound(); k++ )
        cout << matrix1[j][k] << ' ';
    cout << endl;
}
```

Exercise 12.3   Create an array template with bound parameters that is derived from an abstract base class so that arrays with different bounds can be used polymorphically.
We start with an abstract base class template:

```
template< class Type>
class BArray {
public:
    virtual Type& operator[]( int subscrpt ) = 0;
    virtual const Type& operator[]( int subscrpt ) const = 0;
    virtual int topbound() const = 0;
    virtual bool inbounds( int subscrpt ) const = 0;
};
```

Then this is used to derive the concrete array template:

```
template< class Type, int SIZE >
class Array : public BArray<Type> {
public:
    Type& operator[]( int subscrpt );
    const Type& operator[]( int subscrpt ) const;
    int topbound() const;
    bool inbounds( int subscrpt ) const;
private:
    Type data[SIZE];
    void abortcheck( int subscrpt ) const;
};
```

This is almost the same as the solution to the previous exercise but in this case `Array` is derived from `BArray`. Member function implementation is not shown because it is exactly the same as for `Array` in the previous exercise. This arrangement allows the following:

```
void print( const BArray<int>& a )
{
    for ( int i = 0; i <= a.topbound(); i++ )
        cout << a[i] << ' ';
    cout << endl;
}

void main()
{
    Array<int,5> a1;
    print(a1);
}
```

Unfortunately, this does not work with multidimensional arrays quite so well, and only the primary array can be polymorphic:

```
void print( const BArray< Array<int,2> >& a );    // okay
void print( const BArray< BArray<int> >& a );      // error
```

Exercise 12.4   Write a list class template that can store any kind of object. Base it on the integer List class given in §8.10.
The solution is an almost trivial adaptation of the `List` class in §8.10. To write the template, every occurrence of the stored data type `int` is replaced with the template class parameter `Type`. The `Node` class also has to be converted into a template. After this, the class declaration is as follows:

```
template< class Type >
class List {
public:
    List();
        // Create a new list, empty() = true, end() = true
    void before( Type data );
        // Insert new data before current item.
        //  New item becomes current item
        //     If end() true insert at end list
    void after( Type data );
        // Insert new data after current item
        //  New item becomes current item
        //     If end() true insert at end list
    Type current();
        // Data value of current item
```

```
    void next();
       // Make the next item current
    bool end();
       // Past last item?
       // if true current() undefined
    bool empty();
       // List empty?
       // If true, end() = true and current() undefined
    void top();
       // Goto first item if one exists
    void bottom();
       // Goto last item if one exists
    ~List();
       // Clean up
private:
/* class Node<Type>;     // forward reference not needed */
    Node<Type>* theroot;
    Node<Type>* thecurrent;
    Node<Type>* theprevious;
    void clear();          // for destructor
    bool attop_empty();    // At top of list or list empty?
    bool atbottom();       // At bottom of list?
};
```

Here, the only significant difference is that the forward reference to the
Node class is no longer needed. This is because it is now a template, and the
rules for templates are slightly different from those for ordinary classes.
    The Node class now looks like this:

```
template< class Type >
class Node {
public:
    Node( Type data, Node* node = 0 )
       : thedata(data), thenext(node)
       // Initialize a node with 'data' and connect it
       //     to 'node'.
       // If 'node' not given end of list is indicated.
       {}
    Type data()
       // The data value in this node
       {  return thedata;     }
    Node* next()
       // The next node in the list
       //     or zero if there is not one.
       {  return thenext;     }
```

```
   Node* splice( Node* node )
     // Put 'node' into the list after this node.
     //    'node' is connected to the node this node
     //        was connected to.
     {  node->thenext = thenext;
        thenext = node;
        return node;    }
private:
   Type thedata;
   Node* thenext;
};
```

The implementation of this List template is almost the same as for the non-template version. As an example, here are two member functions:

```
template< class Type >
List<Type>::List()
    : theroot(0), thecurrent(0), theprevious(0) {}

template< class Type >
void List<Type>::before( Type data )
{
    if ( attop_empty() )
      // insert at 'theroot'
       theroot = thecurrent = new Node<Type>(data,theroot);
    else
      // insert after 'theprevious'
       thecurrent = theprevious->splice(new
Node<Type>(data));
}
```

Exercise 13.1   Write a template for a bound array class. It should throw an exception if an array instance is accessed with a subscript that is out of range.

The exception class is called XarrayBound. It holds the value of the offending subscript. An instance of this class is thrown in the abortcheck private member function of Array if a subscript is out of range. Apart from this modification to abortcheck, this template class is exactly the same as the solution to Exercise 12.2:

```
class XarrayBound {
public:
   XarrayBound( int asub )
      : badval(asub) {}
   int subscript()
```

255

```
        { return badval; }
private:
    int badval;
};

template< class Type, int SIZE >
class Array {
public:
    Type& operator[]( int subscrpt )
        {  abortcheck(subscrpt);
           return data[subscrpt]; }
    const Type& operator[]( int subscrpt ) const
        {  abortcheck(subscrpt);
           return data[subscrpt]; }
    int topbound() const
        {  return SIZE - 1; }
    bool inbounds( int subscrpt ) const
        {  return bool( subscrpt >=0 && subscrpt < SIZE ); }
private:
    Type data[SIZE];
    void abortcheck( int subscrpt ) const
        {  if ( !inbounds(subscrpt) ) {
               throw XarrayBound(subscrpt);
           } }
};
```

The XarrayBound exception can be caught like this:

```
try {
    myarray1[5] = 99;
}
catch ( XarrayBound error ) {
    cout << "bounds error with subscript "
        << error.subscript() << endl;
}
```


Exercise 13.2 Show how casting can be used to access fully an object with a pointer to its base class. The solution should be based on the classes Store and Storable, both of which are discussed in the question.

First define a couple of classes based on Storable:

```
 class Bread : public Storable {
public:
    Bread( int aprice, string atype )
```

```
      : theprice(aprice), thetype(atype) {}
   double price()
      {  return theprice; }
   string type()
      {  return thetype; }
// ...
private:
   string thetype;
   double theprice;
};

class Coffee : public Storable {
public:
   Coffee( int aprice, string avariety, string abrand )
      : theprice(aprice), thevariety(avariety),
thebrand(abrand) {}
   double price()
      {  return theprice; }
   string brand()
      {  return thebrand; }
// ...
private:
   string thebrand;
   string thevariety;
   double theprice;
};
```

Instances of these could be declared and used with Store like this:

```
Store store;
Bread b1(1,"white"), b2(7,"whole meal"), b3(3,"brown");
Coffee c1(2,"Smith's","Javan"),
       c2(5,"Ponsomby's","Colombian"),
       c3(8,"Brown's","Kenyan");
store.add(&b1);
store.add(&b2);
store.add(&b3);
store.add(&c1);
store.add(&c2);
store.add(&c3);
```

Full access to these instances of Coffee and Bread from a pointer returned from store needs a cast up from their Storable base class using a dynamic cast:

```
cout << "List Coffee" << endl;
```

```
while( !store.end() ) {
    cout << store.current()->price() << " ";
    Coffee* coffee = dynamic_cast<Coffee*>(store.current());
    if ( coffee != 0 )
        cout << coffee->brand() << endl;
    else
        cout << "not coffee" << endl;
    store.next();
}
```

Exercise 13.3 Casting can seriously damage the health of a program. Show how the misuse of casting can produce incorrect results.

The following example illustrates how casting can produce invalid results. This short program compiled without error messages. The first example is a call to a function that expects a `double` parameter but gets a cast `int` argument. The value of the returned argument is nonsense. (When this was tested, it actually crashed the program with a "general protection exception".) The second example shows a valid, and then an invalid, static cast up from a pointer to a base class, to a pointer to a derived class. The actual outcome of running this program is unpredictable.

```
#include <iostream.h>

void change( double& param )
{
    param = param + 100.3;
}

class Base {};

class Derived1 : public Base {
public:
    Derived1(): i(2) {}
    int value() { return i; }
private:
    int i;
};

class Derived2 : public Base {
public:
    Derived2(): d(3.5) {}
    double value() { return d; }
private:
    double d;
};

void main()
```

```
{
   int aninteger = 1234;    // example 1
   change(reinterpret_cast<double&>(aninteger));
   cout << aninteger << endl;

   Derived1 d1;               // example 2
   Derived2 d2;
   Base* pd1 = &d1;
   Base* pd2 = &d2;
   cout << "correct cast up gives value as "
       << static_cast<Derived2*>(pd2)->value() << endl;
   cout << "incorrect cast up gives value as "
       << static_cast<Derived1*>(pd2)->value() << endl;
}
```

Exercise 14.1 Write a program that converts all the **tab** characters in a text file to a specified number of space characters.

```
#include <fstream.h>
#include <string>
#include <stdlib.h>

enum bool { false, true };

//const char REPLACE = ' ';
const char REPLACE = '*';
const int DEFSPACE = 3;

void getargs( int argc, char* argv[],
              string& in, string& out, int& spaces,
              bool& invalid )
{
   invalid = false;
   if ( argc < 3 )
      invalid = true;
   else {
      in = argv[1];
      out = argv[2];
      if ( argc == 3 )
         spaces = DEFSPACE;
      else
         if ( argc == 4 )
            spaces = atoi(argv[3]);
         else
            invalid = true;
```

```
      }
   }

   void printformat( ostream& os )
   {
      os << "Format is:" << endl
         << "DETAB <in file> <out file> [<replace spaces>]"
         << endl;
   }

   void main( int argc, char* argv[] )
   {
      string namein;
      string nameout;
      int spaces;
      bool error;
      getargs(argc,argv,namein,nameout,spaces,error);
      if ( error ) {
         printformat(cout);
         exit(99); // terminate immediately
      }
      ifstream in(namein.c_str());
      ofstream out(nameout.c_str());
      char c;
      int charcount = 0;
      int linecount = 0;
      int tabcount = 0;
      in.get(c);
      while ( !in.eof() ) {
         if ( c == '\n' )
            linecount++;
         else
            charcount++;
         if ( c == '\t' ) {
            tabcount++;
            for ( int i = 0; i < spaces; i++ )
               out.put(REPLACE);
         }
         else
            out.put(c);
         in.get(c);
      }
      in.close();
      out.close();
      cout << "Done with " << tabcount << " tabs replaced" <<
```

```
endl;
    cout << "There were " << charcount
          << " characters and " << (linecount + 1)
          << " lines in this file" << endl;
}
```

Exercise 14.2 Write a program that prints a comma delimited file of names and addresses. Each field should start on a new line, and the address lines should be indented by three spaces.

A simple class called `Indata` is used to manage the incoming data. It has two member functions, one to extract the name and address fields from the file, and one to print them in the required format. The extract function `readfrom` uses `get` and `putback` to check for end of line, so records with a blank last field are managed correctly.

```
#include <fstream.h>
#include <iomanip.h>
#include <stdlib.h>
#include <string>

class Indata {
public:
    void readfrom( ifstream& in )
        {   getline(in,name,',');
            getline(in,addr1,',');
            getline(in,addr2,',');
            char c = in.get();
            if ( c != '\n' ) {
                in.putback(c);
                getline(in,addr3);
            } }
    void printto( ostream& os )
        {   os << name << endl;
            os << setw(3) << "" << addr1 << endl;
            os << setw(3) << "" << addr2 << endl;
            os << setw(3) << "" << addr3 << endl; }
private:
    string name, addr1, addr2, addr3;
};

void main()
{
    ifstream data("addr.dat");
    if ( !data ) {
        cout << "Cannot open data file" << endl;
```

```
        exit(99);
    }
    Indata input;
    input.readfrom(data);
    while ( !data.eof() ) {
        input.printto(cout);
        input.readfrom(data);
    }
}
```

Exercise 14.3 **Take the `List` class given in §8.10, and add marshalling functions.**

The following members are added to the List class:

```
public:
    void readfrom( const string& filename );
    bool goodread();
    void writeto( const string& filename );
private:
    bool readokay;
```

The member functions are implemented like this:

```
void List::readfrom( const string& filename )
{
    ifstream is(filename.c_str());
    if ( !is ) {
        readokay = false;
        return;
    }
    clear();
    int data;
    is >> data;
    while ( !is.fail() ) {
        after(data);
        is >> data;
    }
    if ( is.eof() ) {
        readokay = true;
        top();
    }
    else {
        readokay = false;
        clear();
    }
```

```
   is.close();
}

bool List::goodread()
{
   return readokay;
}

void List::writeto( const string& filename )
{
   ofstream os(filename.c_str());
   Node* oldcurrent = thecurrent;          // preserve state
   Node* oldprevious = theprevious;
   top();
   while ( !end() ) {
      os << current() << endl;
      next();
   }
   thecurrent = oldcurrent;                // restore state
   theprevious = oldprevious;
   os.close();
}
```

APPENDIX B

C++ strings

The C++ string class is called `string`. To use it, the header file `<string>` must be included. Some C++ compilers have a slightly different string class, but the functions described below should be available.

The type `size_t` is used extensively. This is an implementation dependent integral type defined in the standard header `<cstddef>`, or the older `<stddef.h>`. The constant NPOS is the largest representable value of type `size_t`.

Some of the `string` member functions are overloaded on the type of their input string parameters. These parameters have the following form:

- A C++ string

  ```
  const string& str, size_t pos = 0, size_t n = NPOS
  ```

  This is the string beginning at position `pos` in the C++ string `str`, and continuing for n characters, or to the end of `str`, whichever comes first. The parameters `pos` and n have default values that result in the following behaviour. If n is omitted as an argument, the string starts at `pos` and goes to the end of `str`. If both `pos` and n are omitted, the string is all of `str`. An out-of-range error is reported if `pos` is greater than the length of `str`.

- A C string

  ```
  const char s[], size_t n
  const char s[]
  ```

  This is the value of the C string s. This should be an array of `char` holding a sequence of characters terminated with a `'\0'` character. The argument given for s shall not be a null pointer. If n is given as an argument, and s cannot fit into n characters, the string is truncated.

Otherwise, if s is too short, it is padded with spaces. If n is not given as an argument, all of s is used.

- A repeated character

```
char c, size_t rep = 1
```

This is the string composed of the character c repeated rep times. If an argument is not given for rep, the string contains only the character c.

Constructors

- `string();`

The default constructor. It creates an empty string.

```
• string( const string& str, size_t pos = 0,
          size_t n = NPOS );

string( const char s[], size_t n );
string( const char s[] );

string( char c, size_t rep = 1 );
string( unsigned char c, size_t rep = 1 );
string( signed char c, size_t rep = 1 );
```

Create a string and initialize it with the value of the string obtained from the parameters.

- `string( size_t size, capacity cap );`

The type capacity is the enumeration:

```
enum capacity { default_size, reserve };
```

If cap is reserve, the created string is empty, and size is the reserve size for the string. The reserve size, for an unallocated string, contains the estimated size of the string, whereas for an allocated string, it is the currently allocated size. If cap is default_size, a string value is allocated that is size long and filled with ' \0 ' (binary zero) characters.

Assignment

- Member function assign

```
string& assign( const string& str, size_t pos = 0,
                size_t n = NPOS );
string& assign( const char s[], size_t n );
string& assign( const char s[] );
string& assign( char c, size_t rep = 1 );
```

Replace the value of the target `string` with the value of the string obtained from the parameters. This function returns a reference to the `string` object for which it was invoked.

- Member function `operator=`

```
string& operator=( const string& str );
string& operator=( const char* s );
string& operator=( char c );
```

Replace the value of the `string` with the value given by the parameters `str`, `s` or `c`. It returns a reference to the `string` for which the function was invoked. These overloaded operators have the same behaviour as the equivalent `assign` functions.

Concatenation

- Member function `append`

```
string& append( const string& str, size_t pos = 0,
                size_t n = NPOS );
string& append( const char s[], size_t n = NPOS );
string& append( const char s[] );
string& append( char c, size_t rep = 1 );
```

Add the value of the string obtained from the parameters onto the end of the target `string`. This function returns a reference to the `string` object for which it was invoked.

- Member function `operator+=`

```
string& operator+=( const string& str );
string& operator+=( const char s[] );
string& operator+=( char c );
```

This function adds a string value onto the end of the `string` for which this function is invoked, and returns a reference to this object. The behaviour of this operator overload is the same as the equivalent `append` function.

- Non-member function `operator+`

```
string operator+( const string& lhs, const string&rhs );
string operator+( const char lhs[], const string&rhs );
string operator+( char lhs, const string& rhs );
string operator+( const string& lhs, const char rhs[] );
string operator+( const string& lhs, char rhs );
```

This is the *concatenation* operator. This function returns a `string` that has a value calculated by adding the string value of the `rhs` parameter onto the end of the value of the `lhs` parameter. Arguments that are `char` arrays shall not be null pointers.

Substring operations

- Member function `substr`

```
string substr( size_t pos = 0, size_t n = NPOS ) const;
```

Returns a substring without modifying the `string` to which the function was applied. The substring starts at the character position `pos`, and finishes at the end of the `string`, or when the substring is n characters long, whichever is the smaller. If n is omitted, the substring is from character position `pos` to the end of the target `string`. If `pos` and n are both omitted, the value of the returned `string` is the same as the `string` for which `substr` was invoked.

- Member function `remove`

```
string& remove( size_t pos = 0, size_t n = NPOS );
```

Remove at most n characters starting with the character at `pos`. An out-of-range error is reported if `pos` is greater than the length of the target string. If n is omitted, all characters from `pos` to the end are removed. If `pos` and n are both omitted, the *all* characters are removed. A reference to the `string` that this function was applied to is returned.

- Member function `insert`

```
string& insert( size_t pos1, const string& str,
                size_t pos2 = 0, size_t n = NPOS );
string& insert( size_t pos1, const char s[], size_t n );
string& insert( size_t pos1, const char s[] );
string& insert( size_t pos1, char c, size_t rep = 1 );
```

Insert the string given by `str`, s or c, and their associated parameters, into the target `string` starting at character `pos1`. Existing characters in the target string are not overwritten. A reference to the resulting target `string` is returned. An out-of-range error is reported if `pos1` is greater than the length of the target string, and a length error is reported if the resulting string is `NPOS` or more characters long.

- Member function `replace`

```
string& replace( size_t pos1, size_t n1,
                 const string& str,
                 size_t pos2 = 0, size_t n2 = NPOS );

string& replace( size_t pos1, size_t n1,
```

```
                    const char s[], size_t n2 );
string& replace( size_t pos, size_t n1,
                 const char s[] );
string& replace( size_t pos1, size_t n1,
                 char c, size_t rep = 1 );
```

Remove the substring beginning at pos1, continuing for at most n1 characters, and *replace* it with a substring from str beginning with pos2, continuing for at most n2 characters. A reference to the resulting target string is returned. An out-of-range error is reported if pos1 is greater than the length of the target string, and a length error is reported if the resulting string is NPOS or more characters long.

Character access

- Member function get_at

```
char get_at( size_t pos ) const;
```

Returns the character at position pos. An out-of-range error is reported if pos is greater than or equal to the length of the target string.

- Member function put_at

```
void put_at( size_t pos, char c );
```

Changes the value of the character at pos to c. If pos is equal to the length of the target string, the character c is appended. An out-of-range error is reported if pos is greater than the length of the target string.

- Member function operator[]

```
char& operator[]( size_t pos );
char  operator[]( size_t pos ) const;
```

For the non-constant version, if pos is less than the length of the target string a reference to the character at position pos is returned. This reference can be used to modify the character, but it should be used immediately. Any subsequent use of the target string might invalidate the reference. If pos is greater than or equal to the length of the target string, the behaviour is undefined (but some versions report an out-of-range error). The constant version is similar but it does not return a reference, and if pos is equal to the string's length zero is returned. So, as expected, this version of the function cannot be used to modify a string's value.

Utility functions

- Member function `c_str`

```
const char* c_str() const;
```

Returns the value of the target `string` as a C string. This will be an array of `char` containing a sequence of characters terminated with the character `'\0'`. The returned C string must not be treated as valid after any subsequent use of a non-constant member function with the `string` object that provided the string. If its value is required for a longer period than this, a copy should be made with `strcpy` from `<string.h>`.

- Member function `data`

```
const char* data() const;
```

This function is similar to `c_str`, but it does not terminate the character sequence returned in the array of `char` with a `'\0'` character, and it returns a null pointer if the length of the target string is zero. This means that `data` does not return a C string.

- Member function `length`

```
size_t length() const;
```

Returns the number of characters in the string value stored in the target `string`.

- Member function `resize`

```
void resize( size_t n, char c = 0 );
```

Alters the length of the target `string`. If n is less than or equal to the original length, the string is truncated to its first n characters. If n is greater than the original length, characters of value c are appended to make the string n characters long. If an argument for c is not provided, the appended character is `'\0'`.

- Member function `reserve`

```
size_t reserve() const;
void reserve( size_t res_arg );
```

The function `reserve()` returns the reserve size of the target string. The function `reserve(size_t)` changes the reserve size to `res_arg` provided no value has been allocated to the string. Otherwise this function's behaviour is unspecified.

- Member function `copy`

```
size_t copy( char s[], size_t n, size_t pos = 0 );
```

Copies a portion of the target `string` to an array of `char`. The sub-string starts at `pos` and continues for n characters, or until the end of the string. The array s must be large enough to take the substring. The sequence of characters stored in s is not terminated by a ` '\0' ` charac-ter, so it is not a C string. This function returns the length of the result-ing string. It reports an out-of-range error if `pos` is greater than the target `string` length.

Comparison

- Member function `compare`

```
int compare( const string& str, size_t pos = 0,
             size_t n = NPOS ) const;
int compare( const char s[], size_t pos,
             size_t n ) const;
int compare( const char s[], size_t pos = 0 ) const;
int compare( char c, size_t pos = 0,
             size_t rep = 1 ) const;
```

This function compares the target `string` with the string given by the parameters `str` and n, s and n, or c and `rep`. The parameter `pos` gives the start position in the target `string` (not in `str`), and an out-of-range error is reported if `pos` is greater than the length of the target `string`. If `pos` is not given, the comparison uses all of the target `string`. For the strings to be evaluated as equal they must be the same length and have identical character sequences. The order of unequal strings is determined by the ordering of the first unequal character. If the strings being compared are not of equal length, the longer one is considered to be the greater. The values returned by `compare` are:

string relationship	return value
target < parameter	less than 0
target == parameter	0
target > parameter	greater than 0

- Non-member functions `operator==`, `operator!=`, `operator<`, `operator<=`, `operator>` and `operator>=`
  These functions have the following forms, where ◊ is the operation:

```
bool operator◊( const string& lhs, const string&rhs);
bool operator◊( const char[] lhs, const string& rhs);
bool operator◊( char lhs, const string& rhs);
bool operator◊( const string& lhs, const char[] rhs);
bool operatorδ( const string& lhs, char rhs);
```

They all alphabetically compare the string values given by their rhs and lhs parameters. Their behaviour is similar to the standard arithmetic comparison operators. They return true if the condition holds, otherwise they return false.

Search operations

- Member function find

```
size_t find( const string& str, size_t pos = 0 ) const;
size_t find( const char s[], size_t pos,
             size_t n ) const;
size_t find( const char s[], size_t pos = 0 ) const;
size_t find( char c, size_t pos = 0 ) const;
```

Search for the first occurrence of str, s or c in the target string beginning on or after character position pos. If this string is found, the position of its first character is returned, otherwise NPOS is returned. If an argument is not given for pos, the search starts at the beginning of the target string. For the C string version of find, with the parameter n, the string s is truncated or padded with spaces to make it n characters long before the search is performed.

- Member function rfind

```
size_t rfind( const string& str,
              size_t pos = NPOS) const;
size_t rfind( const char s[], size_t pos,
              size_t n) const;
size_t rfind( const char s[], size_t pos = NPOS) const;
size_t rfind( char c, size_t pos = NPOS ) const;
```

Almost the same as find, but this function searches for the *last* occurrence of str, s or c in the target string beginning on or *before* character position pos. The search starts at the end of the target string if an argument is not given for pos.

- Member function find_first_of

```
size_t find_first_of( const string& str,
                      size_t pos = 0 ) const;
size_t find_first_of( const char s[], size_t pos,
                      size_t n ) const;
size_t find_first_of( const char s[],
                      size_t pos = 0 ) const;
size_t find_first_of( char c, size_t pos = 0 ) const;
```

This function treats the string given by `str`, `s` or `c` as a *set* of characters. It returns the location of the *first* character in the target `string` that matches any element in this set. If no match is found, it returns `NPOS`. The search starts at character position `pos`, and proceeds to the end of the target `string`. If `pos` is not given as an argument, the search starts at the beginning of the target `string`. For the C string version of `find_first_of`, with the parameter `n`, the string `s` is truncated or padded with spaces to make it n characters long before the search is performed.

- Member function `find_first_not_of`

```
size_t find_first_not_of( const string& str,
                          size_t pos = 0 ) const;
size_t find_first_not_of( const char s[], size_t pos,
                          size_t n ) const;
size_t find_first_not_of( const char[] s,
                          size_t pos = 0 ) const;
size_t find_first_not_of( char c,
                          size_t pos = 0 ) const;
```

Almost the same as `find_first_of`, but this function searches for the first character in the target `string` that matches *no* elements in the set given by `str`, `s` or `c`.

- Member function `find_last_of`

```
size_t find_last_of( const string& str,
                     size_t pos = NPOS ) const;
size_t find_last_of( const char s[], size_t pos,
                     size_t n ) const;
size_t find_last_of( const char s[],
                     size_t pos = NPOS ) const;
size_t find_last_of( char c, size_t pos = NPOS )
                     const;
```

Almost the same as `find_first_of`, but this function searches for the *last* character in the target string that matches an element in the set given by `str`, `s` or `c`.

- Member function `find_last_not_of`

```
size_t find_last_not_of( const string& str,
                         size_t pos = NPOS ) const;
size_t find_last_not_of( const char s[], size_t pos,
                         size_t n ) const;
```

```
size_t find_last_not_of( const char s[],
                         size_t pos = NPOS ) const;
size_t find_last_not_of( char c,
                         size_t pos = NPOS) const;
```

Almost the same as `find_first_of`, but this function searches for the *last* character in the target `string` that matches *no* element in the set given by `str`, `s` or `c`.

Input and output

- Non-member function `operator>>`

```
istream& operator>>( istream& is, string& str);
```

This *extractor* function gets a `string` value from the input stream `is`, and assigns it to `str`. Input stops when a whitespace character (space, horizontal tab, vertical tab, form-feed or new-line) is encountered, or end of file occurs. The whitespace character is not extracted from the stream. At most `NPOS-1` characters are input. If no characters are input, the `failbit` is set in the input stream. It returns a reference to the input stream.

- Non-member function `getline`

```
istream& getline( istream& is, string& str,
              char delim = '\n' );
```

This function inputs a string value from `is` and assigns the value to `str`. Input stops when the character `delim` is encountered, or end of file occurs. If a `delim` character is not given as an argument, input stops at end of line. The `delim` character is extracted from the stream but it is not appended to the string value. At most `NPOS-1` characters are input, in which case the `failbit` is set for the input stream. If end of file occurs, the `eofbit` is set. It returns a reference to the input stream `is`.

- Non-member function `operator<<`

```
ostream& operator<<( ostream& os, const string&str);
```

This *inserter* function writes the value of `str` to the output stream `os`, and returns a reference to this stream.

APPENDIX C

C++ keywords and operators

Keywords

asm	else	operator	throw
auto	enum	private	true
bool	explicit	protected	try
break	extern	public	typedef
case	false	register	typeid
catch	float	reinterpret_cast	typename
char	for	return	union
class	friend	short	unsigned
const	goto	signed	using
const_cast	if	sizeof	virtual
continue	inline	static	void
default	int	static_cast	volatile
delete	long	struct	wchar_t
do	mutable	switch	while
double	namespace	template	
dynamic_cast	new	this	

Operator summary

Unary operators and assignment operators are right associative. All others are left associative. Each box holds operators with the same precedence. The boxes are in descending order of precedence.

Operator	Description	Example
::	scope resolution	class_name :: member
::	global	:: name
.	member selection	object . member
->	member selection	pointer -> member
[]	subscript	pointer [expr]
()	function call	expr (expr_list)
()	value construction	type (expr_list)
sizeof	size of object	sizeof expr
sizeof	size of type	sizeof (type)
++	post increment	lvalue ++
++	pre increment	++ lvalue
−	post decrement	lvalue −
−	pre decrement	− lvalue
~	complement	~ expr
!	not	! expr
−	unary minus	- expr
+	unary plus	+ expr
&	address of	& lvalue
*	dereference	* expr
new	create	new type
delete	destroy	delete pointer
delete[]	destroy array	delete [] pointer
()	cast	(type) expr
.*	member selection	object . pointer-to-member
->*	member selection	pointer -> pointer_to_member
*	multiply	expr * expr
/	divide	expr / expr
%	modulo	expr % expr
+	add	expr + expr
−	subtract	expr - expr
<<	shift left	expr << expr
>>	shift right	expr >> expr
<	less than	expr < expr
<=	less than or equal	expr <= expr
>	greater than	expr > expr
>=	greater than or equal	expr >= expr
==	equal	expr == expr
!=	not equal	expr != expr

Operator	Description	Example
&	bitwise AND	`expr & expr`
^	bitwise exclusive OR	`expr ^ expr`
|	bitwise inclusive OR	`expr | expr`
&&	logical AND	`expr && expr`
||	logical OR	`expr || expr`
? :	conditional expression	`expr ? expr : expr`
=	simple assignment	`lvalue = expr`
*=	multiply and assign	`lvalue *= expr`
/=	divide and assign	`lvalue /= expr`
%=	modulo and assign	`lvalue %= expr`
+=	add and assign	`lvalue += expr`
-=	subtract and assign	`lvalue -= expr`
<<=	shift left and assign	`lvalue <<= expr`
>>=	shift right and assign	`lvalue >>= expr`
&=	AND and assign	`lvalue &= expr`
|=	inclusive OR and assign	`lvalue |= expr`
^=	exclusive OR and assign	`lvalue ^= expr`
,	comma (sequencing)	`expr , expr`

APPENDIX D
Arithmetic conversions

These lists explain, in detail, the conversions performed on operands during the evaluation of expressions. Knowledge at this low level is not normally needed.

The usual arithmetic conversions
- If either operand is of type `long double`, the other is converted to `long double`.
- Otherwise, if either operand is a `double`, the other is converted to `double`.
- Otherwise, if either operand is `float`, the other is converted to `float`.
- Otherwise, the *integral promotions* are performed on both operands.
- Then, if either operand is `unsigned long` the other is converted to `unsigned long`.
- Otherwise, if one operand is a `long int` and the other `unsigned int`, then if a `long int` can represent all the values of `unsigned int`, the `unsigned int` is converted to a `long int`; otherwise both operands are converted to `unsigned long int`.
- Otherwise, if either operand is `long`, the other is converted to `long`.
- Otherwise, if either operand is `unsigned`, the other is converted to `unsigned`.
- Otherwise, both operands are `int`.

Integral promotions
- An rvalue of type `char`, `signed char`, `unsigned char`, `short int`, or `unsigned short int`, can be converted to an rvalue of `int` if `int` can represent all the values of the source type; otherwise, the source

rvalue can be converted to an rvalue of type `unsigned int`.

- An rvalue of type `wchar_t`[1] or an enumerated type can be converted to an rvalue of the first of the following types that can represent all of the values of the source type: `int`, `unsigned int`, `long`, or `unsigned long`.
- An rvalue for an integral bit-field[2] can be converted to an rvalue of type `int` if `int` can represent all the values of the bit-field; otherwise it can be converted to `unsigned int` if `unsigned int` can represent all the values of the bit-field.
- An rvalue of type `bool` can be converted to an rvalue of type `int`, with `false` becoming zero and `true` becoming one.

Floating point promotions

- An rvalue of type `float` can be converted to an rvalue of type `double`. The value is unchanged.

Notes

1. This is a distinct type that can represent unique codes for all members of the largest supported extended character set.
2. Bitfields allow the specification of very small objects of a given number of bits. They can only be declared as part of a structure, union or class. They are of limited use.

APPENDIX E

C Library functions

This appendix lists some useful utility functions. The list is not complete, and it does not include the standard C++ class and template libraries. For more information about these functions look at the relevant header files on your computer. Alternatively, for more help, consult any good book on ANSI C, such as M. Banahan, D. Brady, & M. Doran, *The C Book, 2nd Edition*, (Addison-Wesley, 1991).

Miscellaneous functions		
abort	Abnormality terminate program	`<stdlib.h>`
atexit	Register function for auto call on exit	`<stdlib.h>`
bsearch	Binary search sorted array	`<stdlib.h>`
exit	Normal exit	`<stdlib.h>`
getenv	Obtain environment information	`<stdlib.h>`
qsort	Sort array	`<stdlib.h>`
rand	Generate a random integer	`<stdlib.h>`
signal	Invoke a function to handle a signal	`<signal.h>`
srand	Seed the random number generator	`<stdlib.h>`
system	Process system command	`<stdlib.h>`
va_arg	Variable argument list access	`<stdarg.h>`
va_end	Variable argument list termination	`<stdarg.h>`
va_start	Variable argument list intitalization	`<stdarg.h>`

Type and conversion functions		
atof	Convert string to double	`<stdlib.h>`
atoi	Convert string to integer	`<stdlib.h>`
atol	Convert string to long	`<stdlib.h>`
isalnum	Alphanumeric character?	`<ctype.h>`
isalpha	Alphabetic character?	`<ctype.h>`
iscntrl	Control character?	`<ctype.h>`
isdigit	Decimal digit?	`<ctype.h>`
isgraph	Printable character but not space?	`<ctype.h>`

281

islower	Lower case alphabetic character?	`<ctype.h>`
isprint	Printable character?	`<ctype.h>`
ispunct	Not alphanumeric or space?	`<ctype.h>`
isspace	White space?	`<ctype.h>`
isupper	Upper case alphabetic character?	`<ctype.h>`
isxdigit	Hexadecimal digit?	`<ctype.h>`
strtod	String to long	`<stdlib.h>`
strtol	String to double	`<stdlib.h>`
strtoul	String to unsigned long	`<stdlib.h>`
tolower	Convert char to lower case	`<ctype.h>`
toupper	Convert char to upper case	`<ctype.h>`

Date and time functions

asctime	Convert time to string	`<time.h>`
clock	Time in 'ticks'	`<time.h>`
ctime	Convert time to string	`<time.h>`
difftime	Difference between two calendar times	`<time.h>`
gmttime	Greenwich mean time	`<time.h>`
localtime	Local time	`<time.h>`
mktime	Calendar time	`<time.h>`
strftime	Convert time to string	`<time.h>`
time	Calendar time	`<time.h>`

Mathematical functions

abs	Absolute value of an int	`<stdlib.h>`
acos	Arccosine	`<math.h>`
asin	Arcsine	`<math.h>`
atan	Arctangent	`<math.h>`
atan2	Principal value of arctangent of y/x	`<math.h>`
atof	Convert string to double	`<stdlib.h>`
atoi	Convert string to integer	`<stdlib.h>`
atol	Convert string to long	`<stdlib.h>`
ceil	Ceiling	`<math.h>`
cos	Cosine	`<math.h>`
cosh	Hyperbolic cosine	`<math.h>`
div	Quotient and remainder of int divide	`<stdlib.h>`
exp	e^x	`<math.h>`
fabs	Absolute value of a double	`<math.h>`
floor	Floor	`<math.h>`
fmod	Floating point remainder of x/y	`<math.h>`
frexp	Floating point number to normalized fraction and integer power of two	`<math.h>`
labs	Absolute value of a long	`<stdlib.h>`
ldexp	$2^y x$	`<math.h>`
ldiv	Quotient and remainder of long divide	`<stdlib.h>`
log	$\ln x$	`<math.h>`
log10	$\log x$	`<math.h>`
modf	Floating point to integer fractional parts	`<math.h>`
pow	x^y	`<math.h>`
rand	Generate a random integer	`<stdlib.h>`
sin	Sine	`<math.h>`
sinh	Hyperbolic sine	`<math.h>`

sqrt	Square root	<math.h>
srand	Seed the random number generator	<stdlib.h>
strtod	String to long	<stdlib.h>
strtol	String to double	<stdlib.h>
strtoul	String to unsigned long	<stdlib.h>
tan	Tangent	<math.h>
tanh	Hyperbolic tangent	<math.h>

Memory functions

calloc	Allocate storage	<stdlib.h>
free	Free storage	<stdlib.h>
malloc	Allocate storage	<stdlib.h>
memchr	Find first of char in memory block	<string.h>
memcmp	Compare blocks of memory	<string.h>
memcpy	Copy block of memory	<string.h>
memmove	Copy block of memory	<string.h>
memset	Set value of memory block	<string.h>
realloc	Change the size of allocated storage	<stdlib.h>

C string functions

asctime	Convert time to string	<time.h>
ctime	Convert time to string	<time.h>
strcat	Concatenate strings	<string.h>
strchr	Find first of char in string	<string.h>
strcmp	Compare strings	<string.h>
strcoll	Compare strings	<string.h>
strcpy	Copy string	<string.h>
strcspn	Find first of char set in string	<string.h>
strerror	String equivalent of errno	<string.h>
strftime	Convert time to string	<time.h>
strlen	Length of string	<string.h>
strncat	Concatenate strings	<string.h>
strncmp	Compare strings	<string.h>
strncpy	Copy string	<string.h>
strpbrk	Find last of char set in string	<string.h>
strrchr	Find last of char in string	<string.h>
strspn	Length of first char set block in string	<string.h>
strstr	Find substring	<string.h>
strtok	Break string into tokens	<string.h>
strxfrm	String transform	<string.h>

Index